Jesus and Israel

One Covenant or Two?

David E. Holwerda

WILLIAM B. EERDMANS PUBLISHING COMPANY
GRAND RAPIDS, MICHIGAN

 APOLLOS
LEICESTER, ENGLAND

© 1995 Wm. B. Eerdmans Publishing Co.
255 Jefferson Ave. S.E., Grand Rapids, Michigan 49503

Published jointly in 1995
in the United States by Wm. B. Eerdmans Publishing Co.
and in the UK by APOLLOS (an imprint of Inter-Varsity Press)
38 De Montfort Street, Leicester LEI 7GP, England

Printed in the United States of America

00 99   7 6 5 4 3 2

Library of Congress Cataloging-in-Publication Data

Holwerda, David E. (David Earl), 1932-
    Jesus and Israel: one covenant or two? / David E. Holwerda.
        p.   cm.
    Includes bibliographical references and index.
    ISBN 0-8028-0685-6 (paper)
    1. Jesus Christ — Views on Judaism. 2. Covenants — Religious aspects —
Christianity. 3. Law (Theology) 4. Judaism (Christian theology) 5. Israel (Christian
theology) 6. Palestine in Christianity. 7. Temple of Jerusalem (Jerusalem) in the
Bible. 8. Christianity and other religions — Judaism. 9. Judaism — Relations —
Christianity.   I. Title.
BT590.J8H68   1994
231.7'6 — dc20   94-20978
                                                              CIP

British Library Cataloguing in Publication Data

A catalogue record for this book is available from the British Library

ISBN 0-85111-439-3

Unless otherwise noted, Scripture quotations are from the New Revised Standard
Version of the Bible *(NRSV),* copyright © 1989 by the Division of Christian Education
of the National Council of the Churches of Christ in the U.S.A., and used by permission.
Scripture quotations noted *RSV* are from the Revised Standard Version of the Bible,
copyrighted 1946, 1952 © 1971, 1973 by the Division of Christian Education of the
National Council of the Churches of Christ in the U.S.A., and used by permission.

JESUS AND ISRAEL

Contents

Preface

My interest in the topic of this book goes back many years to my youth. My mother, brought up in the Reformed Church of America, was committed to a premillennial position on the question of Israel, while my father, a pastor in the Christian Reformed Church, held to the amillennial position common to that tradition. Our discussions of the issues involved occurred during the days of World War II, when even secular scientists positioned the clock of human history at two minutes to twelve because of their fear that the atomic bomb would end it all, and these discussions continued in the years immediately thereafter when the State of Israel was again established. In such an apocalyptic atmosphere, my mother saw numerous "divine" confirmations of her premillennial position. Yet, in the family discussions around the dinner table involving my parents and their six sons, I always felt that the theological arguments in favor of the amillennial position were more convincing. Yet some doubts remained.

Years later, when I was invited to teach some courses in New Testament at Calvin Seminary, I had to create an elective course. I chose to teach on "Promise and Fulfillment," a topic that gave me freedom to roam anywhere in the New Testament and to check out my lingering doubts about the adequacy of the amillennial position. Since that time more than twenty years ago, I have had the privilege of teaching a course on Promise and Fulfillment many times. With a great variety of students we have examined numerous "promise and fulfillment" texts, and some of the results of that effort are found in this book. I could discuss many more texts under that heading, but the ones I have chosen here are sufficient to establish the theological contours of an answer to the question of Jesus and Israel. The position of my youth has been slightly modified, but the basic answer remains more at home among amillennial positions than with most premillennial positions.

While my interest in the relation of Jesus to Israel arose out of questions associated with the amillennial-premillennial debate, this book does not directly address the question of the millennium.[1] An explanation of this omission will also explain the shape of this book: Behind the various eschatological viewpoints labeled as millennial lie certain fundamental theological assumptions that shape the entire perspective. How one answers certain basic questions inevitably determines the shape of everything else. Once one is committed to a certain set of basic answers, the interpretation of most promise-fulfillment texts seems self-evident. Consequently, disagreement among eschatological viewpoints concerning the status and role of Israel is not so much a matter of this or that isolated text as it is a matter of disagreement concerning foundational perspectives. Therefore, each chapter in this book addresses a basic question concerning the relation of Jesus to Israel, and the answers arrived at constitute the basic assumptions of a Reformed theological point of view. The answers are not exhaustive but are in most cases restricted primarily to material found in the Gospels, with the exception of Chapter VI, which is primarily a study of Romans 9–11. Hopefully, this biblical-theological presentation of basic answers will illumine the present debate and demonstrate in part the biblical basis for a Reformed interpretation of the Scriptures.

Although my personal interest in the debate about Jesus and Israel arose in unusual times, the shape of my questions was then quite traditional. Subsequently, the Holocaust and the establishment of the State of Israel have had a radical impact on the shape of the questions in the ongoing debate about Jesus and Israel. Jewish voices, silenced for centuries, demand to be heard. The Christian Church should not be unaware of these voices and should reflect on how it speaks about the

---

1. For various perspectives on the millennium, cf. *The Meaning of the Millennium: Four Views,* ed. R. Clouse (Downers Grove, IL: InterVarsity, 1977).

relationship of Jesus and Israel and what it claims concerning that relationship. In the pages that follow we shall listen, reflect, and carefully examine the New Testament claims.

Many have contributed to the formation of this book. I wish to acknowledge especially the many students who have examined complex biblical texts with such delight and who have made the course in Promise and Fulfillment so stimulating that it was always a joy to teach. I wish to thank also Calvin Seminary and its Board of Trustees for sabbatical leaves that made this book possible. And special thanks are due to our faculty secretary, Jylene Baas, for her indispensable assistance. Without the encouragement and assistance of many, including my family, this book would not have been written.

Books are published into an unknown future. Unanimity of opinion on the theme of Jesus and Israel is not to be expected. At best, those who read with either agreement or disagreement will have their perspectives clarified. For full agreement on all points in dispute, we must await God's promised future. God has his way of surprising us all.

CHAPTER I

Jesus and Israel
in the Twentieth Century

The theme of Jesus and Israel embraces a reality filled with sorrow. From Jesus' weeping over Jerusalem to the apostle Paul's personal anguish over the unbelief of Jewish Israel, the sorrow has continued, even far beyond the limits of the first century. In addition, the parallel theme of the relationship of the Church to Jewish Israel has added many tragedies. The twentieth century has witnessed an unusual degree of sorrow and an unspeakable tragedy. As a consequence it has become a watershed in Christian thinking about the relationship of Jesus to Jewish Israel. Never since the second century have Christian theologians devoted so much energy to rethinking this question as in the present century.

The impetus for this renewed concern arose not simply from within the Church but also from the awful reality of the Holocaust. This horrible attempt of the Third Reich to wipe the Jews off the face of the earth compelled not only the Western nations but also the Church to consider their responsibility for what had happened and to reconsider their attitudes toward Jewish Israel. The establishment of the State of Israel in 1948 has made it possible for Jewish voices, silenced for centuries, to demand a hearing. The Holocaust continues to lend urgency and pathos to their demands. The Church needs to be aware of these voices and to reflect on how it will speak about the relationship of Jesus and Israel and what it can claim concerning that relationship.

1

A Dramatic Change

In order to appreciate the significant changes occurring in the twentieth century, it is important to have some acquaintance with the Church's traditional theological positions concerning Israel. From the early days of the Church the opinion that the Jews had been disinherited as a result of their unbelief was widely held. Many believed that the Jews' role in the history of redemption had come to an end. Already in the middle of the second century, Justin Martyr, in his famous *Dialogue with Trypho,* argued that Christians, not Jews, were the children of Abraham, those who formed the new nation that would inhabit the Holy Land during the millennial reign of Christ. God's covenant with Abraham was in effect established with Gentile Christians, not with Jews. The Jews had been excluded from the purposes of God.[1]

This view expressed became dominant for centuries in the Church, and the Reformation did not significantly change it. Initially, Luther did advocate a change in the way Christians treated Jews. Instead of treating them like dogs, forbidding them to work or to associate with Christians and thus forcing them to become money-lenders and usurers, Luther suggested,

> If we wish to help them, we must practice on them not the papal law but rather the Christian law of love, and accept them in a friendly fashion, allowing them to work and make a living, so that they gain the reason and the opportunity to be with and among us to see and to hear our Christian teaching and life.[2]

At that time Luther believed that the Jews had never been converted because they had never heard the true gospel, but now the recovery of the gospel in the Reformation gave fresh hope for their conversion. But when Jews were convinced neither by his arguments nor by his message,

1. Cf. J. S. Siker, *Disinheriting the Jews: Abraham in Early Christian Controversy* (Louisville: Westminster/John Knox, 1991), pp. 163-184.

2. M. U. Edwards Jr., "Against the Jews," in J. Cohen, ed., *Essential Papers on Judaism and Christianity in Conflict: From Late Antiquity to the Reformation* (New York: New York University, 1991), p. 352. The quotation is from the Weimar Edition of Luther's Works, 11:336.

Luther considered them abandoned by God and changed his previous tolerant advice. Even though he thought that his age stood on the threshold of the return of Christ, Luther lost all hope for the conversion of the Jews. Instead of love and friendship, he advocated harsh repression by Christian princes and magistrates with the expressed hope that such severe discipline might save a few. The Jews were ranked with Turks, fanatics, and papists as agents of Satan in the final assault on the Church before Christ's return. Although many in the Reformation disagreed with Luther's harsh polemic, he advocated the complete elimination of Jewish worship from Christian territories.[3]

Calvin was more like the early Luther in his attitudes toward Jews. While he could readily criticize Jewish interpreters of Scripture for foolishness, stupidity, and blasphemy and even accuse them of fantasy in their materialistic view of the messianic age, he was generally more merciful to Jews than toward Christian heresies.[4] Part of the reason for this was Calvin's positive use of the Old Testament and its law, which led some to accuse Calvin of a Judaizing tendency. But the greater reason for not depriving Jews of their dignity was rooted in his understanding of Romans 11:26:

> Yet, despite the great obstinacy with which they continue to wage war against the gospel, we must not despise them, while we consider that, for the sake of the promise, God's blessing still rests among them.[5]

Calvin's own appreciation of election prevented him from advocating against the Jews the extreme measures common in medieval Christianity. Based on his study of the Old Testament prophets, Calvin was aware that even when Israel was under God's judgment of exile, "election remains inviolable, although its signs do not always appear."[6] Thus, based on Israel's election, Calvin continued to hold to a future conversion of Jewish Israel.

---

3. Cf. W. von Loewenich, *Martin Luther: The Man and His Work* (Minneapolis: Augsburg, 1986), pp. 348-352.

4. Cf. S. W. Baron, "John Calvin and the Jews," in J. Cohen, ed., *op. cit.*, p. 391.

5. *Institutes* IV.16.15.

6. *Institutes* III.21.5.

> When the Gentiles have come in, the Jews will at the same time return from their defection to the obedience of faith. The salvation of the whole Israel of God, which must be drawn from both, will thus be completed, and yet in such a way that the Jews, as the first born in the family of God, may obtain the first place.[7]

Calvin's more moderate attitude toward the Jews was clearly rooted in his theological convictions, but his belief in the future conversion of Jewish Israel never received much emphasis in his theology nor in that of his followers. The major emphasis fell instead on the Church as the New Israel. Within that emphasis, moreover, it became possible for some of Calvin's followers to develop a theology of election that no longer left room for any significant use of "election" with regard to Jewish Israel.

    While the majority view within the Church has been that the Church is the New Israel and that the Jews have lost title to that claim, there has always been present within the Church a minority belief in a premillennial reign of Christ over a converted Jewish Israel. Calvin and others considered this belief a capitulation to Jewish materialistic conceptions of the messianic era, but this premillennial vision has received considerable impetus in the twentieth century from Dispensationalism.[8] In distinction from traditional premillennialism, dispensationalists believe that the title "Israel" should not be applied to the Church but only to Jewish Israel. The Christian Church and Jewish Israel are seen as two entirely distinct and separate peoples of God. When Jewish Israel did not accept Jesus as Messiah, the fulfillment of Old Testament prophecy was interrupted. During this interruption the gospel went out to the Gentiles and the Church was formed, but dispensationalists hold that

---

7. *Commentary on Romans* (Grand Rapids: Eerdmans, 1961), p. 255. While Calvin teaches a future conversion of Jewish Israel, he interprets "all Israel" as referring to both Jewish and Gentile believers.

8. Dispensationalism divides the Scriptures into distinct periods or "dispensations" in each of which God works in a certain way: innocence (Adam before the Fall), conscience (from Adam to Noah), promise (from Abraham to Moses), Mosaic law (from Moses to Christ), grace (from Pentecost to the Rapture), and the millennium. This view originated in the work of John Nelson Darby (1800-1882), a founder of the Plymouth Brethren, and received its greatest impetus from the *Scofield Reference Bible*, which was first published in 1909.

this was not God's original purpose and that it does not fulfill the Old Testament promises for the simple reason that the Church is not Israel. Only after the Church is removed from history by the Rapture and Jesus returns to rule over a converted Jewish nation will the clock of prophecy begin again to move toward fulfillment. This fulfillment will be literal, in Palestine, and experienced by the nation of Israel. The basic premise in this dispensational perspective is that since the promises were given to the literal descendants of Abraham, the promises must be fulfilled in the literal descendants of Abraham. With the reestablishment of the State of Israel in 1948, this view has become very popular among fundamentalist and some evangelical Christians. Books promoting this perspective have sometimes sold literally millions of copies.[9]

The premillennial viewpoint, whether dispensational or classical, has always been a minority position in the Christian Church. The significant challenge today in the mainline Protestant Churches and in Roman Catholicism comes not from premillennialism but from the Holocaust. Since 1945 many denominations, as well as the World Council of Churches, have issued declarations and study documents on the relationship between Christians and Jews.[10] Most of these declarations warn against the anti-Semitism that has infected the Church, encourage support of the present State of Israel (though there are disagreements concerning the reasons for such support), emphasize the common roots of Judaism and Christianity, and affirm the continuing election of Jewish Israel. Even though all affirm this continuing election of Jewish Israel on the basis of Romans 11, there is little unanimity regarding the theological consequences that should be derived from this continuing election. Does it mean that there are two distinct covenants and that, consequently, there should be no Christian proselytizing of Jews? Should the Church conclude that it has no

9. For example, H. Lindsey, *The Late Great Planet Earth* (Grand Rapids: Zondervan, 1970), and more recently J. E. Walvoord, *Armageddon, Oil and the Middle East Crisis* (Grand Rapids: Zondervan, 1990).

10. One of the most recent is the statement adopted by the General Assembly of the Presbyterian Church (USA) in June 1987. For a convenient collection of many such documents together with a brief analysis of their positions, see *The Theology of the Churches and the Jewish People: Statements by the World Council of Churches and Its Member Churches* (Geneva: WCC, 1988).

obligation to evangelize Jews since their conversion and future rests solely in the hands of God?

Clearly, the theological thinking of many Christian churches has undergone dramatic changes, which have raised significant questions concerning Jesus and Jewish Israel, questions that we shall pursue in subsequent chapters. Here it is important to note that this significant theological shift has not been caused merely by debate within the walls of the Church but also by post-Holocaust Jewish-Christian dialogue. The shape of that dialogue can be disturbing, and it presents numerous challenges.

Challenges in Jewish-Christian Dialogue

The question for the twentieth-century Church is now: How should one write or speak about Jesus and Israel after the Holocaust? The haunting memory of the Holocaust looms large over every discussion and claim. Israel is now Israel-after-the-Holocaust, and the contemporary Church encounters modern Israel with a guilty conscience. Although the Church did not directly perpetuate the Holocaust and individual Christians often assisted individual Jews, the Holocaust would not have happened had it not been for the prior history of Christian persecution of the Jews.

Several persons have argued that the Church should not be charged with blame for the Holocaust because anti-Semitism is a purely modern phenomenon divorced from the ancient and medieval worlds. Modern anti-Semitism is rooted in nationalism and racism, and is essentially anti-Christian in character.[11] But most authors, both Christian and Jewish, do not agree. There was in fact a Christian prehistory still at work in the Holocaust.[12] Both the past practices of the Church and its attitudes created a background that could be used directly by Nazi

11. Hannah Arendt is among these. For discussion, see J. Gager, *The Origins of Anti-Semitism* (New York: Oxford University Press, 1983), p. 267; J. Jocz, "Israel After Auschwitz," in *The Witness of the Jews to God,* ed. D. W. Torrance (Edinburgh: Handsel, 1982), p. 65.

12. Cf. Hans Küng, *Judaism: Between Yesterday and Tomorrow* (New York: Crossroad, 1992), pp. 163ff. Cf. also David A. Rausch, *A Legacy of Hatred: Why Christians Must Not Forget the Holocaust* (Grand Rapids: Baker, 1990).

propagandists. Frank Littell speaks for most when he declares that "those who made of Antisemitism a political weapon could mount it upon great barriers of theological and cultural Antisemitism built up by the Churches" and that the Third Reich and its death camps "were not accidental appearances in the heart of Christendom."[13] Hans Küng expresses the common judgment:

> Nazi Anti-Judaism was the work of godless anti-Christian criminals . . . but without the almost two-thousand-year-long pre-history of "Christian" anti-Judaism . . . it would not have been possible. . . . None of the anti-Jewish measures of the Nazis — distinctive clothing, exclusion from professions, . . . forbidding of mixed marriages, expulsions, the concentration camps, massacres, gruesome funeral pyres — was new. All that already existed in the so-called Christian Middle Ages . . . and in the period of the "Christian" reformation. What was new was the racial grounding of these measures. . . .[14]

This long history of Christian civil and religious oppression of the Jews as "God-killers," persons guilty of the unspeakable crime of deicide, meant that Jews were not considered worthy of either respect or civil rights. No wonder then that the Jewish artist Asher Lev in Chaim Potok's novel,[15] though fascinated by the cross as an object of artistic compulsion, finds it almost impossible to fulfill that compulsion because the cross is for the Jew not a symbol of redemption but a horrible sign of oppression. This tragic history of Church-synagogue, Christian-Jew relationships complicates enormously any writing on the subject of Jesus and Israel.

Is it then still possible today to claim that there is an essential connection between Jesus and Israel without being accused of anti-Semitism or anti-Judaism? Can one hold, as does the New Testament,

---

13. F. H. Littell, *The Crucifixion of the Jews* (New York: Harper and Row, 1975), pp. 104, 45.

14. Hans Küng in *Christians and Jews,* ed. H. Küng and W. Kasper (Concilium 8/10; New York: Seabury, 1975), pp. 11f. In a more recent work Küng lists restrictions against Jews found in both the ancient Canon Law of the Church and in the measures adopted by the Nazis. He also describes the failure of the Church to protest Nazi anti-Semitism (*Judaism,* pp. 234f., 245-271).

15. *My Name Is Asher Lev* (New York: Knopf, 1972).

that the relationship of Israel and Jesus is one of promise and fulfillment without being accused of resurrecting claims that inevitably produce anti-Jewish feelings and even provoke homicide against the Jews? While many readers may think that such questions are grossly exaggerated, those acquainted with contemporary Jewish-Christian dialogue in Europe and the United States realize that they are not.

Today in most Western democratic societies the civil and political rights of a religion to maintain itself without external constraint have been granted. It is generally agreed that no one, in particular no government, has the right to constrain or oppress a religion with which one disagrees. Consequently, Christians who live in such societies discover the premodern Christian oppression of the Jews to be an intolerable scandal, a blot upon their consciences. However, is it still permissible — in the light of such a political consensus about the civil rights of all religions — for one religion to assert claims that by their very nature either implicitly or explicitly contain critiques of the claims or status of another religion? Or does religious pluralism as a civil right forbid such a direct challenge concerning the truth of religious claims? Specifically, is it the case that if Christianity continues to make claims about Jesus that imply or entail criticism of the religious validity of certain positions held by Judaism, such claims will inevitably produce consequences that will infringe upon or even deny the political and civil rights of Judaism?

Jewish sensitivities, sharpened by centuries of suffering and by the Holocaust, assert that precisely such will be the result because it has always been so. Although the critique of Judaism by Christianity has always been fundamentally religious in nature, it has usually spilled over into the civil and political arenas and has often led either to forced conversion or to the disinheriting and dispossessing of the Jews. Consequently, after making an impassioned indictment against the Church in which he mentions that "no less than 96 Church councils and 114 popes issued edicts against the Jews . . . treating them as pariahs, and bringing Israel to the brink of destruction,"[16] Pinchas Lapide, a Jewish scholar and a participant in Jewish-Christian dialogue, sets several conditions for continuing the dialogue. He insists that there are three

16. P. Lapide and U. Luz, *Jesus in Two Perspectives: A Jewish-Christian Dialog* (Minneapolis: Augsburg, 1985), p. 12.

errors that form the roots of Christian animosity toward the Jews and that therefore must be rejected by Christians if dialogue with Jews is to be possible at all.

These three "errors" are that Jesus was the Messiah of Israel, that he was rejected by the Jews, and that he in turn has repudiated them.[17] While the third especially is admittedly open to varying interpretations, each of these so-called errors has a basis in the New Testament itself. Even so, and to the extent that they do, Lapide asserts that the New Testament warrant for such positions must be repudiated and that if they are not, Christianity will continue to stimulate anti-Judaic and anti-Semitic sentiments with all their disastrous consequences. Hence Christians may no longer assert that Jesus is the fulfillment of prophecy and is, therefore, the Messiah of Israel. In addition, the parts of the Gospels of Matthew and John which judge Jewish Israel harshly must be repudiated since they are said to be especially to blame for the anti-Jewish tendencies of Christianity. Such repudiation of so-called errors means that Jesus is completely refashioned so that he fits within the religious contours of Judaism.

While it is possible to understand Professor Lapide's demand sympathetically because historically these religious claims on the part of Christianity have produced hatred toward or contempt of the Jewish people, nevertheless, the Christian claim that Jesus is the Messiah is obviously central to the New Testament witness. Hence, his demand entails a curious position, for what he demands of Christianity is in a formal sense identical with what he will not allow it to demand of Judaism, namely, an imposition of one religion's truth claims on another religion. Apparently, Christianity may not assert truth claims that either undermine or contradict Judaism or that even on the basis of the Old Testament claim to be the fulfillment of the hopes of Judaism, while Judaism may insist that the Church modify its understanding of Jesus so that he can fit more comfortably within the framework of Judaism.[18]

17. *Ibid.*, p. 24. The second and third of these "errors" have been spoken of by Jewish authors ever since the work of Jules Isaac. His summary Proposition 21 in *Jesus and Israel* (New York: Holt, Rinehart and Winston, 1971; original French edition, 1948) states concerning the Jewish people: "They did not reject Jesus, they did not crucify him. And Jesus did not reject Israel."

18. *Jesus in Two Perspectives,* pp. 55f. We should note that Professor Lapide would appeal to certain radical forms of higher criticism to justify his position con-

But if dialogue with another religion is accepted, should not one be willing to hear the other's truth claims in full, no matter what the implication may be for one's own? How else can true understanding be achieved? Of course, Lapide's demands stem from the fear that these Christian claims inevitably produce anti-Semitism.

Professor Lapide's various assertions suggest the following position: Christianity can be viewed positively by Judaism as the means that God has used to enable Israel to become a light to the nations through the teaching of Jesus, a Jewish rabbi.[19] But, under the influence of Hellenism, the New Testament and Church dogma have interpreted Jesus in ways that Judaism cannot accept. There are in effect two covenants being used by God and two religions, Judaism and Christianity. But in the final analysis, Judaism possesses the ultimate truth, the validity of which will be established when the Messiah comes. Then even Gentile Christians will have to acknowledge the misunderstandings and heresies contained in the New Testament, for then they will have discovered that the Messiah was not the Christ of Christian faith — though perhaps he could be the "Jesus of history," provided he is understood as a Jesus who fits comfortably within the contours of normative Judaism. Of course, since for Judaism the Messiah is totally unknown, he may prove to be someone totally different. Since Lapide is an articulate representative of Judaism, one would expect him to hold to the truth claims of his own religion. But how should a Christian in dialogue with him respond?

Three Theological Responses

Before delving more deeply into the specific issues of such dialogue, we shall describe briefly the contours of three quite different responses

---

cerning Jesus. Our disagreement with Lapide is also a disagreement with certain claims made by higher criticism, claims that fit better in certain liberal theological traditions than in orthodox or evangelical traditions. Cf. especially "Excursus: The Use of Gospel Criticism," in D. A. Hagner, *The Jewish Reclamation of Jesus* (Grand Rapids: Zondervan, 1984), pp. 72-85.

19. Following in the footsteps of the famous medieval rabbi Moses Maimonides (1135-1204), many Jewish teachers have placed a positive evaluation upon Christianity as serving God's purpose in preparing for the coming of the kingdom.

to the question of Jesus and Israel. It will become obvious that the Holocaust and subsequent Jewish-Christian dialogue have not left Christian theology unaffected. The traditional view that the Christian Church has superseded Jewish Israel, which no longer has a role in God's plan of redemption, is no longer dominant. Even though no consensus has developed on how to evaluate the present position and future role of Jewish Israel, the negative tones prominent in the Church's traditional view have been greatly muted. Our intention in this section is not to enter into extensive debate with these points of view, but rather to present them as evidence of significant change and of the remarkable impact that the Holocaust, the establishment of the State of Israel, and Jewish-Christian dialogue have had on certain Christian theologians.

The theology of **Karl Barth** has had a remarkable impact on subsequent thinking about the relationship of Church and Israel. Although Barth's basic view of Jewish Israel flows directly from his understanding of election, his later more positive emphasis was also influenced by the events we have just mentioned. He sees an essential unity between Church and Synagogue. Jesus Christ is the Elect One, but what is elected in Christ is a community with a twofold form, Israel and the Church: "Israel is the people of the Jews which resists its election; the Church is the gathering of Jews and Gentiles called on the ground of its election."[20] Even though Israel resists its election, it is not thereby rejected but continues to be elect. Thus beneath the historical differentiation of Church and Synagogue lies an essential unity grounded in their election in Christ. Consequently, Barth declares that the present separation is "an ontological impossibility, a wound, a gaping hole in the body of Christ, which is quite intolerable."[21]

Although God's ultimate purpose is that Israel should accept its election in Christ, nevertheless even now in its disobedience God uses Israel in his service. In fact, Barth can say that even now Israel is discharging "exactly the service for which it is elected."[22] For in its resistance Israel provides a necessary, though involuntary, witness to God's judgment, to the nature of fallen humankind in its futile revolt

20. K. Barth, *Church Dogmatics* (Edinburgh: Clark, 1956-75) II/2, 199.
21. *Ibid.* IV/1, 671.
22. *Ibid.* II/2, 209.

against God, and thus even to the burden that God himself removes in Jesus Christ.[23] Even in its self-inflicted judgment Israel testifies to the mercy of the electing God, who continues to maintain Israel in its historical existence. This continuing existence, including the establishment of the modern State of Israel, is for Barth the only credible proof for the existence of God.[24]

Further, this involuntary witness is essential for the Church's authentic existence. If the Church ever becomes estranged from Israel, it will lose its power to witness to human misery and to the cross. For what it costs God to make himself one with the elected community becomes evident in disobedient Israel. Besides, it is only Israel's testimony that prevents the Church from reintroducing the pagan ideas of its own Gentile background into the Christian message.[25] Therefore, if the Church becomes estranged from Jewish Israel, it will inevitably, as happened during the Third Reich, become estranged from its own authentic message.

Barth's view of Jewish Israel is both traditional and novel: traditional in describing Jewish Israel as living under a self-inflicted curse of God, as described in Romans 11, novel in ascribing an ultimately necessary and positive role to Israel's involuntary witness and in considering Jewish Israel's unbelief as already having been overcome in the rejection and election of Jesus Christ. Even in its unbelief Israel is still "the people of its arrived and crucified Messiah, and therefore the people of the secret (concealed from it as yet) Lord of the Church."[26]

What then is the Church's responsibility to Jewish Israel? The Church must never forget Israel's priority, remembering always that the Church is a guest in the house of Israel. Still, because Israel resists its election in Christ, the Church must share with Israel through friendly dialogue the message it possesses. However, this may not be called "missions" because a "mission" is directed toward those who worship

    23. *Ibid.* II/1, 208f.
    24. *Ibid.* II/1, 209; *idem, Dogmatics in Outline* (New York: Harper and Row, 1959), p. 75.
    25. *Church Dogmatics* II/2, 206f., 235.
    26. *Ibid.* II/2, 208. For a more complete analysis of Barth's view, see J. W. Simpson, "The Jews of Today according to Twentieth-Century German Protestant Dogmatics," *Studia Biblica et Theologica* 13 (1983), pp. 195-224.

a false God, and such is not the case with Israel. Yet Barth does not believe that even such friendly dialogue will bring to light the hidden unity. While dialogue may bring about the conversion of a few individuals, Barth believes that the real conversion of true Jews will require, as in the case of the apostle Paul, the direct intervention of God himself. Barth suggests that the real witness necessary to make Israel jealous is not dialogue but authentic living as a community of the King of Israel and the Savior of the world, but he seems to hold out little hope that the unity of Church and Israel will occur by this means either.[27] Thus the conversion of unbelieving Jewish Israel will not be the result of Christian example or Christian proclamation, but only the result of the Lord's return.

Markus Barth followed in the theological footsteps of his father Karl. As an active participant in Jewish-Christian dialogue, he maintained the theological perspective described above. In three books devoted to this topic, familiar themes are repeated: All Jews, even the atheists among them, exist in "indissoluble unity with Jesus Christ." Israel's special function is to remind Gentile Christians that they exist by sheer grace. Israel gives this witness not verbally but by an existence that declares that the "God who tolerates us, the reprobate and the guilty, will also receive you into his people."[28] Markus Barth uses the parable of the Prodigal Son as a paradigm for the relationship of the Church and Israel. Like the elder brother, Israel renders a necessary service in reminding the Church, the younger brother, of his sin and of his salvation by grace. But the younger brother may not reprimand the elder. This is the task of the father, who loves both sons and wants to see both at the banquet table.[29] Thus dialogue is appropriate, but not a mission to Jews with its implicit or explicit reprimands. Still, such dialogue awaits the return of Christ for the resolution of the present mystery of the twofold people of God.[30]

Both Barths develop a positive evaluation of Israel's continuing

27. *Church Dogmatics* IV/1, 671; IV/3/2, 876-878.
28. M. Barth, *Jesus the Jew* (Atlanta: John Knox, 1978), p. 39; *The People of God* (Sheffield: JSOT, 1983), p. 36; cf. *Israel and the Church* (Richmond: John Knox, 1969), p. 74.
29. *Israel and the Church*, pp. 30f.; *The People of God*, p. 44.
30. *Israel and the Church*, pp. 22, 110f.

role in history but continue to maintain the essential Christian claims concerning Jesus Christ. Although the Holocaust is taken seriously and is even associated mysteriously with the cross of Christ, it is not given an independent revelatory status apart from or even alongside the cross.[31] Still, Jewish Israel, though it is elect together with the Church in Christ, receives in the Barthian view an independent role in history that it is predestined to carry out outside and beyond the reach of the Church's proclamation of the gospel of Christ. Jewish Israel remains in a special category until the Lord returns. Nevertheless, here and now Israel is considered a necessary partner in the ecumenical movement as it seeks to restore the unity of God's people on earth.[32] Thus the Barthian perspective maintains the traditional Reformed emphasis on a single covenant of grace and a single people of God but does so in a very nontraditional way. It is not surprising that both Barths adopted a very positive stance toward the State of Israel, viewing it as an expression of the faithfulness of God and as worthy of the Church's support.[33]

While the Barthian revision of the Christian perspective on Israel maintains the traditional Christian claims concerning the finality of the person and work of Christ, others have adopted a far more radical stance. Convinced that certain doctrinal assertions about the finality of Christ are themselves anti-Judaic or even anti-Semitic, they attempt a reinterpretation of these central Christian beliefs. If the Christian Church lacks the courage to accept a radical reinterpretation of basic beliefs, then, these theologians charge, it will not have learned the true lesson of the Holocaust. One such theologian is **Rosemary Ruether**.

After surveying the sad history of Church-Synagogue relations through the centuries, Ruether concludes that the actual root of Christian anti-Judaism is its christology. These New Testament teachings create the problem: Jesus is the true meaning and fulfillment of the Old Testament, he is the Son of God, and he is the Messiah who has already

31. *Jesus the Jew*, p. 39: "Auschwitz meant that we contributed to the crucifixion of Christ."

32. K. Barth, *Church Dogmatics* IV/3/2, 878; M. Barth, *Israel and the Church*, p. 32.

33. For additional expressions of an essentially Barthian viewpoint on Israel and the Church, see the essays by David Torrance, C. E. B. Cranfield, and Thomas Torrance in *The Witness of the Jews to God*, ed. D. W. Torrance (Edinburgh: Handsel, 1982).

appeared in history. Such claims, according to Ruether, necessarily result in anti-Judaism, that is, in the denial of legitimacy to the religious claims of Judaism, which rejects the christology of the New Testament. This anti-Judaism, it is claimed, will in turn produce anti-Semitism.

If one follows this theological direction, what happens to Christianity and its claims? In essence Christianity is transformed into a distinct but parallel form of Judaism. Ruether declares that the fulfillment of Old Testament hopes has not happened and that fulfilled messianism does not yet exist because historical existence is not yet redeemed. The Church cannot say that Jesus *was* the Messiah for that would imply that the final perspective has already occurred in a historical person and then Jesus would no longer be fully human. So in this proposed reinterpretation Jesus is considered to be fully human but with a significance that is no longer final. This human Jesus points to the coming of another and hopes for the coming time of redemption.[34] His resurrection parallels or reduplicates the exodus, but does not fulfill it. Therefore, while Christians may understand their story in the light of Jesus, Jews need not do so. They have their own story, which provides adequate reasons for hope. Consequently, the cross and resurrection of Jesus become at best a particular way of envisioning salvation, but they are not the only way.[35]

Professor Ruether's radical reinterpretation of christology produces a Christianity that is structurally identical with Judaism. Both are religions of hope awaiting a redeemed humanity. Each has its own reason for hope, its own story, and neither needs to share the language of the other. Furthermore, what is said about Judaism and Christianity applies to all other religions as well. According to Ruether, even though

34. The Church has always distinguished the fact that full salvation is still future from the fact that the final reality has already been manifested in the person and work of Christ. Ruether denies that finality can be claimed for either the person or the work of Christ.

35. R. R. Ruether, *Faith and Fratricide: The Theological Roots of Anti-Semitism* (New York: Seabury, 1974), chapter V. Ruether apparently sees the cross and resurrection of Jesus as paradigmatic for Christians only, not for all persons. She thus denies both the uniqueness of Jesus and the universal significance of those events. However, if the resurrection is not just a paradigm but an event in history, the uniqueness of Jesus would be implied and its universal significance undeniable.

every religion is a means of coming into contact with the universal, no particular religion or revelation can claim to be universal. The basic philosophical principle that governs this radical revisioning of Christian teaching is this: The universal cannot be contained within any particular religion or historical person because it is transcendent and awaits all at the end of history. This familiar objection to Christian claims of finality was found already in the ancient Roman world. But to accept it is to say that there is not just one covenant, or even two, but actually many ways to the Father, as many ways as there are religions.[36] Obviously, such a view of religion accomplishes Ruether's goal of rooting out anti-Judaism and anti-Semitism, but it does so at the expense of surrendering the central Christian claims concerning the finality of Jesus' person and work. Are such drastic measures actually necessary to avoid anti-Semitism?

A third response to the question of Church and Israel proposes a totally new paradigm for reading the New Testament texts addressing this issue. Whereas most interpreters have assumed that the New Testament challenges several essential teachings of Judaism, **John Gager** argues that such a traditional reading misreads the context of the New Testament authors.[37]

Gager's general thesis is that there was much sympathy for Judaism in the ancient world and that many Gentiles were attracted at least to aspects of Judaism. Anti-Judaic statements made by both pagans and Christians arose not from any general hatred toward Jews but from concerns about undesired Jewish influence. For example, John Chrysostom, a presbyter in Antioch, gave a series of sermons in A.D. 386 that are filled with tirades against the Synagogue. But his real target was not Judaism but the Judaizing influence exerted on members of his own congregation who were attending Jewish feasts, observing the

---

36. Ruether relativizes the absolute claims concerning Jesus found in the New Testament by a psychologizing reinterpretation. The claims made in the Gospel of John or by Paul are interpreted as a one-sided overreaction to Jewish rejection of Christian claims. While these claims are understandable in their original sociological setting of conflict, the Church can no longer validly make such claims. Cf. *Faith and Fratricide*, pp. 106f., 115f., 231f.

37. Cf. J. Gager, *The Origins of Anti-Semitism: Attitudes Toward Judaism in Pagan and Christian Antiquity* (New York: Oxford University Press, 1983).

Jewish sabbath, submitting to circumcision, using Jewish spells as cures for disease, and honoring the local synagogue as a holy place.[38] These were Gentile Christians attracted to Jewish practices. Gager's general thesis about Christian authors is that "anti-Judaism arises in direct response to a form of Judaizing Christianity."[39] Of course, even though Jews were not the specific target, the hostile tones of invective against the Synagogue frequently produced Christian hostility toward Jews.

This general thesis that the real target of Christian anti-Judaism is Judaizers is then applied to New Testament authors. According to Gager, Paul's conflict with Judaism is focused on a single point: how Gentiles become members of the covenant people. Paul teaches that in Christ Gentiles gain equal status with Jews as members of God's people through a righteousness apart from the law. Therefore, Paul vigorously resists any attempt to subject Gentile believers to the demands of the law. But he does not teach that this righteousness apart from the law is for Jews or that Christ is the end of the law for Jews. These central Pauline themes are directed against Judaizers and applied only to Gentiles. Paul differs from Judaism only in his assertion that Gentiles are not required to keep the Torah (law).[40] Thus Paul is reacting only against Jewish exclusivism, against the insistence that the only way to join Israel is through the Torah. Apart from this single difference, Paul offers no challenge to Jews who follow in the way of Judaism. Gager's summary of Paul's gospel is that Christ is "the fulfillment of God's promises concerning the Gentiles" but "not the climax of the history of God's dealing with Israel."[41]

If this thesis is correct, then the New Testament teaches two covenants, or at least two different ways into a single covenant, one for Jews and the other for Gentiles. But is it possible to restrict Paul's statements to Gentiles only? Many do not think so. It is interesting that at one place Gager agrees that Paul explains Israel's stumbling as caused by their failure "to see that righteousness rests on faith, whether for the

38. Gager, *Origins,* p. 119.
39. *Ibid.,* p. 127.
40. Gager declares that "Torah remains the path of righteousness for Israel; Christ has become the promised way of righteousness for Gentiles" (*ibid.,* p. 247). Gager's thesis is based on the work of Lloyd Gaston, which Gager summarizes on pp. 198-201.
41. *Ibid.,* p. 249.

circumcised or the uncircumcised."[42] On the face of it, this statement looks like a critique of Judaism also and not just of Judaizers who mislead Gentile believers. Of course, Gager would argue both that Paul intends only to remind Jews that faith was always "the proper response to the covenant" and that Paul is not calling Jews to faith in Christ.[43] With the majority of interpreters, however, we shall argue that Paul's teaching of a righteousness based on faith implies a quite different understanding of the interrelationship of sin, law, and salvation than is found in Judaism.

From this brief survey it is obvious that the Holocaust and a sense of Christian responsibility for contributing to it have had a dramatic effect on Christian thinking about Jesus and Israel. The strong desire to avoid anti-Judaism and anti-Semitism has led to bold reinterpretations of the Christian message, reinterpretations that at times violate the boundaries of traditionally orthodox Christianity. With these three examples as background, we shall return to several specific issues in post-Holocaust theology.

Issues in Post-Holocaust Theology

Jewish thinkers such as Pinchas Lapide are not uncomfortable with a two-covenant theology. If there are two distinct covenants, one for Christian Gentiles and one for Jews, and if the Christian covenant implies no obligations of belief for Jews, then there is no objection from the side of Judaism. We have seen that some Christian theologians have in dialogue with Judaism begun to advocate such a two-covenant theology.[44] Having understood Auschwitz (that is, the Holocaust) as a call for another belief, these theologians have attempted to develop a Christian theology that is no longer against Judaism. Christian beliefs that contributed to the Holocaust must be rejected. No longer may Christians theologically deny the right of Jewish Israel to exist as the people of

---

42. *Ibid.,* p. 252.
43. *Ibid.,* p. 224.
44. Some others who have done so are F. Mussner, A. R. Eckhardt, P. Van Buren, and J. Pawlikowski.

God on the basis of the Torah. No longer may Jews be accused of murdering God and consequently of standing under a divine curse. Instead, Judaism and Christianity can exist *theologically* as two different, yet compatible, religions.

While the motives and goals of post-Holocaust Christian theology are laudable — who does not want to eliminate anti-Semitism and hostility? — the transformation suggested is more than a matter of simply adopting differing nuances or rejecting unnecessary or erroneous conclusions traditionally drawn from Christian dogma. Post-Holocaust theology is actually engaged in challenging certain emphases found in the New Testament itself.

The work of **Peter von der Osten-Sacken**, a German theologian, exemplifies the possibilities and difficulties of such a transformation of Christian theology.[45] Considerable effort is expended to demonstrate that much of Jesus' teaching stands in harmony with Jewish teaching, is certainly not anti-Jewish, and affirms the fulfillment, not the abolition, of the law. Thus the easy opposition of law and gospel, which is characteristic of some parts of the Christian tradition, does not do justice to Jesus' own teaching. Furthermore, Jesus himself uses the Old Testament law and prophets as the basis of his critique of certain practices in Judaism. One must certainly agree with much of this attempt to demonstrate Jesus' Jewishness and rootedness in Judaism and the Old Testament.

One of the positive results of Jewish-Christian dialogue has been a renewed Christian recognition of the essential Jewishness of Jesus, a kind of re-Judaizing of Jesus.[46] This development is especially important when seen against the backdrop of the Nazi Aryan myth and the attempts of some modern Christian theologians to substitute philosophical systems in place of Jesus' historical rootedness in Judaism and the Old Testament. Jewish scholars have contributed to this growing awareness of Jesus' Jewishness by producing their own interpretations of the life and teaching of Jesus.[47]

45. Von der Osten-Sacken, *Christian-Jewish Dialogue: Theological Foundations* (Philadelphia: Fortress, 1986).
46. Cf. James H. Charlesworth, ed., *Jesus' Jewishness: Exploring the Place of Jesus within Early Judaism* (New York: American Interfaith Institute, 1991).
47. Jewish scholars such as David Flusser, Geza Vermes, and Ellis Rivkin have

But the attempt to produce a Christian theology that can simply coexist with Judaism requires more than an emphasis upon Jesus' Jewishness. It requires certain reinterpretations or limitations of aspects of New Testament teaching. For example, can one in the light of the New Testament affirm the following?

> For sinners and tax collectors, for the unclean in Israel and — in tendency — for the Gentiles, Jesus is the mediator who brings them into fellowship with God, or under his sovereignty. . . . For Jews, who already follow the way of God through their life with the Torah, Jesus does not have this function.[48]

Such a reinterpretation implies that Jews must recognize that Jesus brings sinners and Gentiles to God and thus carries out Israel's task of being a light to the nations (a position acceptable to many Jewish teachers), but Jews need not become disciples of Jesus. Because the Messiah has not yet appeared to Jewish Israel in the form expected by them, the Church may not demand of Jewish Israel a belief in the crucified Jesus as Messiah.[49] The Jews are the people of God apart from such a Christian belief. Such post-Holocaust theology creates two covenants coexisting as different religions, yet compatible.

A second example concerns the traditional Christian belief in the deity of Jesus Christ. Von der Osten-Sacken observes that the tendency to deify Jesus is seen only in a few parts of the New Testament, especially in the Gospel of John, and he rejects this tendency in favor of a subordinationist christology. In other words, he tries to develop a doctrine of Christ that can be harmonized with Judaism's understanding of monotheism,[50] rather than maintain the trinitarian under-

---

written significant works on the life of Jesus. Of course, major differences remain. Jewish scholars tend to keep Jesus within the limits of Judaism and to reclaim him as a Jewish teacher, prophet, and martyr. Everything in the gospel record that shatters the context of Judaism is usually ascribed to later Christian (Gentile-Hellenistic) origins. For critical responses to this tendency of recent Jewish scholarship, see Küng, *Judaism*, pp. 313-316; D. Harrington, "The Jewishness of Jesus: Facing Some Problems," in Charlesworth, ed., *Jesus' Jewishness*, pp. 121-136.

48. Von der Osten-Sacken, *Christian-Jewish Dialogue*, pp. 58f.
49. *Ibid.*, p. 93.
50. *Ibid.*, p. 130.

standing of monotheism, which affirms that Jesus, as the Incarnate Word, is of one substance with the Father. At best, von der Osten-Sacken can allow that Jesus was appointed to be "God" for the Gentiles if this is understood as analogous to the Jewish tradition, which considered Moses to be "God" for Pharaoh. That is, "God" is a title of function rather than essence. With such a reinterpretation, the only real difference between Jewish and Christian belief is the Christian claim that the future Messiah of Israel will be Jesus when he appears in glory, a Messiah whose cross and resurrection are essential for the redemption of the world. While Professor Lapide can toy with the *possibility* of an identity of the future Messiah with Jesus, since in Judaism the identity of the Messiah is unknown, he cannot accept the Christian understanding of the cross. Within Judaism the cross of Jesus can be viewed only as an instance of the general teaching of the suffering of the righteous. That is, Jesus suffered martyrdom just as many other righteous persons have suffered.

A major reason for the argument that Christian theology must grant the validity of Judaism has been the more recent recognition that Judaism also contains a doctrine of grace. The older criticism of Judaism as based simply on works-righteousness in contrast to Christianity, which is based on salvation by grace alone, is generally recognized to be founded on a simplistic and even inaccurate characterization. Judaism also acknowledges the grace of God in establishing his covenant with Israel.[51] In fact, Professor Lapide asserts that for Judaism salvation is considered to be "God's exclusive prerogative." The Torah is only the guideline for the way of life that God has given and is decidedly "*not* a means of achieving salvation, for Judaism knows of no such means."[52] Judaism, it is claimed, is a religion that stresses salvation by grace alone just as much as Christianity does. But even if one grants the truth that Judaism acknowledges God's grace in the establishment of the covenant, is its understanding of the role and function of grace the same as in Christianity? Is it accurate to suggest that "Israel lives out its relationship to God with the help of the Torah,

51. Cf. E. P. Sanders, *Paul and Palestinian Judaism* (Philadelphia: Fortress, 1977); von der Osten-Sacken, *Christian-Jewish Dialogue*, pp. 28-32.

52. P. Lapide, "The Rabbi from Tarsus," in P. Lapide and P. Stuhlmacher, *Paul: Rabbi and Apostle* (Minneapolis: Augsburg, 1984), pp. 37f.

just as the Christian Church lives out its own relationship with the help of Jesus"?[53]

It is instructive to note that in the same essay in which Professor Lapide claims that Judaism is an advocate of "pure grace," he goes on to criticize Paul for adopting the belief of "marginal Jewish circles" on original sin because such belief means that salvation is passively received, a view emphatically rejected by Judaism. Instead, Judaism believes that human beings are "active partners and free co-workers" and that salvation is in effect their own responsibility. The Pauline and subsequent Augustinian view of salvation is clearly rejected by Lapide as contrary to Judaism:

> The key word in the Jewish teaching about God is reconciliation, which must start with human beings if it is to reach God. Not redemption which comes from above . . . but repentance and contrition which come from below, rising like a well-spring out of the heart towards God.[54]

Obviously, such a view represents a significantly different understanding of both the necessity and function of grace in granting salvation than the view found in the New Testament and in the Christian Church. And Rabbi Lapide's position is not unique to himself but stands in direct continuity with traditional Judaism. As evidence we point to E. E. Urbach's discussion of the traditional Jewish teaching that it is repentance that brings about redemption/salvation. Urbach notes that for Paul this is not so because it is the Redeemer who puts transgressions away (Romans 11:26, a position Urbach describes as antinomian). In contrast to Pauline teaching, Urbach summarizes traditional rabbinic teaching: "If repentance alone makes redemption possible and brings it near, then there is no need for the messianic sufferings."[55]

---

53. Von der Osten-Sacken, *Christian-Jewish Dialogue,* p. 32.

54. P. Lapide, "The Rabbi from Tarsus," p. 46. In a similar vein, Samuel Sandmel, a Jewish rabbi much interested in Jewish-Christian dialogue, wrote: "We believe that man must make his own atonement, not have atonement wrought for him." *We Jews and Jesus* (London: Victor Gollancz, 1965), pp. 46f.

55. E. E. Urbach, *The Sages: Their Concepts and Beliefs* (Jerusalem: Magnes, 1979), p. 671.

Thus, even if one grants that Judaism also speaks of grace in connection with the establishment of the covenant and the giving of the Torah, it is equally obvious that the Jewish understanding of the nature, necessity, and role of grace in salvation is so significantly different that it cancels out the need for a suffering Messiah. Not only does Judaism reject the claims to deity on the part of Jesus, it also rejects the necessity of the cross because salvation on the basis of Torah is within one's own grasp. Hence a Jesus acceptable to Judaism can be a Jesus who functions only as a teacher of law and wisdom but not as Savior and Lord.

Is it possible, then, for these two religions each simply to grant the theological validity of the other as required in a two-covenant theology? They can do so only by assuming that the salvation of Jews and of Gentiles are two completely different processes. The difficulty with that assumption is that both Judaism and Christianity make universal claims about the human condition and thus in essence necessarily disagree with each other.

This disagreement is heightened by the fact that both Judaism and Christianity claim the Old Testament — the *Tanach* of the Jews — as the divinely given warrant for their respective positions. Understandably, Judaism bristles at distinctively Christian interpretations of the Old Testament because they consider the Tanach to be the canonical scriptures that God gave to them, whose interpretation only they really know. But for the Christian, as it was for the apostle Paul who converted from Judaism, the Old Testament can only be properly understood in the light of the revelation that occurred in the person and work of Jesus Christ. This revelation not only brought about an understanding of the Old Testament that at key points differs from that found in Judaism, but it also claims that this new understanding is not merely a reinterpretation but a revelation of the original intention in the mind of God. Obviously, neither side grants the view of the other equal validity. To do so would be to contradict one's own religious commitments at their deepest level.

In this connection it is important to be clear about terminology. Often in Jewish-Christian dialogue one hears certain Christian theologians speak of the Old Testament as Jewish or as part of the Jewish tradition. For example, von der Osten-Sacken speaks of Jesus criticizing certain Jewish practices as "a judgment made on [the basis of] the foundations of Judaism itself," or as an answer "out of the Jewish tradition itself," because Jesus bases his critical judgments on the Old Testament.[56] Is clarity enhanced by the use of such terminology? While Judaism is able to accept some of Jesus' criticisms based on the Old Testament, it cannot accept the interpretation of the Old Testament that undergirds claims about Jesus' status made by himself or others. To claim that Christian use of the Old Testament is in fact a use of *Jewish* tradition turns Judaism on its head. Clarity can be enhanced only by recognizing that both Judaism and Christianity claim Tanach–Old Testament as the basis for their essential teachings and that, therefore, it is not useful to refer to the Old Testament as Jewish (if that implies Judaism). Instead, Judaism and Christianity are in fact at key points competing interpretations of the proper meaning of the Old Testament. Both arise from it, but each disagrees with the other concerning its divine intention. There seems to be no way around that reality.

How then does one write about Jesus and Israel in this last decade of the twentieth century? While I am aware of contemporary Jewish sensitivities sharpened by the Holocaust, I am unable to follow in the footsteps of those theologians who revise Christian teaching by rejecting parts of the New Testament as inconsistencies, outright errors, or claims made in the heat of the controversy during the original separation of Church from Synagogue, claims that are no longer valid.[57] I would hope that as the perspectives of the New Testament unfold in this book that none of these perspectives will be interpreted as anti-Semitic or even as anti-Judaism, at least not in the civil or political sense of anti-Judaism. This book will be a sustained argument about the centrality of Jesus in the fulfillment of the Old Testament and thus will unavoidably be an implicit argument with Judaism on several key issues. Without a drastic reshaping of the New Testament, I do not see how that can be avoided.

56. Von der Osten-Sacken, *Christian-Jewish Dialogue,* p. 54. See also J. Pawlikowski, *Jesus and the Theology of Israel* (Wilmington: Glazier, 1980), pp. 12f., for a similar use of "Judaism" to represent Israel and the Old Testament.

57. Erich Grässer correctly asks whether the two ways of salvation assumed by the "two-covenant" theologians can be justified by the New Testament. He thinks they cannot because such a theology assumes that recent historical events, that is, the Holocaust, are revelatory acts of God on a par with the cross of Christ, because God has one people, not two, and because there is one mediator and thus allegiance to Torah cannot bypass Christ. "Zwei Heilswege?" in *Der Alte Bund im Neuen* (Tübingen: Mohr, 1985), pp. 212-230.

Of course, those who hold to the New Testament teaching must take care that neither their teaching nor their rhetoric produces contempt for the Jewish people.

Von der Osten-Sacken asserts that "a theology of proclamation is anti-Jewish or hostile to the Jews if it sees the life of the Jewish people in its present relationship to God solely under the sign of judgment or death (or both), interpreting the promise as having lost its present-day efficacy."[58] The key term in this description of "anti-Jewish" is the word "solely." Since I hold with the apostle Paul that the category of election still applies to the Jewish people, even those who do not now believe in Jesus, I agree that one cannot speak solely of judgment and death.[59] But in contrast with much contemporary two-covenant theology, I believe that the biblical category of judgment continues to be important. Of course, speaking of judgment, as do the Gospels and Paul, raises contemporary suspicions of being anti-Jewish. But those who believe in the cross of Christ should certainly know that the judgments of God cannot be used directly to justify either human judgments or contempt for others.

Rabbi David Flusser suggests that Christian theologians should not be too concerned about religious or theological positions held by Judaism since "it was not a religion that was chosen but a group of human beings, not the Jewish religion but Israel."[60] While I agree that it is necessary to distinguish the Jewish people (Israel) from the Jewish religion (Judaism), I do not believe that anyone can isolate the Jewish people as Israel from essential confessional beliefs. Both the Old Testament teaching on the relationship of covenant and people and the comparable New Testament understanding of what it means to be Israel imply that neither race nor physical descent provides a sufficient basis for understanding the identity of Israel.[61] Therefore this book focuses on religious or confessional claims and will ask: Who is Jesus? What

---

58. Von der Osten-Sacken, *Christian-Jewish Dialogue*, p. 14.

59. This difficult issue is discussed below in chapter VI.

60. D. Flusser, "Forward: Reflections of a Jew on a Christian Theology of Judaism," in C. Thoma, *A Christian Theology of Judaism* (New York: Paulist, 1980), p. 91.

61. The question of the biblical definition of "Israel" runs through each chapter of the present volume, but it is most explicit in chapters II and VI.

is his relationship to Israel and to the Old Testament with its law and its promises? What is his relationship to the promises concerning the temple, the land, and Jerusalem? What — according to the New Testament — should both Jews and Gentiles think of him?

CHAPTER II

Jesus and Israel:
A Question of Identity

W ho is Israel? Should that even be a question? For many it is not. The answer for them is plain, almost self-evident. Israel refers to the Jews, either to the Jews in the State of Israel or to Jews wherever they are found. And everybody knows who a Jew is. It is simply a matter of ancestry or religion or of some combination of the two. But is it that easy? The Old Testament prophets and the debate going on in Judaism today indicate that it is not.

Israel in history has always been like a question waiting for an answer. Whenever those who claimed to be Israel assumed that Israel was a fixed and static entity, a people self-evident to all, the prophets issued strong warnings. The promises given to Israel were not like automatic guarantees to be received apart from faith and obedience. Consequently, because of Israel's historical disobedience, the prophets announced that in the end it will be the remnant who is saved (Isaiah 10:20-23; Amos 9; Micah 7:18). Therefore, "not all Israelites truly belong to Israel" (Romans 9:6) is not only a Pauline teaching but a summary of the prophetic warnings of the entire Old Testament. Claiming Abraham as father was never a sufficient basis for claiming the covenant promises, for "God is able from these stones to raise up children to Abraham" (Matthew 3:9). Israel in history is a question awaiting the answer that corresponds to Israel's calling.

The shape of that answer is a subject of vigorous debate in contemporary Judaism.[1] There the form of the question is: Who is a Jew? The answers vary greatly and contradict each other. Some claim that a Jew is one who is born a Jew, while others assert that no one can be born a Jew because being a Jew is a matter of decision, a matter of religion or of fulfilling a messianic purpose. Defining "Israel" or "Jew" is, then, an extremely difficult task.

One of the most troublesome issues confronting the modern State of Israel has been the question, who is a Jew? Israel's Law of Return grants automatic citizenship to any immigrant who was born of a Jewish mother or who has converted to Judaism. The criterion of parentage has been easier to apply. Under it, even a Jewish atheist remains a Jew. The conversion criterion has been more difficult to apply because Orthodox Jews demand that conversion be according to the halakah (laws) as interpreted by Orthodoxy. Since the government basically follows Orthodox precepts in such matters as marriages and conversions, even though only about 15% of Israelis are even observant, much less Orthodox, this issue continues to be a divisive cause of heated political debate and controversial court cases. Still as recently as 1986, the Israeli Supreme Court has not granted the Orthodox position. Instead, it has ruled that any immigrant not born of a Jewish mother but converted to Judaism according to any of its recognized forms must be granted the right of citizenship. Because it is a modern secular state embracing religious and non-religious Jews, Israel has thus found it difficult to say with precision who is a Jew.[2]

The contemporary dispute about who is a Jew has its roots in the traditional Jewish answer. Even though the element of ethnicity has always played a significant role in defining a Jew, the traditional understanding also emphasized allegiance to the Torah. From the destruction of Jerusalem in A.D. 70 until the modern period, being a Jew meant adherence to rabbinic Judaism, devotion to the study of the law, and observing the 613 precepts. That this was the norm can be deduced from the requirements for conversion to Judaism. The convert was

---

1. Cf. J. Jocz, *The Jewish People and Jesus Christ After Auschwitz* (Grand Rapids: Baker, 1981).

2. *Encyclopedia Judaica* (New York: 1971-72) IX, p. 395; *Time Magazine*, January 19, 1987, p. 75.

required to accept the Torah, including the Oral Law, that is, the rabbinic interpretation of the law, and to be circumcised if a male, and to be immersed. One who became a Jew was expected to live in accord with halakhah, the Jewish legal system or way of life. Nevertheless, the traditional definition taught that neither apostasy from the Jewish way of life nor heretical belief could negate a person's identity as a Jew. Even if one denied the divine character of the Torah, the coming resurrection, or God's involvement in human affairs, one would not thereby cease to be a Jew. Of course, such heresy would subject one to rabbinic judgment, to exclusion from the synagogue, and even to social ostracism. And it was declared that the heretic or apostate would not receive the blessings promised in the life to come. In spite of all this, the saying held true: Once a Jew always a Jew.[3] To make this point in an extreme manner: If one were stoned for blasphemy, that very judgment would stand as proof that the person so judged was still a Jew, for stoning did not apply to blasphemy by non-Jews. Hence Jewishness, though closely related to the beliefs and practices of Judaism, must be distinguished from Judaism. Since the uniformity of modern Judaism has been fragmented, this distinction becomes even more significant as secular and atheistic Jews argue for a definition broad enough to include them.

Today many scholars (including Jewish scholars) point out that rabbinic Judaism was not always the norm. Prior to A.D. 70 and the destruction of Jerusalem, Judaism was highly variegated and comprised a "great medley of cross-currents."[4] First-century Judaism contained many different understandings of what it meant to be a Jew. In fact, some argue that even Christianity is a form of Judaism — not, of course, a form of rabbinic Judaism because, in opposing Pharisaism, Christianity was opposing the essence of what became rabbinic Judaism. But Christianity can be seen as a continuation of messianic or prophetic

---

3. This summary is based upon L. A. Schiffman, *Who Was a Jew? Rabbinic and Halakhic Perspectives on the Jewish-Christian Schism* (Hoboken: KTAV, 1985).

4. P. Sigal lists fourteen groups and suggests that there were probably many more. *The Emergence of Contemporary Judaism* (Pittsburgh: Pickwick, 1980) I, p. 383.

5. Even a Jewish rabbi, Philip Sigal, can claim that "Both [Paul and Jesus] taught a form of Judaism which was understandable within the messianic context in which they preached, but was not persuasive to those who did not believe the Messiah had manifested himself." *Emergence of Contemporary Judaism* I, p. 377.

Judaism.[5] Such is the claim today of Messianic Jews, that is, Jewish Christians who have not assimilated to Gentile forms of Christianity. They claim to be, in fact, "completed" Jews, though they reject rabbinic Judaism. Belief in Jesus the Messiah completes their Jewishness.

Who then is a Jew? Since there is no unanimity of opinion among contemporary Jews, one who is not a Jew should not attempt to resolve that matter. Therefore, I prefer a different form of the question. Messianic Jews like to say that in asking Who is Jesus? one is asking Who is a Jew?[6] But I would rather suggest that in asking Who is Jesus? one is asking Who is Israel? This altered form of the question does not deny the legitimacy of the Messianic Jewish viewpoint, which asserts that the true definition of what it means to be a Jew can be found in Jesus only. I could agree with that claim from my Christian point of view. But there are two reasons for preferring to ask Who is Israel? First, the term "Jew" is ambiguous. Though it can be defined as synonymous with the biblical concept of Israel (and is so defined by Messianic Jews), "Jew" or "Jewish" in fact embraces religious and secular Jews and is also used of Judaism as a religious, social, and political reality. Therefore, both in the Bible and in contemporary usage, "Jew" and "Jewish" are the terms usually applied to these realities by outsiders.[7] Second, though the Bible can fill the term "Jew" with spiritual significance (as in Romans 2:29), "Jew" is usually used more neutrally to designate simply a people or a nation or even, in the case of the Gospel of John, the official opponents of Jesus. The Bible uses "Israel" as the more common designation of the true people of God, his elect community, the people of his covenant.

If Israel is the elect people, those with whom God has entered into covenant, who then is this Israel? If God has made covenants with Israel and has promised that people all the covenant blessings, how must Israel be defined? Who will actually inherit the promises? The entire Scripture, both Old and New Testaments, is a record of God's activity in creating and defining Israel and thereby answering our question.

That question is basic in interpreting prophecy. Obviously, the

6. For example, J. Jocz, *The Jewish People,* p. 126.
7. Cf. *Theological Dictionary of the New Testament* (Grand Rapids: Eerdmans, 1964-76) III, pp. 356ff.; *Encyclopedia Judaica* X, p. 22.

people to whom God makes promises must be the people who receive the fulfillment of the promises. The Israel of promise must be the Israel of fulfillment. Therefore, it should come as no surprise that the New Testament begins at this point. The Gospel of Matthew, both in its structure and in its themes, is an extended answer to this question, Who is Israel?

A Genealogical Answer

Lists of ancestors, of begetters and begats, seem like a boring way to begin a book, yet the New Testament begins with a genealogy! That should give us pause, and our feelings of boredom should not become a license for skipping over the genealogy to discover what Matthew really wants to say about Jesus. What he really wants to say is said beginning in this carefully constructed genealogy. Matthew's choice of which ancestors of Jesus to mention establishes the particular significance that he ascribes to Jesus. In the ancient world genealogies were used not only to record social and personal relationships but also to establish religious and political claims. Consequently, in reading an ancient genealogy, we must discover the purpose and understand the function for which it was composed.[8] Since no ancient genealogy is a complete record — it was always necessary to narrow the list down to a selection of names — various genealogies could be composed for one person depending on the claims or perspectives intended. Thus Luke's genealogy of Jesus, with its focus on Jesus as the Son of Adam, the beginning of the new humanity, differs from Matthew's. Matthew has his own perspective on the meaning and significance of Jesus.

Genealogies survey centuries in a few lines. Thousands of years of history are compressed and given focus by a genealogical tree. So the Gospel of Matthew begins with a focused survey of the history that explains the significance of Jesus and establishes his claims. The title given to the genealogy is "The Book of the Origin (or Generations) of Jesus Christ, the Son of David, the Son of Abraham." Since that title,

8. Cf. R. R. Wilson, "The Old Testament Genealogies and Recent Research," *Journal of Biblical Literature* 94 (1975), pp. 164-189.

"The Book of the Origin," is found also in Genesis 2:4, where it is used of the creation of heaven and earth, and in Genesis 5:1, where it is used of the descendants of Adam, some interpreters suggest that Matthew intended to declare by that title that with the coming of Jesus a new creation had occurred or at least a new humanity had begun.[9] Although such claims are made explicitly by Luke and Paul, Matthew has a more limited focus. He proclaims Jesus as the Son of David and the Son of Abraham. Such sonship undoubtedly has significance for a new creation and a new humanity (cf. Matthew 28:18-20), but here Matthew is thinking not of a parallel to Genesis 2 and 5 but of a fulfillment of Genesis 12 and II Samuel 7. Indeed a new age has begun, but it is new because after centuries of Israel's failure the covenant promises of God to Abraham and David are finding fulfillment in their Son, Jesus Christ.

God's covenant with Abraham lays the foundation for the entire ensuing history of redemption recorded in the Scriptures. So Matthew begins his genealogy of Jesus at that point. God promised Abraham, "I will make of you a great nation, and I will bless you, and make your name great, so that you will be a blessing. I will bless those who bless you, and the one who curses you I will curse; and in you all the families of the earth shall be blessed" (Genesis 12:2f.). Later God renewed that promise in covenant form and explicitly included Abraham's descendants (17:7) and declared that through Abraham's "offspring shall all the nations of the earth gain blessing for themselves" (22:18).

By linking Jesus to Abraham, Matthew declares that God's promise of blessing for the nations is now being fulfilled through Jesus. The early hint of this fulfilled promise is given in the coming of the magi to worship Jesus (Matthew 2). Later Jesus prophetically announces that "many will come from east and west and will eat with Abraham and Isaac and Jacob in the kingdom of heaven" (8:11). Then at the conclu-

---

9. Cf. W. D. Davies, *The Setting of the Sermon on the Mount* (Cambridge: Cambridge University Press, 1964), pp. 67ff.; D. Hill, *The Gospel of Matthew* (Grand Rapids: Eerdmans, 1981), pp. 74f. F. D. Bruner suggests that the opening title may even be telescopic, "serving as three titles at once: 'The Book of Genesis' (Matt 1–28), 'The Book of the Birth Stories' (Matt 1–2), and 'The Book of the Genealogy' (Matt 1:1-17)." *The Christbook: A Historical-Theological Commentary: Matthew 1–12* (Waco: Word, 1987), p. 2.

sion of the Gospel Jesus commissions his disciples to "make disciples of all nations" (28:19). Through Jesus, the Son of Abraham, all nations are being blessed and the promise to Abraham is being fulfilled.

If Jesus is the one through whom the promise is being fulfilled, then he can lay claim to being Abraham's true descendant, the one who is what a descendant of Abraham is supposed to be. Jesus, then, is true Israel, the one who does everything that Israel was supposed to do and who is everything that Israel was supposed to be. Historical Israel had failed, and the promises had not come to fulfillment through the Israelites. Instead, the prophets had decreed judgment and exile, and Isaiah had declared that, though Israel had become as numerous as "the sand of the sea," only a remnant would return (Isaiah 10:22). Now Matthew proclaims that the judgment of Israel by exile finds its answer and hope in the birth of Jesus ("from the deportation to Babylon to the Messiah, fourteen generations," Matthew 1:17). Jesus is the remnant who represents the hope and rebirth of Israel announced by the prophets. He is Israel, Abraham's Son.

A second Old Testament promise is equally important for the shape and scope of Matthew's genealogy. God promised David that his house and kingdom would be secure forever and that the throne of his offspring would be established forever (II Samuel 7:8-16). Although this covenant with David is subordinate to God's covenant with Abraham, the fulfillment of this promise to David becomes the means by which the promise to Abraham is fulfilled. The promised Son of David will be the representative embodiment of Israel through whom the nations will be blessed. The prophet Isaiah said as much already when he described the rebirth of Israel as occurring through "a shoot . . . from the stump of Jesse" (Isaiah 11:1). The Son of David, as Israel's king, represents true Israel. Therefore, the genealogy of Jesus in Matthew is a Davidic genealogy.[10] The royal lineage from Judah (Genesis 49:8-12) to Jesus interests Matthew: Though he compresses the genealogy to indicate that the kings of Israel had failed and that the exile had effaced

---

10. Many have suggested that Matthew's schematic division of Jesus' genealogy into three sets of fourteen (1:17) may also contain a hint of its Davidic character since the numerical value of David's name in Hebrew (the consonants *d, w,* and *d*) is fourteen ($d = 4$, $w = 6$).

the visible signs of the kingdom, still the promise to David had not failed because it finds fulfillment in Jesus, David's Son. David's Son is the Son of God (II Samuel 7:14), and his throne is eternal.

The focus of Matthew's genealogy is clear. The significance of Jesus is deeply rooted in the history of Old Testament Israel, so deeply that the blessings promised to Old Testament Israel find their fulfillment only through him. He is Israel, the representative embodiment of true Israel and Israel's king. Undergirding this understanding of Jesus lies the biblical idea of corporate person, the idea that one person can represent a group or a nation and that the nation can be representatively embodied in one person. Consequently, the sin of one can be the sin of many (for example, the sin of Adam or the sin of Achan) and the righteousness of one can be the righteousness of many (Isaiah 53:11). From this perspective of corporate person, Israel as the people of God in search of its destiny finds its answer in the One who is both true Israel and Israel's king, the Son of Abraham and the Son of David.

The focused claim of Matthew's genealogy is clear, but is not the basis of the claim a bit surprising? Can the answer to the question "Who is Israel?" be established merely by a genealogical record, even if it is a royal genealogy? The prophets always declared that a genealogical claim is by itself insufficient to establish the identity of Israel. John the Baptist warned, "Do not presume to say to yourselves, 'We have Abraham as our ancestor'; for I tell you, God is able from these stones to raise up children to Abraham" (Matthew 3:9). God's promises are for Israel, but Israel is not established simply by birthright. The blessings are not automatically guaranteed by preserving the purity of an Israelite or Jewish gene pool or an impeccable family tree.[11] Much more is involved — and this is hinted at in Matthew's genealogy of Jesus.

This hint comes with the women listed in Jesus' family tree. The mere fact that women are included is astonishing since it was not customary, but even more astonishing are the women chosen to be

---

11. E. A. Speiser, a Jewish commentator, asserts the contrary: "The ultimate purpose of biblical genealogies was to establish the superior strain of the line through which the biblical way of life was transmitted from generation to generation. In other words, the integrity of the mission was to be safeguarded in transmission, the purity of the content protected by the quality of the container." *Genesis* (Anchor Bible; Garden City: Doubleday, 1964), pp. 93f. Matthew disagrees with that emphasis.

included. They are not the four famous matriarchs of Judaism — Sarah, Rebekah, Rachel, and Leah — but four women who are foreigners and not especially "holy": Tamar and Rahab the Canaanites, Ruth the Moabite, and Bathsheba, the wife of a Hittite. At the very least, Matthew is saying that the true descendants of Abraham are not preserved by their purity of descent. As the people of God, Israel was always intended to be and to become a universal people, not limited by racial purity. These four women testify to God's initiative in incorporating outsiders into Israel and to his astonishingly strange providence in placing these women into the royal lineage in which lay the hope of Israel. Thus even in this genealogical record the emphasis falls not on human initiative and planning but on God's intervention as it overcomes human obstacles and historical dilemmas on behalf of the Messiah who was to come. God decides who belongs to Israel.[12]

God's election shapes the genealogy of true Israel, and that election becomes especially apparent in the fifth woman mentioned, "Mary, of whom Jesus was born, who is called the Messiah" (Matthew 1:16). The genealogy notes a "holy irregularity" in describing Jesus' ancestry. Joseph is simply "the husband of Mary," not the begetter of Jesus. Jesus was born of Mary. Thus the claims made for Jesus on the basis of descent through Joseph are legal claims because Joseph is his *legal* father. The nature of this "holy irregularity" is not disclosed in the genealogy but in the story that follows: Jesus was conceived in Mary by the Holy Spirit (1:18, 20). There is a discontinuity within the continuities of his genealogy. Therefore, though he is linked to the history of his people and is comprehensible only within the interconnectedness of that history, yet he is beyond history, beyond its potentialities and possibilities. He is more than his ancestry could produce. He represents the intervention of God, the creative work of the Holy Spirit, which was active once in creation and promised again in the messianic salvation of the end time.[13] God provided what human history could not.

12. R. Brown allows a subordinate emphasis on these four women as foreigners but favors the proposal that stresses the irregular or even scandalous union of these four with their husbands together with the initiative taken by these women. They foreshadow, then, the scandal and initiative of Mary. *The Birth of the Messiah* (Garden City: Doubleday, 1977), pp. 73f.

13. Cf. Davies, *Setting of the Sermon on the Mount,* p. 71.

Israel came into being in the mysterious election of God and depends for its continuing existence on God's gracious and miraculous actions. Therefore, the definition of Israel can never be merely a matter of proper genealogical connections, even when God chooses to use such connections. Matthew's genealogy of Jesus demonstrates that in the end, and often along the way, the genealogical connections to Abraham were insufficient and that God had to intervene to preserve a people for himself. Jesus Christ is that intervention on our behalf. In his person and in his work, Jesus is all that Israel was meant to be because in Jesus God himself takes the place of his covenant partner in order to secure the continuity of his covenant with Israel. Jesus is Emmanuel, God-with-us. Consequently, the definition of true Israel is forever shaped by this action. Israel can never again be defined apart from Jesus Christ.

Matthew's genealogy of Jesus signals that a new beginning has been inaugurated, a new era in Israel's history and a new era in the history of the world, for in Jesus God's centuries-old promises to Abraham and David have entered upon their historical fulfillment. After centuries of oppression and disappointment, of disobedience and failure in mission, Israel is renewed and the nations will be blessed. Through his providential guidance and miraculous grace, God has answered the question, "Who is Israel?"

A Geographical Answer

Can geography shed light on the question Who is Israel? Normally we would not expect a significant answer from that direction. But because the promises and actions of God in the Old Testament are closely associated with nations, certain geographical areas, such as Egypt, become prophetically significant. Egypt was the classic land of refuge for God's Old Testament people, as well as the classic oppressor of Israel. Once God's astonishing acts of providence had placed the patriarch Joseph in Egypt "in order to preserve a numerous people" (Genesis 50:20), so now again his faithful providence leads another Joseph to Egypt to protect the life of another who is Israel (Matthew 2:13-15). Egypt serves God's providence once again as a haven from the storms raging in Palestine. But Egypt had also been Israel's great oppressor, and God had intervened by signs and wonders to lead Israel out of Egypt into the promised land. So now, once again, Jesus is prophetically called forth out of Egypt with overtones of a new exodus, one that will finally bring to an end the oppression of God's people and fulfill the promises God made to Israel.

Thus Old Testament stories associated with Egypt shape Matthew's presentation of the story of Jesus. What happened once in Israel's history happens again as God brings the history of Israel to its promised fulfillment. Persons, events, and even places that were important in the redemptive history of the past become important again in the redemptive history of the present because what happened in the past provides types of the person and life of Jesus.[14] Thus there are resemblances between the birth stories of Moses and Jesus. Both were threatened by a king's decree at birth. Just as Moses' birth story in Exodus 2 is significant for the life and salvation of Old Testament Israel, so Jesus' birth story in Matthew 2 is significant for the life and salvation of a renewed Israel. Like Moses, Jesus is protected by God so that an exodus out of bondage can occur. There are thus echoes of a Moses' typology in Matthew 2, but even so the figure of Moses does not loom large in Matthew's account.[15] Nowhere does Matthew quote specific proof texts linking Jesus directly to Moses. Matthew is interested not so much in Moses as in the Israel that Moses represents.

This focus on Israel is seen clearly in the word of prophecy that Matthew attaches to the story of the flight into Egypt (Matthew 2:14f.). On the surface his use of Hosea 11:1 for this event in Jesus' life seems out of place. The story is about a flight into Egypt, about a safe haven, about God's providential protection, but the verse from Hosea is about the original exodus from Egypt, about escape from slavery, about God's

---

14. A. B. Mickelsen defines typology as "a correspondence in one or more respects between a person, event, or thing in the Old Testament and a person, event, or thing closer to or contemporaneous with a New Testament writer. . . . The correspondence is present because God controls history." *Interpreting the Bible* (Grand Rapids: Eerdmans, 1963), p. 237. L. Goppelt argues that a "heightening" of the type in its fulfillment in the antitype is an essential ingredient in biblical typology. *Typos: The Typological Interpretation of the Old Testament in the New* (Grand Rapids: Eerdmans, 1982), p. 18.

15. Cf. B. Childs, *The Book of Exodus* (Philadelphia: Westminster, 1974), pp. 21-26.

providential deliverance. Why does Matthew attach a prophetic word about the exodus from Egypt to a story about an entrance into Egypt? Perhaps the answer lies in the symbolism of Egypt in the history of redemption. Egypt is remembered as the land of bondage from which God's people came forth to enter upon a new life of freedom. Even though in these early chapters of Matthew the presence of the cross in Jesus' life is seen in Herod's massacre of the infants and in the necessary flight into Egypt and not in oppression by Egypt,[16] still Jesus must come forth from Egypt as did Israel of old. God had promised that his people would once again be reborn, renewed, and restored in a new exodus.

Matthew's use of Hosea 11:1 is indeed remarkable. Without the addition of this verse to the story, the theme of God's providential care would be a sufficient interpretation of Jesus' brief stay in Egypt,[17] but the quotation from this text about the exodus sheds surprisingly new light on the significance of the story. Matthew intends Hosea 11:1, understood in its original context, to be the key to the story.

Most readers are surprised when they turn to Hosea 11:1 and read: "When Israel was a child, I loved him, and out of Egypt I called my son." This verse does not look like a prophecy about the future. Instead it refers to an event in Israel's past, to the original exodus from Egypt. How can Matthew use this verse referring to Israel's past as a prophetic word coming to fulfillment in Jesus' life?[18] The answer is found in the

16. The presence of the cross in the early life of Jesus is clearly seen by John Calvin: "We must still remember God's purpose, to keep His Son, from the beginning under the elements of the cross, as this was to be His means of redeeming the Church." *Harmony of the Gospels* (Grand Rapids: Eerdmans, 1972) I, p. 104.

17. R. H. Gundry favors such an interpretation even with the addition of Hosea 11:1. He argues that "The clause immediately preceding the present quotation stresses residence in Egypt till Herod's death, not departure from Egypt after Herod's death. Therefore Matthew is not highlighting Jesus' later departure as a new Exodus, but God's preservation of Jesus in Egypt as a sign of his divine sonship; God cares for Jesus as a father cares for his son." *Matthew: A Commentary on His Literary and Theological Art* (Grand Rapids: Eerdmans, 1982), p. 34. Such an interpretation, however, does not adequately take into account the literal meaning of Hosea 11:1 or its context.

18. Some scholars, in fact, accuse Matthew of ignoring the meaning and context of Hosea 11:1 and Jeremiah 31:15 (which is quoted in Matthew 2:18). Cf. S. L. Edgar, "Respect for Context in Quotations from the Old Testament," *New Testament Studies* 9 (1962), pp. 55-62. Others assert that "Matthew was only doing what Jewish teachers regularly did when he used prophecy this way," and that that way of using prophecy

way New Testament authors quote Old Testament texts. Frequently, texts are quoted as indicators of entire Old Testament contexts. The New Testament author selects a key verse with the understanding that this key verse carries with it into the New Testament the meaning it had in the original Old Testament context.[19] The verse quoted is not to be interpreted in isolation from its Old Testament context, and the context of Hosea 11:1 contains a promise for the future.

How can we discover this future implicitly contained in the reference to the past in Hosea 11:1? Hosea 11 is a formal complaint that God lodges against Israel, his son, because Israel has failed to respond to his love. Even though Israel had experienced God's liberating love in the exodus from Egypt, Israel spurned that love in favor of the fertility cult associated with the worship of Baal. For all the good that Israel had received Baal received the credit (v. 2). God's intention expressed in the exodus had not taken shape in history because of Israel's disobedience, and judgment had to be ordained, a new oppression, a return to Egypt, as it were, under the guise of exile to Assyria (v. 5). The first exodus from bondage ends in bondage renewed.

But Israel's disobedience followed by God's judgments cannot be the end of the matter. Because Israel's existence and security are based on God's love, a love so deep and so compassionate, God cannot and will not finally destroy his son (Hosea 11:8f.). Instead, God's love overcomes his wrath and, consequently, Israel's future return and security are assured.[20] Exile is not God's final word pronounced upon his son's disobedience. Return from exile is promised, a return from the land of Egypt (v. 11). Thus Hosea 11:1 speaks of a first exodus in order

---

is something that we can no longer legitimately do. Cf. W. Barclay, *Introduction to the First Three Gospels* (Philadelphia: Westminster, 1975), p. 163.

19. In his influential book *According to the Scriptures* (New York: Scribner, 1953), C. H. Dodd wrote: "Sections of the Old Testament Scriptures were understood by the Christian evangelists as *wholes,* and particular verses or sentences were sometimes quoted from them rather as pointers to the whole context than as constituting testimonials in and for themselves" (p. 126). Similarly, A. T. Hanson writes, "often we cannot appreciate the point they are making unless we study the context also." *The Living Utterances of God: The New Testament Exegesis of the Old* (London: Darton, Longman, and Todd, 1983), p. 38.

20. Cf. H. Wolff, *Hosea* (Philadelphia: Fortress, 1974), pp. 203f.

to point to a second. Because Israel's disobedience after the first exodus thwarted God's intention to create on earth "a priestly kingdom and a holy nation," God's chosen people (Exodus 19:6; cf. Deuteronomy 10:15), a new exodus must occur following judgment, a new exodus by which God will create on earth his true people, his obedient son. Thus God recalls the first exodus in Hosea 11:1 in order to promise a second. The first exodus and the second are intimately related in the love of God, because their intention is the same. The past is recalled to assure a future that will renew the past.

A question still remains. What is the future that Hosea announces? Was not Hosea's promise of a new exodus fulfilled when Israel returned from exile in 538 B.C.? Those who returned thought so initially, but subsequent history proved otherwise. Even though Israel returned from exile, its people continued to live under foreign domination. The hopes for the freedom promised by God always fell short of realization. The Maccabean revolt gained a brief period of political independence (142-63 B.C.) and stimulated high hope that finally God's promises were being realized, but the cruelty and inadequacy of the Maccabean descendants (the Hasmonean rulers) turned hope into despair, and Israel fell once more under foreign rule as Palestine became part of the Roman Empire. At the time of Jesus, Rome still ruled, and Israel knew that the promises of a new exodus had not yet been fulfilled. Certainly the prophets had promised more than Israel had yet experienced. True liberation and freedom awaited a new future, a new exodus from "Egypt."[21]

Jesus' stay in Egypt is the sign that the new future has begun. By declaring Hosea 11:1 fulfilled in this event, Matthew proclaims not only that Jesus is Israel, God's beloved Son, but also that the long awaited exodus has begun. By itself this story is only a symbol of the reality that Matthew wishes to proclaim. For it is finally through the cross that Jesus is acknowledged as God's Son and through the resurrection that Israel is gathered. But the shadow of the cross and the hint of promised deliverance are already contained in this early event in the life of Jesus.[22] In him the history of Israel is relived and fulfilled.

21. "Egypt" is the biblical symbol of the oppressor of God's people, whether it be the Assyria of Hosea 11:5 or those who crucified the Lord, as they are referred to in Revelation 11:8.

22. F. D. Bruner captures the thought succinctly: "Jesus goes down into Egypt

A second prophecy containing a geographical reference further indicates how Jesus relives and fulfills the history of Israel.[23] Matthew establishes a connection between Herod's killing of the infants and the earlier death and oppression of Israel in exile.[24] The prophet Jeremiah spoke of that exile and described its pathos poetically:

> A voice is heard in Ramah,
>   lamentation and bitter weeping.
> Rachel is weeping for her children;
>   she refuses to be comforted for her children,
> because they are no more.
>
> (Jeremiah 31:15)

Ramah was the scene of national grief as the captives of Judah and Jerusalem were gathered in chains to be sent in exile to Babylon (Jeremiah 40:1). Rachel, the favorite mother of Israel, had died centuries earlier and had been buried on the way from Bethel to Bethlehem-Ephrath, not far from Ramah. As Israel journeys into exile, the prophet "hears" Rachel weeping over the loss of her children. But the Lord instructs Rachel to stop weeping because "there is hope for your future" and her children will return (31:16-17). Israel did return from exile, but the oppression of the enemy continued unabated. Therefore, Matthew, like Jeremiah, hears Rachel still weeping over the loss of her children:

---

land (in a kind of prefigured crucifixion) and is brought up out again (in a kind of geographical resurrection) in order to inaugurate the New Exodus of the people of God, the definitive exodus, the exodus that will count this time for everyone." *The Christbook*, p. 59.

23. Speaking of the places mentioned in these two prophecies quoted in Matthew 2, Brown suggests that they "offer a theological history of Israel in geographical miniature. Just as Jesus sums up the history of the people named in his genealogy, so his earlier career sums up the history of these prophetically significant places." *Birth of the Messiah*, p. 217.

24. Some interpreters suggest that Matthew quotes this prophecy because of an association of Rachel's tomb with Ephrath (Genesis 35:19; 48:7) and Matthew's interest in Bethlehem. But when Matthew cites the prophecy about Bethlehem-Ephrath in 2:6, he omits the reference to Ephrath. Thus the connection seems not to be based on this association but rather on a typological relationship in which Jesus as the representative of corporate Israel relives Israel's history in order to accomplish its hopes. Cf. Gundry, *Matthew*, p. 36.

In Herod's slaughter of the infants the oppression and destruction of Israel still continues.[25] The hope promised to Rachel had not yet been fully realized. Matthew quotes Jeremiah 31:15 not only to establish the continuity of Israel's grief but also to signal the fulfillment of Israel's hope contained in its context. Jesus escapes the slaughter, and therein lies the fulfillment of Israel's hope. Since Jesus is now Israel, Abraham's true seed and God's true Son, God's promise to Rachel of a restored family is now on its way to fulfillment. The hope promised for her future is now being realized.[26] Jesus relives Israel's history and thereby restores Israel.

An Answer from Heaven

Direct answers from heaven are unusual even in the Bible. Matthew records only two instances of a voice from heaven, and in both instances the pronouncement is the same: "This is my Son, the Beloved, with whom I am well pleased," the second time with the command "listen to him!" (Matthew 3:17; 17:5). How should we understand this heavenly pronouncement concerning Jesus? The words of the pronouncement clearly echo Old Testament passages. But which passages? And what identity is given to Jesus by the heavenly voice?

The voice is, the first time, a response to the baptism of Jesus given because Jesus' baptism is an act of messianic fulfillment. John

25. Matthew exchanges his common introductory formula, "in order to fulfill," for "then was fulfilled what was spoken by the prophet Jeremiah." The slaughter of the infants was not required by prophecy, but its occurrence did continue the state of affairs described in Jeremiah 31:15. This continuation implies that the earlier return from exile was not the fulfillment of the promised hope.

26. B. Lindars characterizes Jeremiah 31:15 as "a prophecy of the reversal of grief." *New Testament Apologetic* (London: SCM, 1961), p. 218. A similar positive understanding of Matthew's use of this prophecy ("present sorrow is not the end of God's purpose") is found in R. V. G. Tasker, *The Old Testament in the New Testament* (Grand Rapids: Eerdmans, 1963), p. 44, and in Tasker's *The Gospel According to St. Matthew* (Grand Rapids: Eerdmans, 1961), pp. 43f. And J. B. Meier comments, "For the moment, innocent children die so that Jesus may be saved, but only so that the innocent Jesus may later die to save his people from their sins." *Matthew* (Wilmington: Glazier, 1980), p. 14.

was reluctant to baptize Jesus, but Jesus replied, "It is proper for us in this way to fulfill all righteousness" (Matthew 3:15). Because John's baptism symbolized God's standard of righteousness, sinners had to repent before being baptized. But Jesus had no sin and no need of repentance. Instead, Jesus declared that he would fulfill the righteousness symbolized by John's baptism. That is, he would actively carry out that righteousness in his life and thereby establish the righteousness of God's kingdom on earth.[27] In response to this action and declaration by Jesus, God sent the Spirit to qualify Jesus for his messianic task and then announced from heaven: "This is my Son, the Beloved, with whom I am well pleased."

Almost everyone agrees that this voice echoes Isaiah 42:1: "Here is my servant, whom I uphold, my chosen, in whom my soul delights," a verse that Matthew quotes later in a translation which parallels the voice from heaven, "my *beloved,* with whom my soul is well pleased" (Matthew 12:18). Thus it would appear from Matthew that the voice from heaven indeed echoes Isaiah 42:1. God promises in Isaiah 42 that he will place his spirit on this servant to qualify him for his messianic work and declares that this servant is his elect one, called in righteousness to bring the salvation of the covenant to the peoples of the world. Therefore, it seems obvious that the story of Jesus' baptism is intended to proclaim Jesus as God's anointed servant.

But who is this servant described by Isaiah? From the descriptions of the Servant of Yahweh found in various passages of Isaiah (Isaiah 42:1ff.; 44:1ff.; 52:13ff.), the best interpretation is one that identifies the servant as referring in some sense both to Israel and to one who by representing Israel renews Israel.[28] Thus, because the voice from heaven echoes Isaiah 42:1, it intends to identify Jesus as God's anointed servant,

27. D. Hill rightly argues on the basis of Matthew 21:32, which speaks of John the Baptist coming "in the way of righteousness," that "in the context of Jesus' baptism, the word 'righteousness' refers to the righteousness of life demanded of those who accepted that baptism." *The Gospel of Matthew* (Grand Rapids: Eerdmans, 1981), p. 96.

28. Though some scholars favor the individual reference and others the corporate reference, the majority would agree with John Bright's description of the servant figure: "The figure of the servant oscillates between the individual and the group. . . . the Servant? He is Israel; he is the true and loyal Israel; he is the great Servant who will be leader of the servant people — all in one!" *The Kingdom of God* (Nashville: Abingdon, 1953), pp. 150f.

his beloved Israel-Servant, who is well pleasing to God because of the righteousness that he fulfills.

The voice from heaven also echoes Psalm 2:7: "You are my son; today I have begotten you."[29] Psalm 2 is a royal psalm that announces the enthronement of the king of Israel in his universal rule over the nations of the world. This psalm reflects the covenant with David, in which God promises concerning David's descendant: "I will be a father to him, and he shall be a son to me" (II Samuel 7:14). This Davidic king of Israel, destined to become the ruler of the nations, is God's Son. Hence the voice from heaven announces that Jesus is this Davidic king whose throne is everlasting and whose kingdom embraces the nations of the world. However, the rule of this Messianic king will not be inaugurated with wrath and fire as John the Baptist expected, but by a humble servant who walks in the way of righteousness.

In the Gospel of Matthew, these two questions coincide: Who is Jesus? and Who is Israel? Jesus is Israel, and Israel is Jesus. From the genealogy to the voice from heaven, Matthew proclaims Jesus as Israel's king who fulfills the role assigned to Israel, God's servant. Because Old Testament Israel had not fulfilled its calling and righteousness had not sprung forth before all nations (Isaiah 61:11), God himself acted to place on earth the one who is both truly Israel and Israel's king so that the righteousness of his kingdom would be established.

A Wilderness Answer

The wilderness was important in the life of Israel since there Israel had been tested. Now that Jesus has been identified as Israel, he too must be tested. The test involves the basic question whether, as God's Son, he will love God with all his heart, soul, and strength (Deuteronomy

---

29. O. Cullmann and J. Jeremias have argued that the voice echoes only Isaiah 42:1 and that the word for "servant" can be translated also as "son." Cf. O. Cullmann, *The Christology of the New Testament* (Philadelphia: Westminster, 1959), p. 16; J. Jeremias, *Abba* (Göttingen: VandenHoeck und Ruprecht, 1966), pp. 191-216. But their argument is not convincing. Cf. I. H. Marshall, "Son of God or Servant of Yahweh? — A Reconsideration of Mark 1:11," *New Testament Studies* 15 (1969), pp. 326-336.

6:5). Will Jesus be faithful to the covenant that God made with Israel and perfectly keep God's commandments? To discover the answer the Spirit leads Jesus into the wilderness to be tempted as Israel was tempted. Jesus relives Israel's wilderness experience to demonstrate "what was in [his] heart" (Deuteronomy 8:2).

The evidence for this understanding of Matthew's temptation story is found both in its placement after the announcement of the voice from heaven and in the many parallels between the situation of Jesus and the situation of Israel in the wilderness. The story follows immediately after God's public declaration that Jesus is his Son, Israel's king, and the one who takes Israel's place. Thus as obedient Israel, the Israel who is well pleasing to God, Jesus is brought by the Spirit into the wilderness, and the temptations by Satan assume this publicly declared sonship: "If" — that is, since — "you are the Son of God. . . ."

In the wilderness Jesus fasts forty days and forty nights, a time which may reflect the forty years of Israel's wandering in the wilderness (Deuteronomy 8:2).[30] Just as Israel underwent a period of testing before entering the promised land, so Jesus undergoes a similar period of testing before the kingdom can appear in and through his ministry. And the temptations Jesus encounters in the wilderness are identical to Israel's wilderness temptations. Consequently, Jesus chooses to reject the temptations by quoting texts from Deuteronomy 6 and 8, which are part of a lengthy sermon in which Moses rehearses Israel's history of sin and failure during the wanderings in the wilderness and uses that history to admonish Israel and to encourage obedient living when Israel enters the promised land. Thus Jesus must be tempted as Israel had once been tempted to see whether he is in fact obedient Israel, the Son with whom the Father is well pleased.[31]

30. B. Gerhardsson suggests that the difference between "forty days" and "forty years" may be accounted for on the principle of one day for one year (Numbers 14:34; Ezekiel 4:5) and by the consideration that, since the object of the temptation is an individual and not a people, "it is natural for the period to be forty days and not forty years." *The Testing of God's Son* (Lund: Gleerup, 1966), pp. 41-43. Others prefer a comparison with Moses' fasting on Mount Sinai (Exodus 34:28). This is possible since Moses as Israel's leader also represented Israel, but the focus of Matthew's temptation story is primarily on the Jesus-Israel connection.

31. There has been a long debate over interpretation of the temptations between those favoring a messianic purpose in each temptation and others favoring a paradig-

The first temptation is focused on the question of how the true child of God must live. The child of God lives from the Word of God, both from the revealed and written Word of God and from the word of God's command by which he supplies the necessities of life. Living from "every word that comes from the mouth of God" reflects undivided, wholehearted trust in God for everything. Originally the gift of manna in the wilderness had been intended to teach such a lesson, but it was a lesson Israel never understood (Deuteronomy 8:3). Instead, the Israelites understood manna as miracle bread, simply a substitute for the bread they used to make, a poor substitute at that and a reason for complaint. But manna was a sacrament of life, and eating it was intended to be a confession that "one does not live by bread alone, but by every word that comes from the mouth of the LORD" (Deuteronomy 8:3). Jesus understood this sacrament of life. He obeyed God implicitly, trusting God wholeheartedly for the standards and provisions of life. This is how obedient Israel lives in the world.

The second temptation involved testing God to see whether God is faithful in keeping his covenant promises. Such a reversal of testing is always a sin. God may test his children to see what is in their hearts (Exodus 16:4; Deuteronomy 8:2), but his children may never test him to see what is in his heart, since such testing amounts to unbelief, a lack of trust, an implicit denial of God's faithfulness. If Jesus were to act on Satan's suggestion that he throw himself down from the temple, even if he did so on the basis of God's covenant promises (Psalm 91:11f.), his action would be motivated by unbelief, by a failure to trust the presence and faithfulness of God in his life. Once Israel had so tested God in the wilderness. The people needed water, complained against Moses, and "tested the LORD, saying, 'Is the LORD among us or not?' " (Exodus 17:7). The Israelites no longer believed that the Lord was with them in the wilderness and demanded some evidence that God had not forsaken them. Satan suggests that Jesus demand similar visible evidence of the presence and faithfulness of God, but as true Israel Jesus knows the commandment,

---

matic purpose (that is, Jesus' temptations are examples for any pious person). But since Jesus as God's Son is both Israel and Israel's king, there is no need to choose between these interpretations. There are applications of the temptations both to Jesus as Messiah and to Jesus as true Israel, and in both cases sonship is the key.

"Do not put the Lord your God to the test" (Matthew 4:7; Deuteronomy 6:16). God's commandments through Moses are faithfully kept by Jesus, and Jesus demonstrates that he is ready even to lose his life rather than by some desperate act to challenge God to save him. Jesus lives as the Israel with whom God is well pleased.

The third temptation asks Jesus to achieve control of the world by worshipping God's rival. Had Jesus bowed down and worshipped Satan, he would have been doing what Israel did after entering the promised land. There the Israelites worshipped Baal because they thought that Baal was the source of their prosperity (Hosea 2). They ignored the warning that such worship of the gods of the land would lead not to possession of the land but to destruction. The promised land and its prosperity were gifts promised by God in his covenant with Abraham, Isaac, and Jacob, gifts of the God who brought Israel out of the land of Egypt. Israel was obligated to worship him alone (Deuteronomy 6:10-15). As God's obedient Son, Jesus knew this promise and its condition, that by serving and worshiping God alone he would inherit the world and its kingdoms as a gift from God (Matthew 28:18). World sovereignty had been promised to Israel and Israel's king, and Jesus is on the way to achieving it.

Thus in the temptations Jesus relived Israel's wilderness experiences, but where Israel failed, Jesus succeeded.[32] By being tested, Jesus proved himself faithful to God, and God, without being tested, proved himself faithful to his Son by sending angels to minister to him. Thus Satan's defeat began and what had to precede the arrival of God's kingdom had itself been set in place: Jesus indeed loves God with all his heart, soul, and strength. The promises once given to Israel can now be fulfilled.

32. This typological interpretation of Matthew's temptation story (Israel as the type and Jesus as the greater antitype) is a more recent but widely accepted understanding. It is not found in Calvin, who sees a parallel between the fasting of Moses and the fasting of Jesus but not a Jesus-Israel typology. Nor is it even in W. Hendriksen, *Exposition of the Gospel of Matthew* (Grand Rapids: Baker, 1973), who focuses more on dogmatic issues and on an Adam-Christ typology. A basic work that established the Jesus-Israel typology is Gerhardsson's *The Testing of God's Son*. See also J. A. T. Robinson, *Twelve New Testament Studies* (London: SCM, 1962), pp. 53-60; R. T. France, *Jesus and the Old Testament* (Downers Grove: InterVarsity, 1971), pp. 50-53; and the commentaries by Hill and Meier cited above.

Promises Fulfilled

The kingdom of God is at hand! That exciting note of fulfillment is heard immediately after Satan's defeat. Centuries of patient waiting have come to an end, and the blessings promised long ago can now, finally, be poured out on God's people. Jesus' ministry inaugurates a kingdom, God's kingdom, a kingdom not made with human hands, a kingdom of peace and justice that will stand forever (Daniel 2).

The prophets had promised a future in which God would rule, healing would occur, sin and evil would be overcome, God's people would be gathered, and righteousness would spring forth before the nations (Ezekiel 34; Isaiah 61).[33] Jesus announces the arrival of that future: "Repent, for the kingdom of heaven is at hand" (Matthew 4:17, *NRSV* margin). In fact, "if it is by the Spirit of God that I cast out demons, then the kingdom of God has come to you" (Matthew 12:28). God's kingdom is not only near, it is here, for the miracles of Jesus manifest the sin-revoking, healing presence of God, and the word of Jesus reveals the dynamic power of the word of God, which brings into being what is spoken. Through the word of the kingdom, sown like a seed, the kingdom of God is taking root in the soil of human history (Matthew 13:18ff.). In Jesus the blessings of the kingdom are being poured out and promises are being fulfilled! "Repent, for the kingdom of heaven is at hand!"

To guarantee that no one would miss that note of fulfillment, Matthew immediately places Jesus' ministry in Galilee in the light of prophecy fulfilled, quoting Isaiah 9:1f. (Matthew 4:15f.):

> Land of Zebulun, land of Naphtali,
> > on the road by the sea, across the Jordan,
> > > Galilee of the Gentiles —

---

33. G. E. Ladd gives a useful definition of the kingdom of God: "the redemptive reign of God dynamically active to establish his rule among men. . . . [It] involves two great movements: fulfillment within history, and consummation at the end of history." *A Theology of the New Testament* (Grand Rapids: Eerdmans, 1974), p. 91. Matthew usually refers to God's kingdom as "the kingdom of heaven" while the other Gospels speak exclusively of "the kingdom of God." "Heaven" designates the place where God dwells and is a common Jewish circumlocution for "God." The meaning of the two phrases is the same.

the people who sat in darkness
    have seen a great light,
and for those who sat in the region and shadow of death
    light has dawned.[34]

Jesus began his ministry in a place no one had expected. Isaiah 9:1f. had never been interpreted in Judaism as a messianic prophecy. Instead the "light" was understood as a reference to the oral Torah preserved in Judaism.[35] But at the point when Jesus withdraws into Galilee after the arrest of John the Baptist, Matthew proclaims a twofold connection between this prophecy and Jesus. First, the prophecy promises light and salvation to people living *in Galilee*.[36] Second, the context of Isaiah 9:1f. promises that this salvation will be brought by the promised Son of David, who will establish the eternal kingdom. Thus that Jesus ministered in Galilee is not noted just as a matter of geography but also as a revelation that the zeal of Yahweh is now at work in history establishing the rule of justice and righteousness of the promised Davidic kingdom (Isaiah 9:6f.).

Originally Isaiah had prophesied that Zebulun and Naphtali would be brought into contempt. This occurred in 734-32 B.C. when Tiglath-Pileser, the Assyrian king, conquered the northern territories of Israel and assimilated them into his empire. From that time on Galilee became a melting pot of the nations, a mixture of Jews and Gentiles considered by Judea and Jerusalem to be an impure race, a people far removed from the purity of the law. Aristobulus I, a Jew and a descendant of the Maccabees, had conquered these territories north of Judea in 101 B.C.

---

34. To account for the textual differences between Matthew's translation and both the Hebrew and Septuagint forms of the Old Testament text, G. M. Soares Prabhu's explanation seems best: Like other Jewish interpreters (the Targumists) "the author of Mt 4,14-16 would have freely translated his original to bring out what he believed was its true meaning." *The Formula Quotations in the Infancy Narratives of Matthew* (Rome: Biblical Institute Press, 1976), p. 104.

35. Cf. (H. Strack and) P. Billerbeck, *Kommentar Zum Neuen Testament Aus Talmud und Midrash* I (Munich: Beck, 1922), p. 162.

36. The precise reference of the place names is disputed, especially whether "toward the sea" and "across the Jordan" are to be interpreted as adverbially modifying Zebulun and Naphtali or as designating separate territories. Cf. Soares Prabhu, *op. cit.*, pp. 97f.

and had forcibly subjected the inhabitants to circumcision and thus to the "yoke of the Torah."[37] But at the time of the New Testament, Jews still considered the inhabitants ceremonially unclean because they did not properly observe the stipulations of the law. They were a people living in darkness, a darkness that symbolizes sitting "in the region and shadow of death."

But Isaiah had also prophesied that "in the latter time" God would "make glorious the way of the sea, the land beyond the Jordan, Galilee of the nations" (Isaiah 9:1). Perhaps in the return from exile there was already a slight beginning of the fulfillment of this prophecy,[38] but nothing that happened to Galilee from the time of the return from exile until the time of Jesus remotely measured up to the glorious horizon announced by Isaiah. He saw the final glorious action of God in which God would glorify himself by fulfilling the promises and restoring his people in unity and peace under the scion of David.[39] The light dawning on that horizon begins in the ministry of Jesus in Galilee.

The light of the dawning kingdom begins to shine in Galilee but is not restricted to Galilee. Both the original prophecy and fulfillment have a scope that embraces more than the literal territory of Galilee. The prophecy announces the coming of the eternal kingdom of the Son of David, a kingdom universal in its extent. And the fulfillment, which begins in "Galilee of the Gentiles," continues in the extension of Jesus' authority over all people as his disciples "make disciples of all nations" (Matthew 28:19).[40] Contrary to Jewish expectation this kingdom does not arrive in its fullness all at once. There is a future that has not yet arrived, in which the forces of evil will be definitively removed from the earth (Matthew 13:40-43).[41] Jesus is the dawning of a new day, a

37. Cf. B. Reicke, *The New Testament Era* (Philadelphia: Fortress, 1968), pp. 68f.

38. Calvin so interprets it: "The beginning of this light, its dawning as it were, came at the return of the people from Babylon." *Harmony of the Gospels* I, p. 153. But "dawning" is Matthew's interpretation of Jesus' activity, not Isaiah's original term.

39. Cf. O. Kaiser, *Isaiah 1–12: A Commentary* (Philadelphia: Westminster, 1972), p. 125.

40. The reference to "Galilee of the *Gentiles*" (Matthew 4:15) announces by anticipation the future mission to the Gentiles. Cf. U. Luz, *Das Evangelium nach Matthäus* (Zurich: Benziger, 1985) I, p. 171.

41. J. D. Kingsbury argues that the tension between the kingdom as present and

day that begins in his ministry in Galilee and to the entire house of Israel, continues in the ministry of his disciples to the nations of the world, and climaxes in the events surrounding the final coming of the Son of Man, which will enable the righteous to shine like the sun in the kingdom of their Father. Thus the "gospel of the kingdom" introduced in Matthew 4 is an anticipatory summary of the entire Gospel of Matthew since its content is nothing other than the deeds Jesus performs and the words he speaks.[42]

A central theme of the Old Testament expectation of the coming kingdom is the gathering of the people, a gathering that will include the nations of the world. This gathering of the people is central also to Matthew's announcement that the kingdom is at hand. One of Jesus' first actions is the calling of disciples to follow him, to whom he says, "I will make you fish for people" (Matthew 4:19). Here the disciples are incorporated into the ministry of Jesus as his agents, whose task will be to gather people into his eschatological kingdom. "Fish for people" is a kingdom metaphor: "The kingdom of heaven is like a net that was thrown into the sea and caught fish of every kind" (Matthew 13:47). The disciples are given the task of gathering the people of God as citizens of his kingdom.

A similar perspective is contained in the designation of Simon as the one "called Peter" (Matthew 4:18), with its anticipation of Matthew 16:18: "And I tell you, you are Peter, and on this rock I will build my church." Though it is thus ascribed especially to Peter, the task of all the disciples as those who confess faith in Jesus (16:16) will be to gather the church, the people of God, who are seen here as the remnant of Israel or as true Israel.[43] The arrival of the kingdom makes necessary and possible the gathering of the people of God (16:19).

---

the kingdom as future is contained already in Jesus' announcement that the kingdom is at hand: "On the one hand, it connotes that the kingdom is indeed near, so near that in the person of the earthly and exalted Son of God the authority (power) of God impinges upon the present and decisively qualifies it. On the other hand, it connotes that the kingdom has not arrived, for God has not yet miraculously consummated his rule in all power and outward splendor." *Matthew* (Philadelphia: Fortress, 1986), p. 68.

42. Cf. Luz, *op. cit.,* p. 182.

43. K. L. Schmidt argues that "church" here refers to the divine community of the Old Testament or to a separate group that "represents the remnant of Israel on which depends the continued life of all Israel as the people of God." Thus the church represents true Israel. *Theological Dictionary of the New Testament* III, pp. 524-526.

This task of gathering God's people is begun first by Jesus himself. Both at the beginning and at the conclusion of Jesus' Galilean ministry Matthew describes a scene in which crowds come to Jesus and receive the blessings of the kingdom. Remarkably, at the beginning of the ministry, in Matthew 4:25, the crowds come not only from Galilee and the Decapolis, but also from Judea, Jerusalem, and beyond the Jordan: The crowds represent the whole of Israel. The people of God are being gathered and blessed, the sick are healed, and all hear and are astonished at the authority of Jesus' word (Matthew 7:28).[44]

The second gathering scene is found in Matthew 15:29-31. Here again Jesus goes up onto a mountain, and crowds bring him sick people, whom Jesus heals. Matthew records that "the crowd was amazed when they saw the mute speaking, the maimed whole, the lame walking, and the blind seeing. And they praised the God of Israel." This description of Jesus' ministry contains a clear allusion to Isaiah 35:5f., where the prophet refers to nearly the same four categories:

> Then the eyes of the blind shall be opened,
>   and the ears of the deaf unstopped;
> then the lame shall leap like a deer,
>   and the tongue of the speechless sing for joy.

These are the blessings promised to Israel as they moved on the highway to eschatological Zion (Isaiah 35:8ff.). The crowd gathered around Jesus "praised the God of Israel" because they were experiencing the compassion and mercy of the promised kingdom. They were being gathered by the Davidic Shepherd-King (Ezekiel 34), who came for "the lost sheep of the house of Israel" (Matthew 15:24), a shepherd who "had compassion for them, because they were harassed and helpless, like sheep without a shepherd" (Matthew 9:36), a Shepherd-King who had compassion on their hunger and fed them on the mountains of Israel (Matthew 15:29ff.; Ezekiel 34:13f.).

Although the focus of Jesus' earthly ministry was restricted to "the house of Israel," there is a fascinating hint concerning the gathering

44. For this theme of the gathering of the crowds in Matthew, cf. T. L. Donaldson, *Jesus on the Mountain: A Study in Matthaean Theology* (Sheffield: JSOT, 1985), chapter 8.

of the Gentiles. This hint occurs in the story of the Canaanite woman, which immediately precedes the scene of the gathering of the crowds in Matthew 15. This Gentile woman begs Jesus to have mercy on her by casting a demon out of her daughter. To her Jesus gives an apparently hopeless reply: "I was sent only to the lost sheep of the house of Israel," and "it is not fair to take the children's food and throw it to the dogs" (Matthew 15:24, 26). In spite of her apparently hopeless position, this woman persists by pleading that "even the dogs eat the crumbs that fall from their masters' table." Because of her "great faith" her daughter was healed. Here a Gentile woman and her daughter share in the compassion of the Davidic Shepherd-King, he who heals and feeds his people, even though she receives only scraps from the table and not the overflowing abundance with which Israel is fed (15:37). For a Gentile to be so blessed is an exception during Jesus' earthly ministry, but it will not be thereafter.

The Gospel of Matthew contains much more about promises fulfilled, but the theme presented in summary through the perspectives of Matthew 4 is sufficiently clear. The promised kingdom and its Davidic king have arrived, and the scattered flock is being gathered, healed, and miraculously fed. The blessings prophesied for the citizens of this renewed Israel are pronounced on the disciples in the Beatitudes, and the righteousness that must spring forth before the nations is expected from them (Matthew 5). So in gathering disciples Jesus is reestablishing Israel on earth, filling them with the promised blessings, and expecting them to take on themselves his "easy yoke" of God's way of righteousness.

Rejection and Election

If Jesus is God's beloved Son, the one who represents and takes the place of chosen Israel, what is the status of Old Testament Israel? If the promises given to Israel are fulfilled in Jesus and if in Jesus the kingdom of God has appeared, the eternal kingdom promised to David by which God rules his people Israel, what happens to those who do not accept the testimony of Jesus? If Jesus is Emmanuel, the prophesied presence of God with his people, what happens to those "heirs of the kingdom" who do not acknowledge that presence?

Matthew's answer is very clear: Continued possession of promises cannot be maintained apart from the faith that God gives to his people. Alongside Matthew's positive theme of the fulfillment of promises to Israel there is a negative theme of fulfillment of judgment on the Israel that does not believe. The climax of this theme of judgment is found in chapters 11–13, where the rejection of Jesus by unbelieving Israel becomes evident. Even though Israel had been confronted by the presence of the kingdom in the teaching of Jesus (Matthew 5–7), had seen its power over sin and nature manifested in the miracles of Jesus (ch. 8–9), and had been invited into the kingdom by the mission of the disciples (ch. 10), most of Israel remained unconvinced and unbelieving. They were, said Jesus, an "evil generation," always asking for signs and refusing to believe (12:39).

The consequences of such unbelief are spelled out in Matthew 13. Answering the question why he spoke in parables, Jesus said to his disciples: "To you it has been given to know the secrets of the kingdom of heaven, but to them it has not been given" (v. 11). Knowledge of the secrets or mysteries of the kingdom is the key to understanding the parables, and such knowledge is a gift from God.

What is this mystery of the kingdom? The background for Jesus' use of "mystery" is found especially in Daniel 2, where the word is used of the mystery of the future kingdom of God. In general, "mystery" refers to the hidden plan of God, which has been revealed in part to the Old Testament prophets.[45] Because the prophets were granted some insight into the plan of God, the Old Testament reveals some knowledge of the mysteries of the kingdom. However, the full revelation of the mystery occurs in the preaching and ministry of Jesus, which is the fulfillment of the Old Testament promise.

But that fulfillment contains some surprises about God's plan. The parables of the kingdom in Matthew 13 reveal the surprising nature of that kingdom and the unexpected manner of its coming. The kingdom comes not with the blast of a trumpet announcing the total destruction of evil, as many had expected. Instead, it comes like a seed that is sown and that encounters all sorts of obstacles. It is present in human history even while evil still exists because it is a kingdom that manifests the patient mercy of

45. Cf. R. Brown, *The Semitic Background of the Term "Mystery" in the New Testament* (Philadelphia: Fortress, 1968).

God, a kingdom of love and forgiveness. But this hidden kingdom will someday be completely victorious, and evil will be totally destroyed on the day of judgment at the close of the age. Because this kingdom of God coexists in history with the kingdom of Satan, its presence is not self-evident. Faith is necessary to see its presence. Faith in Jesus opens one's eyes to the presence of the kingdom of God. Just as Jesus' victory passed through weakness, suffering, and death to resurrection, life, and power, so also the kingdom that he brings appears at first hidden in apparent weakness until it finally emerges in full glory and power. Faith is required to know that mystery, and only disciples have that faith.

Judgment falls on those who do not believe. Even though, as the Old Testament people of God, Israel possessed the mysteries of the kingdom in the law and the prophets, they did not understand the mysteries. They had a different understanding of the kingdom of God, a kingdom of political might and power defeating the enemies of Israel and overwhelming the forces of evil, and, as a result, they did not believe that the kingdom of God had arrived in the person and ministry of Jesus. Consequently, their privileged position as the heirs of the kingdom would be taken from them: "For to those who have, more will be given, and they will have an abundance; but from those who have nothing, even what they have will be taken away" (Matthew 13:12).[46]

Because of this failure to comprehend, Israel loses what it had and continues to manifest the judgment that Isaiah pronounced on his own unbelieving generation (Matthew 13:14):

> You will indeed listen, but never understand,
>   and you will indeed look, but never perceive.

Instead, the position of privilege in Israel now belongs to the disciples (vv. 16f.):

> But blessed are your eyes, for they see, and your ears, for they hear. Truly I tell you, many prophets and righteous people longed to see

46. Cf. R. Stein, *An Introduction to the Parables of Jesus* (Philadelphia: Westminster, 1981), chapter 2; B. VanElderen, "The Purpose of the Parables according to Matt. 13:10-17," in *New Dimensions in New Testament Study,* ed. R. Longenecker and M. C. Tenney (Grand Rapids: Eerdmans, 1974), pp. 180-190.

what you see, but did not see it, and to hear what you hear, but did not hear it.

The same loss of privilege is pronounced on unbelieving Israel in the parable of the vineyard. The vineyard represents Israel, from whom the Lord expects fruit, but the servants in the vineyard abuse the master's servants and kill his son. Consequently, the kingdom of God will be taken from them and "given to a people that produces the fruits of the kingdom" (Matthew 21:43). Here again Matthew announces that unbelieving Israel will lose its privileged position as "heirs of the kingdom" (8:10-12), and others will receive that privileged status with its accompanying task of producing the fruit of the kingdom. That is always the task of true Israel, doing the will of God (7:21) and performing the greater righteousness (5:20). Such is the fruit that God desires. Therefore, according to Matthew, those who believe in Jesus and comprehend the mysteries of the kingdom, those who accept Jesus' word and follow his teaching are the recipients of the privileged status and task of Old Testament Israel.[47]

Epilogue

Who then is Israel? The answer is never simply a matter of ancestry. Consequently, the central issue in the New Testament is not really Jew versus Gentile. Instead, Israel is the people chosen by God and called to respond in faith and obedience. Israel is the people on whom the Lord sets his love (Deuteronomy 7:7).

Such also is Matthew's teaching. Jesus, a literal descendant of Abraham, himself a Jew, is the Israel who is the object of God's love. He is chosen by God and responds in perfect obedience, fulfilling the law and the prophets (Matthew 5:17) and all righteousness (3:15). Since

---

47. H. Frankenmölle argues that although the church receives the status and task of Israel, the church does not become Israel since for Matthew "Israel" refers exclusively to those who are disobedient. *Jahwe-Bund und Kirche Christi* (Münster: Aschendorff, 1984), p. 261. But this position does not do justice to the clear implications of Matthew's Gospel since Jesus represents the positive line of obedient Israel, as do those who believe in him.

Jesus is the corporate representative of Israel, God now recognizes as Israel all who respond in faith and obedience to the presence and will of God revealed in Jesus.[48] Of course, the first to so respond are in fact Jews. Jesus' condemnation of Israel is not a blanket condemnation of all Jews but only of those who do not believe. The crowds that follow him do not receive from him the same radical judgment as is pronounced on the leaders of the nation.[49] Instead, Jesus has compassion on the crowds as "sheep without a shepherd" and declares to his disciples that "the harvest is plentiful" (Matthew 9:36-38). So long as they do not reject Jesus, the possibility of becoming Jesus' disciples remains open to the people. Will they accept the definition of Israel and the fulfillment of the promises revealed in Jesus? Will they acknowledge the presence of God and the arrival of the kingdom in the person and ministry of Jesus? Will they comprehend the mystery of the kingdom? That was and continues to be the only question that decides the identity of Israel: Not ancestry but faith, not human achievement but God's gift, calling, and election, acknowledged in Jesus, son of Abraham, son of David, Son of God.

If the church is Israel, then the church is not just an interim arrangement but a people standing in continuity with Old Testament Israel and carrying out Israel's mission in the world. Israel's central calling was to be a light to the nations (Isaiah 42:6). As God's anointed servant, Jesus fulfills that task of Israel and commissions his disciples to be the light of the world (Matthew 5:14-16). They are that light not only by preaching the gospel of the kingdom to the whole world, by baptizing disciples, and by "teaching them to obey everything that I have commanded you" (28:19-20), but also by doing good works (5:16),

48. This theme of the continuity between Jesus and Israel was of great significance for Matthew's original audience. Though scholars still dispute whether Matthew's audience, composed mainly of Jewish but also some Gentile Christians, had already separated from the synagogue, that audience would have been aware that the majority of Jewish Israel had not believed in Jesus. Consequently, they needed assurance that the rupture with Jewish Israel was not a failure of the promises of God. Matthew's focus on Jesus as the fulfillment of the promises made to Israel is designed to provide that assurance.

49. Matthew clearly distinguishes the crowds from both the disciples and the Jewish leaders. Cf. J. D. Kingsbury, *The Parables of Jesus in Matthew 13* (Richmond: John Knox, 1969), pp. 24-28; Donaldson, *Jesus on the Mountain,* pp. 114f.

doing the will of God (7:21), and walking in the way of righteousness that was lived and taught by Jesus (5:20). The law of God for his people has not simply disappeared; rather, it has been renewed by Jesus according to its original intention (5:17ff.).[50] Israel can be the light of the world only by walking in the way of righteousness. Only in this way will Isaiah's prophecy continue to be fulfilled (Isaiah 61:11):

> For as the earth brings forth its shoots,
>   and as a garden causes what is sown in it to spring up,
> so the Lord GOD will cause righteousness and praise
>   to spring up before all the nations.

---

50. This topic is discussed below in chapter V.

CHAPTER III

Jesus and the Temple:
A Question of Essence

Must a temple be built in Jerusalem? Does prophecy require that a temple of stone be built by human hands on the site of the previous temples in Jerusalem? Many answer Yes: The building of the temple will be the last great fulfillment of prophecy before the return of Christ. Others answer No: Jesus is himself the fulfillment of the Old Testament prophecies concerning the temple so that if a temple should be erected on the site of the previous temples it will be because of misunderstanding and unbelief, not because prophecy demands it.[1]

Christians are not the only ones who disagree about the rebuilding of the temple. Modern Jews do also. Traditional Jewish prayers include a petition for the rebuilding of the temple. The third benediction in the ancient prayer after meals prays for "the great and holy house over which Thy name has been called." Originally this was a prayer for the continuation of the existence of the temple, but after the temple's destruction, the prayer was for the rebuilding of the temple. Some pious Jews recite prayers, the hatzot, each midnight for the rebuilding of the

---

1. The affirmative is held by those following a dispensationalist or premillennial position, for example, H. Lindsey, *The Late Great Planet Earth* (Grand Rapids: Zondervan, 1970), p. 56. The negative is held by those following a nonmillennial position, for example, E. P. Clowney, "The Final Temple," in *Prophecy in the Making,* ed. C. F. H. Henry (Carol Stream, IL: Creation House, 1971), chapter 4; A. Hoekema, *The Bible and the Future* (Grand Rapids: Eerdmans, 1979), pp. 203-205.

temple. And the synagogue prayer called the Eighteen Benedictions begs God to reinstate the temple service and to return the divine presence to Zion. It adds this petition: "May it be Thy will that the temple be rebuilt soon in our days." Thus traditional Judaism has continued to pray for the rebuilding of the temple. Reform Judaism, however, has omitted these prayers for the rebuilding of the temple and the restitution of the sacrificial system.[2]

Even though traditional Judaism has longed for the rebuilding of the temple throughout the centuries, Judaism's emphasis on the works of the law significantly modified the role and the necessity of a temple in Jersualem. This is apparent already in the ancient story of a rabbi's reply to his pupil, who was bemoaning the loss of the temple:

> A story is told about Rabban Johanan ben Zakkai that he was walking along the road when Rabbi Joshua ran after him and said to him: Woe to us because the house of our life has been destroyed, the place which used to atone for our sins. He answered: Do not be afraid. We have another atonement instead of it. He asked: What is it? Johanan answered: "For I desire loving kindness and not sacrifice" (Hos. 6:6).[3]

Deeds of mercy or fulfilling what the law requires actually accomplishes redemption. Sacrifices are not necessary. Thus the temple may still be desired as a fulfillment of divine promise, as a sign of divine Presence and, consequently, as a sign of Israel's election, but in Judaism the temple is not needed as a place of atonement.[4] All that is required for

2. Cf. "Temple," *Encyclopedia of the Jewish Religion* (New York: Adana, 1986).
3. A. J. Saldarini, *The Fathers according to Rabbi Nathan (Abot De Rabbi Nathan)* (Leiden: Brill, 1975), p. 75.
4. J. O. Haberman writes, "Nowhere is there a greater gap between Jewish and Christian thought than in the redeeming power of righteousness. To the Jew, the commandments of Torah are both sacrament and salvation." And commenting on Paul's distinction between a righteousness of faith and a righteousness of works, Haberman states: "If such a distinction had to be made, rabbinic sages would affirm the efficacy of righteous works even in the absence of true faith." "Righteousness," in *Contemporary Jewish Religious Thought,* ed. A. A. Cohen and P. Mendes-Flohr (New York: Scribner, 1987). Perhaps the absence of an essay on the temple in this large volume indicates the subordinate role of the temple in contemporary Judaism and the ability of Judaism to define itself theologically without focusing significantly on the temple.

redemption to occur is repentance and good works. Such has been the traditional teaching of rabbinic Judaism.[5]

Under the impact of the Holocaust, contemporary Judaism has added the emphasis that "righteousness must be universalized" because it has become obvious that Israel cannot stand alone in its devotion to Torah. All the nations must be united in the "Torah way of life," but how this will happen — whether by Israel's teaching or by divine intervention — remains part of the messianic mystery.[6] Thus in contemporary Judaism, as in traditional rabbinic Judaism, the emphasis continues to fall not on a righteousness achieved apart from the law by faith, but on achieving righteousness through keeping the law of God. Obviously, the temple as a place of atonement is no longer essential for Judaism, and the temple is understood differently in Judaism from the way it is understood in the New Testament.

The question facing us in this chapter is not first of all whether a temple *will* be built in Jerusalem. Much happens in human history that need not happen. It is conceivable that a temple could be built in Jerusalem, though since a Muslim sacred place, the Dome of the Rock, is on the temple site, the rebuilding of a temple would create an almost unthinkable religious and political situation.[7] The question facing us is whether Old Testament prophecy requires that a temple now be built in Jerusalem. In order to understand such prophecy it is important to understand the history and the purpose of the temple in the Old Testament.

The Temple in the Old Testament and Judaism

The history of the temple in the Old Testament is a fascinating and disappointing story, fascinating because the temple was where God's glory dwelled in the midst of Israel, disappointing because, through a

5. Cf. G. F. Moore, *Judaism* I (Cambridge: Harvard, 1927), pp. 500ff.; E. E. Urbach, *The Sages: Their Concepts and Beliefs* (Jerusalem: Magnes, 1979), pp. 666ff.
6. Haberman, *op. cit.,* p. 839.
7. H. Lindsey acknowledges this and quotes an Israeli historian to the effect that God would handle this problem, perhaps by destroying the Dome of the Rock with an earthquake (*The Late Great Planet Earth,* p. 57).

total misunderstanding of the presence of Israel's covenant God, the temple became the source of idolatry in Israel. The story of the temple really begins with David collecting materials and Solomon building the first temple in Jersualem, but before the temple there was a tent and a tabernacle.

Following Israel's sin of worshipping the golden calf, Moses erected a tent outside the camp and called it "the tent of meeting" (Exodus 33:7). There God and Moses met. When the pillar of cloud descended to the tent, God spoke with Moses and all Israel worshipped. The tent was placed outside the camp to symbolize the removal of God's presence from the midst of the camp because of Israel's sin. Yet the significance of this tent is like that of the tabernacle erected in the midst of Israel since the tabernacle was also called the "tent of meeting" (40:2). Both tent and tabernacle symbolized the presence of God with Israel (33:14), the fact, that is, that God had chosen to dwell in the midst of Israel (25:8; 29:45).

This tent/tabernacle was not only a place of meeting and revelation, it was also a place of atonement. If God, the holy God, were to dwell in the midst of Israel, an unclean, unholy, and sinful people, atonement had to be made by sin offering and burnt offering. The elaborate ceremony of the Day of Atonement (Leviticus 16) symbolizes the forgiveness and removal of sin so that a holy God can meet with a holy people and continue to dwell in their midst. Thus the tabernacle with its ark of the covenant and mercy seat, its altars and lavers symbolized for Israel the necessity and possibility of atonement. Israel was called to be holy because the God who dwelt in the midst of Israel was holy (Leviticus 19:2).

The change from tabernacle to temple occurred after Israel settled in the land of Canaan. Strikingly, when David first proposed to build a house for God to match his own house of cedar, God surprised both David and Nathan the prophet by refusing the proposal. God preferred to dwell in the tent because the tent symbolized God's journey with his people, a journey that would not be complete until God had brought his people to their place of rest, a place where they would be free from the oppression and violence of their enemies. Only then would God be able to settle down and dwell in a fixed place. Instead of accepting David's offer, God promised that he would build a house for David and that one from that house would build the house for God (cf. II Samuel 7:1-17; I Chronicles 17:1-15). Two houses would be built, David's house and God's house, and amazingly in the end — in Jesus — these two houses would become one. But that is to run ahead of the story.

A time of peace arrived under Solomon, and Solomon built the temple. The temple was patterned after the tabernacle and took over its functions. Like the tabernacle the temple was the place of atonement and the place of God's presence. Though Solomon acknowledged that the temple could never contain God's presence, since even the highest heaven could not, still he prayed that the temple might be the place of which God had said "My name shall be there" (I Kings 8:29). God's name represents his presence, and God promised Solomon, "I have consecrated this house that you have built, and put my name there forever; my eyes and my heart will be there for all time" (9:3). God promised to be present in the temple to hear and respond to the requests of his people. So the temple became the place of the presence of God and the place of sin offerings to make atonement for Israel. Since Solomon was David's son, Solomon's temple was also the beginning of the fulfillment of God's promise to David in II Samuel 7:10-14, but it was not its final fulfillment. For already in I Kings 9:8 God warned Solomon about the possibility that "this house will become a heap of ruins."

Solomon's temple did, in fact, become a heap of ruins because Israel misunderstood the presence of its covenant God. The people thought that God's presence was automatically guaranteed by the temple in Jerusalem. Since the creator of heaven and earth dwelled in the holy city, surely that city and its temple could never be destroyed by any earthly creature or foreign army. When the prophet Jeremiah warned the people to amend their ways or be destroyed, they chanted in his face: "This is the temple of the LORD, the temple of the LORD, the temple of the LORD" (Jeremiah 7:4). The temple had become for them a guarantee of safety, an idol in fact.

Idolatry was no recent heresy on Israel's part. When the people assumed that their security was guaranteed by the temple and that repentance was not necessary, Jeremiah reminded them of the fate of the tabernacle at Shiloh. Already then in the early days of its existence

Israel had misunderstood the presence of God. When Israel was defeated by the Philistines, the people properly concluded that God was not with them. But then the elders and the people thought that they could compel God to be present and to fight for them, merely by bringing the ark of the covenant to the battlefield. Like pagans they thought that the ark controlled the presence of God. The Philistines were terrified by the sight of the ark on the battlefield, since the Israelites' God had already defeated the mighty Egyptians, and in their pagan thought the ark was an idol, a representation of God that controlled and guaranteed his presence. Yet Israel was defeated and even the ark was taken — a lesson for Israel concerning the absence of God because of Israel's disobedience. The Philistines also had to be taught a lesson. So God returned to the ark to demonstrate his power over the Philistines and their gods, and the Philistines concluded that indeed they could not handle the God of Israel. This, said Jeremiah, was an important lesson concerning the presence of God, a lesson Israel should never forget but always did. God promises to be present among his people only within the context of the covenant. The ark is the ark of the *covenant,* not a pagan idol. When the covenant is broken, God is absent. When sacrifices are viewed merely as a commanded ritual guaranteeing atonement and not as a means to holiness, then God can no longer dwell in the midst of a sinful and disobedient people. Tabernacles, temples, and even the ark of the covenant cannot guarantee the presence of God. When God departs, these are only buildings and artifacts made by human hands and capable of being destroyed by human hands.

Strangely the temple built in fulfillment of God's promise became an obstacle to the prophets of God because the prophets insisted on covenant obedience but Israel found security in an idol. So Shiloh, the place of the tabernacle, was destroyed, and Solomon's temple was destroyed as well. To make sure that Israel understood the lesson about the absence of God and did not falsely conclude that the destruction of Jerusalem and the temple was evidence of the superiority of the gods of Babylon, God gave a vision to the prophet Ezekiel. In that vision God revealed how the glory of the Lord, which like the name of God was a representation of God's presence, had departed from the temple and from the city (Ezekiel 10:18f.; 11:22-25). Consequently, the temple was no longer the holy temple and the city was no longer the holy city.

Holiness is the result of God's presence, but with his absence the city and the temple became like any other city or temple on the face of the earth. Jerusalem and the temple were destroyed and burned by the armies of Nebuchadnezzar. They did, in fact, become "a heap of ruins."

But the history of the temple does not end with its destruction. God keeps covenant even when his people do not. He is faithful and fulfills his promises. So the promise to David in II Samuel 7 continues, and a house will be built where God's name and glory will dwell in the midst of his people. The visions given to Ezekiel did not end with explanations of destruction but with a vision of a magnificent future of a perfect temple in the midst of a perfect city. This ideal temple of Israel's future will be filled with the glory of God, and God "will reside among the people of Israel forever" (Ezekiel 43:1-7). Ezekiel's vision is focused on the presence of God, and even the name of the city reflects that focus: "The LORD is There" (48:35). A marvelous future is coming, a perfect city, a holy God dwelling in the midst of a holy people.

Ezekiel's vision of an ideal temple or mountain was never literally fulfilled in Israel's history. The second temple, built after the return from exile, lacked the glory of Ezekiel's vision. In fact, it did not even equal Solomon's temple in glory. The old men who remembered the first temple wept at the sight of the second (Ezra 3:12). Yet the second temple had messianic significance. It was to some degree a fulfillment of God's promise that he would dwell in the midst of his people (Zechariah 2:10), and Joshua, the high priest, and Zerubbabel, the Davidic prince, together function as anticipations of the messianic figure called the "Branch," who was to "build the temple of the LORD" (Zechariah 6:12f.). Thus the second temple built after exile is both a fulfillment of promises made earlier and an anticipation of the more complete fulfillment that would occur in the days of the Messiah.[8]

Within the history recorded in the Old Testament the promises concerning the temple are not completely realized. Fulfillment occurs, but the reality achieved is less than what was promised. The second temple is not yet the house that the son of David will erect for God, nor is the present son of David, Zerubbabel, the occupant of the eternal throne (II Samuel 7:13). The promised house of David and the promised

8. Cf. R. L. Smith, *Micah-Malachi* (Waco: Word, 1984).

house of God must still be erected in history. Thus the Old Testament anticipates a future beyond its own horizons.

What happens between the testaments? Jewish belief in the period between the Old and the New Testaments continues to share the Old Testament expectation of a future, more glorious temple. The second temple is not considered the final temple, but instead will someday be folded up, and the Lord will build a "new house greater and loftier than the first one."[9] The community living by the Dead Sea at Qumran rejected the temple in Jerusalem as corrupt and was waiting for the house that the Lord himself would build in the last days.[10] The dominant belief during the period of the second temple was that God himself would be the builder of this new house. Apparently, after the destruction of the first temple and the disappointment with the second temple, there developed a fascination with the words from Exodus 15:17, "the sanctuary, O LORD, that your hands have established." Only a temple erected by God himself would fulfill the promises and last forever, not temples built by human hands.[11] Temples built by human hands could be destroyed by human sin, but the one built by God would be a purified

9. I Enoch 90:28f., in *The Old Testament Pseudepigrapha* I, ed. J. H. Charlesworth (Garden City: Doubleday, 1983).

10. 4QFlorilegium (T. H. Gaster, *The Dead Sea Scriptures* [Garden City: Doubleday, 1976], pp. 446-448). The texts considered important for this expectation were II Samuel 7:10-14 and Exodus 15:17f. By quoting Exodus 15:17, the Qumran community demonstrates that in its belief II Samuel 7:10 does not refer to the Solomonic temple but to the final eschatological sanctuary. Cf. G. J. Brooke, *Exegesis at Qumran: 4QFlorilegium in Its Jewish Context* (Sheffield: JSOT, 1985), pp. 134ff.

11. This fascination with Exodus 15:17 is found not only in Qumran but also in rabbinic teaching. For example, in the Mekilta of R. Ishmael there is this interpretation of the verse:

> The sanctuary, O Lord, which thy hands established: How precious is the Temple in the sight of Him Who Spoke and the World Came to Be! For when the Holy One, blessed be He, created this world, only with one hand did He create it, as it is said, 'Yea, My hand both laid the foundation of the earth' (Isa. 48:13). But when He comes to build the Temple, it will be, as it were, with His two hands, as it is said, 'Thy sanctuary, O Lord, which Thy *hands* establish, when the Lord will reign.' When will *that* be? When Thou shalt build it with thy two hands!"

J. Goldin, *The Song at the Sea* (New Haven: Yale University Press, 1971), pp. 237f. Though the Mekilta is from the second century A.D., the teaching is undoubtedly older. Cf. Goldin, pp. 11f.

temple that would last forever. Although the dominant expectation was that God would build his temple, there was also the belief that the Messiah would build it. The messianic promises of both II Samuel 7:10-14 and Zechariah 6:12 continue to influence Jewish expectations.[12]

At the time of Jesus, even though Herod had remodeled and greatly expanded the second temple, no one in Judaism ever dreamed of identifying that temple with the promises of the Old Testament. In Jewish hopes the temple was more than a building, however beautiful it may be, and Herod's temple was extraordinarily beautiful. Rather, the temple lay at the center of a constellation of promises and hopes: the Glory of God dwelling in the midst of Israel, the rebirth and gathering of Israel, the gathering of the Gentiles, holiness, peace, unity, and security. King Herod could supply architectural plans and marble slabs, but only God himself could fulfill the hopes associated with the temple. At the time of Jesus, Israel was still waiting for the fulfillment of the promises.

Jesus and the Temple

What was Jesus' attitude toward the temple? Did he support the temple, its priests and its sacrifices? Did he show reverence and respect for it as the place of God's presence and as the place of atonement for Israel's sins?

The Gospels reveal two attitudes on the part of Jesus.[13] When he was twelve years old and discussing issues with the teachers of Israel, he referred to the temple as "my Father's house" (Luke 2:49). At various times in his public ministry he spoke of the temple as "the house of God" (Matthew 12:4), "a house of prayer for all the nations" (Mark 11:17), and in the parable of the publican and the Pharisee as the place of prayer (Luke 18:10). In his teaching about taking oaths, he refers to Jerusalem as "the city of the great King" (Matthew 5:35) and

12. Although L. Gaston, *No Stone On Another* (Leiden: Brill, 1970), pp. 105ff., has argued that there was no explicit hope for a new temple built by the Messiah, the evidence clearly supports the contrary. Cf. D. Juel, *Messiah and Temple* (Missoula: Scholars, 1977), chapter 9; E. P. Sanders, *Jesus and Judaism* (Philadelphia: Fortress, 1985), chapter 2.

13. Cf. Y. Congar, *The Mystery of the Temple* (London: Burns and Oates, 1962), pp. 112ff.

to the temple as the place where God dwells (Matthew 23:21). In illustrating the meaning of the commandment against murder, Jesus spoke of leaving one's gift at the altar in order first to be reconciled to a brother and then returning to offer the gift (Matthew 5:23f.). In addition, Jesus himself went to Jerusalem to celebrate the great feasts.

Clearly, Jesus showed respect for the temple in Jerusalem, but strikingly nowhere do the Gospels inform us that he offered any sacrifices there. He is found in the temple precincts teaching and healing, but never do the Gospels say that he went to the temple to pray or to offer sacrifice. On any direct involvement in the cultic practices of the temple on the part of Jesus the gospel record is strangely silent.

But it is not silent concerning the coming destruction and replacement of the temple. Jesus condemns the chief priests and elders for having turned the temple into "a den of robbers" (Mark 11:17) and "a marketplace" (John 2:16). Because of the sins of the leaders and the people Jesus announced the coming destruction of Jerusalem (Matthew 23:37ff.) and the temple (Mark 13). Moreover, he was more than a prophet announcing judgment: he was the prophesied Messiah through whom the age of fulfillment was beginning. Not only would the temple be destroyed, it would be replaced by Jesus and his ministry.

Interesting light is shed on Jesus' twofold attitude toward the temple by the story of the temple tax (Matthew 17:24ff.). According to Peter, Jesus paid the temple tax, but the reason Jesus gave for doing so was quite astonishing. He denied any basic obligation to pay the tax. The tax was used to support the temple services, and in Exodus 30:16 it is called "atonement money" because it supports all the services of the temple and all the sacrifices, including "the sin offerings to make atonement for Israel" (Nehemiah 10:33). By denying any obligation to pay the tax, Jesus is denying any obligation to pay for the sacrifices offered there. But in order to avoid giving offense, he paid the tax. He paid freely but without obligation. He showed no disrespect for the temple, but was aware of a certain provisionality about the temple as a place of atonement because he had a relationship to God as King, as do his disciples, which is not dependent on the temple service.

Jesus is the one who "will save his people from their sins" (Matthew 1:21). As such, he has the authority to forgive sins (Mark 2:10) and the power by touch and word to make the unclean clean (Mark

1:41; John 15:3). "Something greater than the temple is here" (Matthew 12:6), the Son of God, who has the power to make others the children of God. As free children of the King they are not obligated to pay the tax,[14] but, lest others be offended, the tax is freely paid. Therefore Jesus does not disapprove of the temple and its sacrificial service, but he clearly puts them in their place.[15]

Jesus' entire public ministry is actually a fulfillment of what the temple symbolized. He forgives sins directly, apart from sin offerings, guilt offerings, and the ritual of the Day of Atonement. He touches the unclean, lepers, and corpses, and is touched by the unclean, the woman with the hemorrhage, and remarkably uncleanness does not win by contaminating Jesus, but instead the unclean becomes clean. Jesus eats with sinners and tax collectors and thereby identifies with sinners, whom he calls to repentance. He enters the house of Zacchaeus and according to Jewish law thus contracts uncleanness, but "when he emerges from Zacchaeus' house to face the accusing crowd, it is not he who is unclean but Zacchaeus who is 'a son of Abraham.' "[16] Cleanliness, forgiveness, and healing formerly received through the symbolism of ritual law and temple sacrifice are now gifts of Jesus' word and healing touch. The temple had not yet reached its appointed end during Jesus' ministry, but surely something greater than the temple had entered human history, and the end of the temple could not be long delayed. The temple and its sacrifices were a sign pointing to "the Lamb of God who takes away the sin of the world" (John 1:29). When the Lamb appeared and atonement in fulfillment of the sign was accomplished, the significance of the sign was at an end. Fulfillment implies no disrespect for the sign, and Jesus showed no disrespect for the temple.

The story of the cleansing of the temple combines Jesus' attitude of respect for the temple and his awareness of messianic fulfillment and

14. "Freedom is the hallmark of such sons: freedom from the temple tax, and therefore freedom in principle from the temple and from the law which imposed the tax." J. P. Meier, *Matthew* (Wilmington: Glazier, 1980), p. 197.

15. Cf. B. Gerhardsson, "Sacrificial Service and Atonement in the Gospel of Matthew," *Reconciliation and Hope,* ed. R. Banks (Grand Rapids: Eerdmans, 1974), p. 28.

16. N. T. Wright, "Jesus, Israel, and the Cross," *SBL Seminar Papers,* 1985, p. 83.

displacement of the temple. His symbolic action is rich in meaning, and the attempt to discover a single intention in it is misguided. The traditional interpretation sees in Jesus' action a restoration of the purity of the temple. Obviously that is part of the story. Mark's statement that Jesus "would not allow anyone to carry anything through the temple" (Mark 11:16) parallels Jewish respect for the holiness of the temple.[17] The cleansing, however, occurred only in the Court of the Gentiles, an area not considered especially holy, and thus it is conceivable that Jesus' action symbolizes an extension of the holy area in accordance with the eschatological expectations associated with the future temple (Zechariah 14). By removing merchandising from the temple Jesus was restoring its purity and pronouncing a prophetic judgment on present practice, but for what purpose?

The purpose is clearly eschatological. Jesus was not simply a prophetic reformer trying to reestablish the purity of the existing temple. He had been acclaimed as the son of David, the messianic figure commissioned to build the house for God, as he came into Jerusalem. Thus his action of cleansing the temple was associated with the dawning of this new era.[18] The evidence for this eschatological interpretation is contained in Jesus' quotations from the Old Testament. Both Matthew and Mark quote Isaiah 56:7, "My house shall be called a house of prayer for all the nations" (Mark 11:17; Matthew 21:13; Matthew omits the last phrase), and John refers to Zechariah 14:21, which promises a future temple in which there will be no traders (John 2:16). Both Isaiah and Zechariah are speaking of the future eschatological temple, the gathering place of all nations, who will pray and worship in the Lord's house. But the temple in Jesus' day did not measure up to this eschatological vision because of the sins of those in charge of temple worship. Therefore, a new temple is on the horizon, a temple that will be what prophecy

17. A man "may not enter into the Temple Mount with his staff or his sandal or his wallet, or with dust upon his feet, nor may he make of it a short by-path." Berakoth 9:5. H. Danby, *The Mishnah* (London: Oxford University Press, 1933), p. 10.

18. There were Jewish expectations of a renewal of the temple as a preparation for the messianic age. R. E. Dowda states, "In a general way, then, the temple reform and renewal were associated with the inauguration of a new era, at least in some of the literature, as preparatory to the beginning of the messianic age." *The Cleansing of the Temple in the Synoptic Gospels* (dissertation, Duke University, 1972), p. 239.

said it must be, and the present temple, which robbed the Gentiles of their right and oppressed the poor like "a den of robbers" (Jeremiah 7:11), will fall under judgment, just as the first temple fell into ruins. Jesus' action pointed to this new and greater temple filled with a new and greater community of those who worship God.[19]

Did Jesus' action also directly symbolize the destruction of the temple and the cessation of sacrifice? Many have suggested that it did, but the evidence is not compelling.[20] Although it is difficult to delimit the meaning of symbolic actions, it should be noted that Jesus did not interfere with the temple ritual, which was being carried on in the inner courts, nor do the Old Testament references directly suggest the cessation of sacrifice. There may be a hint of coming destruction in the "den of robbers" quotation from Jeremiah 7:11; at least, there is the prophetic warning that if because of the sins of the people the temple does not manifest the characteristics of the final temple, it will be destroyed. However, in Mark the real note of coming judgment and destruction is found in the cursing of the fig tree (Mark 11:12-14, 20).[21]

The theme of the messianic replacement of the temple becomes

---

19. Jesus' disciples understood the action of the "cleansing" as pointing toward "eschatological renewal centered on Mount Zion and on an eschatologically renewed or rebuilt temple." J. D. G. Dunn, *Unity and Diversity in the New Testament* (Philadelphia: Westminster, 1977), p. 324. Cf. also E. Lohmeyer, *The Lord of the Temple* (Edinburgh: Oliver and Boyd, 1961), p. 42; R. H. Lightfoot, *The Gospel Message of St. Mark* (London: Oxford University Press, 1962), pp. 63ff.; R. J. McKelvey, *The New Temple* (Oxford: Oxford University Press, 1969), pp. 66, 71ff.

20. E. P. Sanders, for example, grants that if one uses the Old Testament quotations as the clue to Jesus' intention, then Jesus was interested in the purity of the temple. But since many scholars reject these quotations as the later interpretations of the evangelists, Sanders favors the view that Jesus' act was a direct symbol of the cessation of sacrifice and the destruction of the temple. *Jesus and Judaism* (Philadelphia: Fortress, 1985), chapter 1.

21. This correlation of the cursing of the fig tree and the cleansing of the temple has been developed by W. R. Telford, *The Barren Temple and the Withered Tree* (Sheffield: JSOT, 1980). Although he grants that cleansing and an eschatological sign may have influenced the disciples' understanding, Telford does not interpret Jesus' action as messianic purification of the cultus but as judgment announcing destruction. Telford concentrates on the fig tree, on Jeremiah 7:11, and on the saying concerning the removal of the mountain (Mark 11:23), which he interprets as referring to the removal of the temple mount. He virtually ignores the quotation from Isaiah 56:7. This passage is not a prophecy of judgment and destruction.

more explicit as Jesus' ministry approaches its conclusion. Once the messianic king has entered his city, the establishment of the messianic temple cannot be far behind. Immediately Jesus claims authority over the temple and is challenged by the existing authorities, but since his authority is from God he cannot be successfully challenged (Mark 11:27ff.). Of course, the leaders create an apparently successful challenge by placing him on trial and crucifying him as the one who would destroy the temple (Mark 14:58; 15:29), but paradoxically Jesus' death destroys the temple. The tearing of the temple curtain announces the approaching destruction of the temple and its end as the place of the presence of God and as the place of atonement for Israel.[22] Its replacement is a temple not made with hands (Mark 14:58).[23]

What is this temple not made with hands? Does the Gospel of Mark inform us concerning its nature? Although in Paul the phrase contrasts the spiritual with the fleshly or physical order and in Hebrews the heavenly with the earthly order, in Mark it is more likely that the phrase simply contrasts what God builds with what human beings build. As in Jewish messianic belief, the reference is to the temple that God would build with *his* hands. This temple fulfills the promise in II Samuel 7 and was thought by some Jews to be the new community of Israel. For example, the Qumran community believed that they were the temple and may even have explicitly taught that the temple promised in II Samuel 7 was to be a "sanctuary of humans."[24] But quite apart from

22. The curtain has been commonly understood in the light of Hebrews 9 and 10 as referring to the curtain concealing the Holy of Holies. Ultimately this is a correct understanding of the significance of Jesus' death, but there was in the days of Herod also an outer curtain over the doors separating the sanctuary from the forecourt. Some early Church Fathers thought it was this curtain that was torn and understood its tearing as a symbol of destruction. Cf. D. Juel, *Messiah and Temple* (Missoula: Scholars, 1977), pp. 140ff.

23. Mark calls the testimony that Jesus referred to such an eschatological temple false and says that the witnesses did not agree (Mark 14:55-59). It was false in the sense that Jesus never said that he would destroy the temple and perhaps false also in the sense that the witnesses understood the rebuilding as a magical rebuilding of a temple of stone in three days; yet, on another level, the false testimony speaks the truth: Jesus' death destroys the temple and his resurrection rebuilds it.

24. All agree that the Qumran community viewed itself as the temple and its works as atonement for Israel. Cf. B. Gärtner, *Temple and Community in Qumran* (Cambridge: Cambridge University Press, 1965). There is disagreement whether Qum-

Qumran, it does appear that Mark expects his readers to think of II Samuel 7. For immediately after the charge is made about building a temple without hands, the high priest asks whether Jesus is the Messiah, who is the Son of God (Mark 14:61). It is II Samuel 7 that describes the son of David, the Messiah who will build God's house, as "God's son." Therefore, Mark considers the temple built without hands to be the promised house that God and the son of David will build, a house that will include the regathering of scattered Israel under the Davidic Shepherd-Prince (II Samuel 7:8-11).

Does the Gospel of Mark contain any hint that this temple not made with hands is a new community? There is such a hint if one observes the intended connection between two passages in Mark. At the close of the Gospel there is a recollection of Jesus' earlier promise that he would go before his disciples to Galilee (Mark 16:7). The earlier promise is in Mark 14:27f.:

> You will all become deserters; for it is written,
>   "I will strike the shepherd,
>   and the sheep will be scattered"
> But after I am raised up, I will go before you to Galilee.

Although the Old Testament quotation is from Zechariah 13:7 and not II Samuel 7, both the oracles of Zechariah and the prophecy of II Samuel 7 contain the promise of the Davidic Shepherd-Prince who will gather the people of Israel and establish them in peace. The disciples, scattered by the death of Jesus and very much afraid, are instructed to go to Galilee to meet this Davidic Shepherd-Prince of Israel, whose task is to establish them as the new Israel. Mark does not say explicitly that the temple built without hands is this new community of Israel, but the hint is there.

---

ran spoke of the messianic temple as a "sanctuary of humans." For the affirmative, cf. G. J. Brooke, *Exegesis at Qumran,* pp. 92ff.; and for the negative, D. Juel, *Messiah and Temple,* chapter 8.

Jesus and Ezekiel's Temple of Glory

Ezekiel prophesies a future temple filled with the glory of the Lord, who promises to dwell in the midst of his people forever (Ezekiel 43:5, 7). The Gospel of John proclaims the One in whom the glory of God becomes flesh and dwells among his people (John 1:14). Surely there is a connection. If the Old Testament temple exists only to express God's desire to dwell with his people (Isaiah 66:1f.), then Jesus is the fulfillment of God's desire. The essential truth of Ezekiel's temple has become reality apart from a building of stone. That may seem like a surprising twist in the fulfillment of prophecy, but with Stephen and the prophet Isaiah we should know that "the Most High does not dwell in houses made with human hands" (Acts 7:48). God dwells in Jesus and in us (John 14:23), and the reality of Ezekiel's temple exists throughout the world.

On that high note of fulfillment the Gospel of John begins. The Word of God, who was God and through whom all things were created, "became flesh and lived," that is "tabernacled," "among us, and we have seen his glory, the glory as of the Father's only son, full of grace and truth" (John 1:14). What was once present in the tabernacle in the wilderness and in the temple in Jerusalem now "tabernacles" among us in Jesus Christ. God has kept his promise and has demonstrated that he is the merciful God "abounding in steadfast love [grace] and faithfulness [truth]" (Exodus 34:6). The truthfulness of God is his faithfulness in keeping his covenant promises.[25] God promised that he would dwell with his people, and Jesus is the incarnate proof that God is faithful who keeps his covenant promises. Jesus is the appearance of the glory that is full of grace and truth. What God promised in the Old Testament covenant and symbolized in the temple is now accomplished in Jesus Christ. The grace and truth of God have been fully expressed.

When fulfillment happens, the institutions that were types or symbols of that reality are no longer necessary. They are displaced by the

25. Cf. G. E. Ladd, *The Pattern of New Testament Truth* (Grand Rapids: Eerdmans, 1968), pp. 77-80. Even though John does not use the common word for grace found in the earlier Septuagint translations, he clearly has the Old Testament covenant in mind. Cf. R. Schnackenburg, *The Gospel According to John* I (New York: Seabury, 1980), pp. 272f.

reality they symbolize. Jesus' body is the new temple because Jesus is both the place of atonement and the place of God's presence. He is "the Lamb of God who takes away the sin of the world" (John 1:29), the passover sacrifice (19:36), and the One in whom God is so fully present that he can say: "whoever has seen me has seen the Father" (14:9). Temples of stone can no longer compete, and Jesus need not be a magician who would try to rebuild in three days what others had taken forty-six years to build (2:20f.). Jesus did not come to turn Ezekiel's architectural blueprints into the most magnificent temple ever constructed by human hands. That the Messiah was supposed to do this was the misunderstanding of Jesus' opponents, a misunderstanding shared by his own disciples until the resurrection opened their minds. Ezekiel's temple of glory is Jesus, a truth revealed in the incarnation, proclaimed in Jesus' teaching, and made understandable by his resurrection (2:21f.). An era had come to an end.

Not only did the temple lose its significance in the resurrection of Jesus, but the sacred mountain on which the temple was built did as well. Such was Jesus' astonishing message to the Samaritan woman. When she understood that Jesus was a prophet, since he knew all about her past life, she asked him to resolve the most important dilemma separating the Samaritans and the Jews: Which mountain was the sacred mountain (John 4:20)? The Samaritans claimed that Mount Gerizim was the sacred place that God had designated for his temple, and in the fourth century B.C. they had built a temple there.[26] But the Jews claimed that Mount Zion was the place designated by God. Since, according to Moses, there was only one sacred mountain and hence only one temple (Deuteronomy 12:5, 11; Psalm 24:3), which was the proper mountain and the sacred temple in which God dwelt? Conflict over that question had separated Samaritan from Jew for centuries. Both claimed obedience to Moses, but both could not be right.

Jesus' reply to this woman was totally unexpected. No one, either Jew or Samaritan, could have anticipated it. Your dilemma, he says, has completely disappeared, since the possibility of worshipping God is far greater than the two options set forth in your question. If merely for

26. For the Samaritan argument based on Deuteronomy, see R. Brown, *The Gospel According to John* I (New York: Doubleday, 1966), p. 171.

historical reasons you want to know the answer, then it is the case that "You [Samaritans] worship what you do not know; we [Jews] worship what we know, for salvation is from the Jews" (John 4:22). In other words, the temple in Jerusalem was, in fact, the proper temple, and Mount Zion was the sacred mountain designated by Moses. But all that no longer matters, since "the hour is coming when you will worship the Father neither on this mountain nor in Jerusalem." Instead, "the hour . . . is now when true worshipers will worship the Father in spirit and truth" (vv. 21, 23).

Such an answer reveals that Jesus is more than a prophet providing insight into a difficult question. He is the Messiah, the Savior of the world, inaugurating the fulfillment of the promises. The Old Testament era of a sacred mountain with a sacred temple has come to an abrupt end. Now in the time of fulfillment holiness is no longer tied to sacred times and sacred places. True worship is simply worship in spirit and in truth.

The Old Testament had already prophesied such worship (Zechariah 14:20f.). When the final Day of the Lord would come, it would no longer be just the pots and the bowls of the temple that were holy. Instead, all the pots and pans in the kitchens of Jerusalem and Judah would be holy, and the slogan "Holy to the LORD" would be inscribed on the bells of horses pulling chariots and wagons through the streets of Jerusalem. In other words, holiness would spill out of the temple and embrace the whole of human life. All of life and all its activities would come to be holy.

Now that day had come. Specific sacred places no longer mattered. In fact, there are no specific sacred places, no Holy Land, no sacred building, no sacred utensil for worship. Consequently, no pilgrimage to the holy temple on a holy mountain is required. Instead, every land is or can be holy, every building, every time or place, every utensil is or can be sacred. Worship is now universal, tied to no special sacred time or sacred place. Worship is possible in any place at any time. All that is required for true worship is the Spirit and the truth. Jesus is the truth (John 14:6), and he gives the Spirit to all who believe in him (7:39). Thus the only requirements for genuine worship in the age of fulfillment are that one be in Jesus and have received the Spirit. Temples of stone and sacred mountains have lost their significance because God no longer dwells there to make such places sacred. God is present in Jesus and in the Spirit, a presence that can be experienced and worshiped any place in the world. Jesus' reply to the Samaritan woman announces the radical end of the Old Testament temple era.

How does this radical end of the Old Testament temple era influence the fulfillment of Ezekiel's prophecy of a future temple? As we have already seen, Ezekiel's temple promise of the glory of God dwelling in the midst of his people is fulfilled in Jesus. The Gospel of John also announces that the blessings that were to flow from Ezekiel's temple of glory now flow from Jesus Christ. Ezekiel prophesied that a river would flow from the temple and renew life (Ezekiel 47). Jesus announces that the rivers of living water now flow from him, and he invites all to drink (John 7:37-39). Are Ezekiel and Jesus speaking of the same river? If they are, how do we know?

The Gospel of John presents Jesus as the fulfillment of the feasts, the holy days, and the institutions of the Old Testament.[27] Most of the major festivals at the time of Jesus contained within themselves the promise of the Messiah. Since Jesus issued the invitation to come to him to drink during the Feast of Tabernacles (John 7:2), it is important to discover how Jesus fulfills the messianic expectations associated with this feast.

The dedication of Solomon's temple took place during the Feast of Tabernacles (I Kings 8:2), and since then a special relationship had existed between the temple and this feast. This relationship is seen also in Zechariah's prophesies concerning the final Day of the Lord. Besides announcing the coming triumphal entry of the messianic king into Jerusalem (Zechariah 9:9), the opening of a fountain to cleanse Jerusalem from sin and uncleanness (13:1), and the flowing of living waters from Jerusalem (14:8), Zechariah also proclaims an ideal Feast of Tabernacles to be celebrated by peoples from all nations coming to the

---

27. For example, besides the temple Jesus fulfills the expectations associated with the sabbath (John 5), the Passover (John 6), the Feast of Tabernacles (John 7), and the Feast of Dedication (John 10), as well as the more generalized messianic hopes of Judaism (John 3) and Samaritanism (John 4). This understanding of the structure and purpose of the Gospel of John has become quite common and is found in the commentaries and other works on the Gospel by C. H. Dodd, R. Brown, R. Schnackenburg, B. Lindars, C. K. Barrett, L. Morris, and others.

renewed eschatological temple (14:16-21). This future messianic era will witness the final purified temple and all the blessings associated with the celebration of the Feast of Tabernacles.

What were those blessings? A water ceremony lay at the heart of the celebration of the Feast of Tabernacles. Each day of the feast the priests would circle the altar and pour out a libation of water drawn from the pool of Siloam, and on the seventh day this ceremony was performed seven times. The pouring of water on the altar was a prayer for rain for future crops as the harvest was celebrated at the Feast of Tabernacles. But at the time of Jesus it had also become a prayer for the promised outpouring of the Holy Spirit. In the Old Testament there are references to a river of living water. It was believed to have flowed first from the rock in the wilderness, and it was prophesied that it would flow from the temple in Jerusalem (Ezekiel 47) and from Jerusalem itself (Zechariah 14:8). This river of life was understood as the promised outpouring of the Holy Spirit, and it was for the outpouring of this river of life that Jews prayed at the Feast of Tabernacles.[28]

Thus, at that memorable Feast of Tabernacles Jesus proclaims that he fulfills their expectations and is the answer to their prayers. The river of life prophesied by Ezekiel and Zechariah had already begun to flow, and now it was possible to drink of it. As the new temple of glory, Jesus is the source of all blessings, and after his glorification he will give the Holy Spirit to all who believe in him (John 7:37-39). When that gift is received, believers will also have within them "a spring of water gushing up to eternal life" (4:14). The blessings of renewal and refreshment, of healing and life, are already flowing from the temple.

Of course, Ezekiel's prophecy has not yet arrived at its complete fulfillment. Such fulfillment will occur when the new Jerusalem descends from heaven to earth, since in that city there is no temple but a river flows "from the throne of God and of the Lamb," a river bringing life and healing to the nations (Revelation 22:1f.). Although this

---

28. For this interpretation and the rabbinic evidence on which it is based, see C. H. Dodd, *The Interpretation of the Fourth Gospel* (Cambridge: Cambridge University Press, 1955), pp. 348ff.; Brown, *The Gospel According to John* I, pp. 320ff.; Schnackenburg, *The Gospel of John* II, pp. 155ff.

complete fulfillment is still future, we need not wait until then to drink from that river of life. Already it is flowing from "the Lamb of God who takes away the sin of the world" and who gives the Spirit to all who believe. The rivers of John 7:38 and Revelation 22:1f. are one and the same, Ezekiel's river, a symbol of the life-giving presence of God, the Holy Spirit. Thus the fulfillment of Ezekiel's vision began at that memorable Feast of Tabernacles, continues wherever the Spirit is poured out, and will be completed when the heavenly Jerusalem becomes the new Jerusalem. Jesus is Ezekiel's temple of glory both now and in the future.

What happened to this temple of glory after Jesus' departure to the Father? Did the glory of God depart? Is there no longer any visible sign of God's presence with his people? The Gospel of John announces the continuation of fulfillment in the disciples of Jesus. In his prayer to the Father, Jesus announces that "the glory that you have given me I have given them, so that they may be one, as we are one, I in them and you in me, that they may become completely one, so that the world may know that you have sent me and have loved them even as you have loved me" (John 17:22f.). The disciples take the place of Jesus. Just as Jesus, because of his unity with the Father, was the manifestation of the glory of God, so now the disciples, because of their unity with Jesus and the Father, become the visible evidence of the ongoing presence of God in the world. They will be that visible sign of God's presence only as they live in unity with each other.

Such was the intention for the presence of God's glory from the beginning. It was intended to create a true community of men and women who love God and their neighbors. The law and the prophets proclaim that without such a presence of God there can be no true community. So Ezekiel saw a temple of glory in the midst of a new city and prophesied that God would dwell in the midst of his people so that they would become this genuine community. Now, in Jesus, God dwells with his people and creates out of Jesus' disciples this new community of people who love one another (John 13:34f.). At the center of this community the glory of God becomes visible. Ezekiel's temple is fulfilled in Jesus and his disciples.

The Temple as Community

Although the Gospels have much to say about the temple, their focus
falls on Jesus, who fulfills the purpose and the functions of the temple.
The old era is coming to an end, and in the new era Jesus is the place
of atonement and of the presence of God. He is the temple, and he
builds it. Yet nowhere do the Gospels say explicitly that the disciples
are the temple. The Gospels contain hints in this direction, and the
Johannine language about the glory of God is almost explicit temple
language. Still, none of the Gospels ever says directly that the disciples
are the temple.

For such explicit teaching one must turn to the New Testament
Epistles. On significant occasions Paul addresses the Church as God's
temple, the holy temple, because God's Spirit dwells in them: "You are
God's temple" (I Corinthians 3:16f.). The holy temple is no longer a
building but a community.[29] In a chapter devoted to the unity of Jew
and Gentile in Christ, Paul caps his discussion by describing all believers as "built upon the foundation of the apostles and prophets, with
Christ Jesus himself as the cornerstone. In him the whole structure is
joined together and grows into a holy temple in the Lord; in whom you
also are built together spiritually into a dwelling place for God" (Ephesians 2:20-22). The temple is a metaphor of unity, the unity of believers
with one another in Christ that exists because of the indwelling presence
of God in the Spirit. In addition, the language of Paul contains a clear
allusion to Isaiah 28:16, where God announces his work of salvation
and calls Israel to believe:

> See, I am laying in Zion a foundation stone,
>   a tested stone,
> a precious cornerstone, a sure foundation.

God was already erecting his new edifice in Jerusalem in the Old
Testament era, and the Old Testament manifestations of that edifice of

29. In English translation the community theme is not self-evident because "you"
can be either singular or plural. However, in the original Greek "you" is plural. Paul
is addressing the entire congregation (in fact, all Christians) who constitute together a
single temple.

salvation — whether the king (Psalm 118) or the temple — find their fulfillment in the building of which Jesus Christ is the cornerstone. As Isaiah saw a temple situated on this foundation stone in Zion, a temple in which Jews and Gentiles serve the Lord, so Paul announces the fulfillment of that vision in the new temple in the Lord. The worldwide community of believers in Christ is the superstructure erected on the foundation that God laid in Zion, and the ancient prophetic vision of a universal temple is being fulfilled.[30]

Fulfillment of the Old Testament promises concerning the temple is the theme of II Corinthians 6:16–7:1. There the apostle asserts the claim that "we are the temple of the living God," and he grounds that unique status of the Church in the fulfillment of Old Testament promises: "we have these promises." The basic promise finding fulfillment is expressed in Leviticus 26:11f.: "I will place my dwelling in your midst. . . . And I will walk among you, and will be your God, and you shall be my people." That promise was initially fulfilled by God's dwelling in the tabernacle and the temple, but now that symbolic presence became actualized in the new temple, the new people of God. That early promise is renewed in Ezekiel 37:27, where, after the exile, God promises to build an eternal sanctuary in the midst of the people to sanctify them: "My dwelling place shall be with them; and I will be their God, and they shall be my people." Such Old Testament promises given originally to Israel are claimed by the apostle as possessions of the New Testament Church. He may be suggesting that the fulfillment is even richer than the promise, since God not only walks among us but dwells *in* us (II Corinthians 6:16). God has welcomed his people as promised (Ezekiel 20:34) and has become a Father to his sons and daughters. This last promise comes from II Samuel 7:14, where it applied first of all to the king as God's son (daughters are not yet mentioned), but through the king who represents Israel all Israel was included. Now in Christ that promise extends to all sons and daughters who confess God as Father through Jesus Christ.[31] Amazingly, the house that God promised to build for David now turns out to be the house that

30. Cf. R. J. McKelvey, *The New Temple: The Church in the New Testament* (Oxford: Oxford University Press, 1969), chapters 7-8.
31. Cf. C. K. Barrett, *The Second Epistle to the Corinthians* (New York: Harper and Row, 1973).

David's son builds for God! The restored house of David (Acts 15:15ff.) is the new temple, and its cornerstone is Christ. All who believe in Christ, who is David's son and God's Son, enter into David's house and God's house. And the promises are fulfilled.

The consequence of this fulfillment of the promises is holiness, holiness as both a gift and a task. Holiness is primarily a gift of the presence of God. The temple is holy because God dwells there. God's people are holy because they are the temple in which God lives. But holiness is also a requirement for retaining the presence of God. Therefore, Paul quotes also from the commands given to the priests when the people of Judea departed from Babylon (Isaiah 52:11; II Corinthians 6:17). Just as the priests who bore the vessels of the Lord had to leave behind everything that was unclean and purify themselves because the Lord would be accompanying them on their journey, so now believers, those who are the temple, must separate themselves from iniquity, darkness, idolatry, and unbelief. Because of the holiness of God dwelling in them, they are exhorted to cleanse themselves "from every defilement of body and of spirit" and to make "holiness perfect in the fear of God" (II Corinthians 7:1). They are like priests in the temple, who must be holy because God is holy. Holiness is a gift, but it must become perfectly expressed in the lives of God's people. Holiness applies to people, no longer to a building, and temple service no longer refers to ritual acts but to life itself.[32]

Can Both Be True?

Can the temple be both a building and a community of people? Is it possible to hold that the temple indeed finds fulfillment in the New Testament body of believers and still maintain that the building features of Ezekiel's prophecy must also be literally fulfilled? One could point out that in the Qumran community, which existed at the time of Christ, such beliefs were held simultaneously. While viewing their own community as the temple and applying to themselves the rules that applied to the priests, they still expected a new temple to be built by the

32. For similar teaching see I Peter 2:4-10.

Messiah.[33] Certainly on the basis of the Old Testament and Judaism,[34] it would be possible to hold both understandings of the temple.

But can both be held in the light of the fulfillment in Jesus Christ? What significance could a temple building have? If the significance of the Old Testament temple was in its sacrificial ritual as the means of atonement, then from a New Testament perspective the temple as a God-ordained means of atonement is exhaustively fulfilled in the once-for-all atonement of Christ. If the significance of the temple was in its Holy Place as the symbolic presence of God, then from a New Testament perspective that symbolic presence finds its actual fulfillment in Jesus Christ. In the light of such complete fulfillment, could a rebuilt temple of stone regain its Old Testament significance?[35] If, as Jesus declared to the Samaritan woman, sacred space is no longer geographically delimited, what significance could a geographically delimited temple have as the dwelling place of God? It is conceivable that a temple could be built again on Mt. Zion — though with a Muslim sacred building located on the site the obstacles are formidable — but if a temple should be built would Mt. Zion again become the holy mountain? The New Testament proclaims the fulfillment in Christ of all the essential characteristics of the Old Testament temple, and thus it appears that a limited temple on a specific holy mountain has been displaced by a universal temple in Christ. The only perspective that still awaits complete fulfillment is the coalescense of temple and city, that is, the arrival of the city that is itself the temple. God's history of redemption is moving toward that goal. That is the subject of our next chapter.

33. Cf. R. McKelvey, *The New Temple,* p. 53; L. Gaston, *No Stone On Another,* p. 174.

34. The Pharisees also believed that "the whole world was a divine Temple in which each man served as priest," but also accepted the temple in Jerusalem. C. L. Finkelstein, *The Pharisees: The Sociological Background of Their Faith* (Philadelphia: Jewish Publication Society, 1963), p. XXXIX.

35. C. L. Feinberg gives the traditional dispensational suggestion concerning the significance of a rebuilt temple: The sacrifices in the rebuilt temple would be only a memorial of the completed work of Christ. He then argues that if the Church has a memorial of the finished redemption in the Lord's Supper, why should not Israel have a visible memorial of that same redemption? "The Rebuilding of the Temple," in *Prophecy in the Making,* ed. C. F. H. Henry (Carol Stream, IL: Creation House, 1971), chapter 5. But on a New Testament basis how could one argue that the Lord's Supper is not the prescribed memorial also for Jews?

CHAPTER IV

Jesus and the Land:
A Question of Time and Place

The biblical message is very earthy. At its center lies a concern about land, about the earth. From creation to consummation the question is: Who possesses the earth, how can it be possessed, and when? The consistent biblical answer is: The meek shall inherit the earth (Matthew 5:5; Psalm 37:11). The inheritance promised to those who enter the kingdom of God inaugurated by Jesus Christ includes a renewed earth. The gospel of salvation never becomes so spiritual that it loses its rootedness in creation, and its belief in the resurrection of the body remains absolutely foundational. Without the resurrection of the body the gospel is in fact without meaning. God created humankind out of the dust of the earth and for life on this earth. Therefore, God now redeems human beings for life in a renewed body on a renewed earth. Human beings require land under their feet. Therefore, redemption does not dissolve but rather renews the creation.

When God established his covenant with Abraham, he included a promise of land. God called Abraham to go to the land that God would show him (Genesis 12:1). After the covenant ceremony in which God passed between the pieces of the divided animals, God promised Abraham, "To your descendants I give this land" (15:18). Again when Abraham was ninety-nine years old, God renewed the covenant promise: "I will give to you, and to your offspring after you, the land where you are now an alien, all the land of Canaan, for a perpetual holding; and I will be their God" (17:8). Thus the covenant with Abraham was tied to this earth and concerned inheritance of it. The promise of the land is central to the promise of salvation.

This promise of the land has haunted Jewish consciousness for centuries. Forced from the land in A.D. 70 — from the land promised to Abraham, Isaac, and Jacob — the Jews have wandered over the face of the earth as exiles and sojourners in foreign lands. The very uncertainties and dread caused by the loss of the land, which Moses had announced as consequences of disobedience to the covenant, became their daily experience:

> The LORD will scatter you among all peoples. . . . Among those nations you shall find no ease, no resting place for the sole of your foot. There the LORD will give you a trembling heart, failing eyes, and a languishing spirit. Your life shall hang in doubt before you; night and day you shall be in dread, with no assurance of your life. (Deuteronomy 28:64-66)

No wonder that the promise of the land given to their ancestors captured the Jewish religious consciousness, since again and again they have experienced the dread of life outside The Land. Their mourning for that land was expressed as mourning for Jerusalem, since that city, the City of David, which was once the City of God, symbolized the hopes of the covenant. Three times a day and at sabbath worship and festivals, Jewish prayers remember Zion:

> Merciful Father,
>   Deal kindly with Zion,
> Rebuild the walls of Jerusalem.
> Truly, in thee alone we trust,
>   High and exalted King and God, eternal God![1]

Return to Jerusalem became the central hope: "Next year in Jerusalem." Over the many centuries of sojourn in foreign lands, Jerusalem and the

---

1. A sabbath prayer for the synagogue as the ark is opened so that the Torah scrolls can be taken out. Cf. A. J. Heschel, *Israel: An Echo of Eternity* (New York: Farrar, Straus, and Giroux, 1969), pp. 43f.

land were never forgotten. Even at the joyous occasion of a wedding celebration, a glass is broken in remembrance of the destruction of Jerusalem. "If I forget you, O Jerusalem . . ." (Psalm 137:5). The Jerusalem of dust and stones lingered on in the soul of Judaism as a longing and hope.

Jews have remembered that the biblical message, for all its heavenly splendor and its focus on God as the source of all good and the originator of salvation, is focused on the earth, on the land, on a city. Expressing that Jewish perspective, Rabbi Heschel affirmed:

> The love of this land was due to an imperative, not to an instinct, not to a sentiment. There is a covenant, an engagement of the people to the land. . . . To abandon the land would make a mockery of all our longings, prayer, and commitments. To abandon the land would be to repudiate the Bible.[2]

In contrast to this Jewish faith, the faith of many Christians has been more heaven-oriented than land-oriented. The biblical themes of land and city have been spiritualized and focused elsewhere than on this earth. Is this the inevitable result of New Testament teaching? Is the land or this earth no longer important? Strikingly, since the return of the Jews to Palestine, the biblical theme of the land has caught the attention of Christian theologians. There is a renewed recognition that "the land is a central, if not *the central theme* of biblical faith" and that as a consequence "it will no longer do to talk about Yahweh and his people but we must speak about Yahweh and his people *and his land*."[3] It has been acknowledged that "of all the promises made to the patriarchs it was that of the land that was most prominent and decisive,"[4] and that the land as promised and given by God stood at "the center of Israel's faith and thought in all the historical epochs of the Old Testa-

---

2. Heschel, *Israel*, p. 44.
3. W. Brueggemann, *The Land* (Philadelphia: Fortress, 1977), pp. 3, 126.
4. W. D. Davies, *The Gospel and the Land* (Berkeley: University of California Press, 1974), p. 24. G. von Rad claims the same significance for the land in the first six books of the Old Testament: "In the whole of the Hexateuch there is probably no more important idea than that expressed in terms of the land promised and later granted by Yahweh." *The Problem of the Hexateuch and Other Essays* (London: Oliver and Boyd, 1966), p. 79.

ment period.''[5] Obviously one cannot tell the story of God's covenant
with his people without telling the story of The Land.

Still, is this focus on land more an Old Testament emphasis than
a New Testament theme? Does the fulfillment proclaimed by the New
Testament embrace also the land and the earth? Or does the New
Testament head off in a different direction so that the theme of the land
is set aside? Should Christians affirm with Rabbi Orlinsky that the land
is the *essence* of the covenant and that "were it not for the Land that
God promised on oath to Abraham and to Isaac and to Jacob and to
their heirs forever, there would be no covenant"?[6] Or does that exag-
gerate the significance of the land? Clearly, if the theme of the promised
land is central to the Old Testament — and no one would dispute that
it is — then the fulfillment of that promise is an important question to
be addressed to the New Testament. How is the promise of the land
fulfilled, or how will it be fulfilled? If the answer is to be understood,
it is necessary first to examine the promise of the land and its significance in the Old Testament before turning to the New Testament.

The Land: An Irrevocable Promise

We have already noted that in the Bible the promises of salvation have
an unbreakable tie to the land. From the call of Abraham (Genesis 12)
to his conflict with Lot (Genesis 13), from Abraham's concern about
an heir (Genesis 15) to the promise of the birth of Isaac (Genesis 17),
God promises again and again to give the land to Abraham and his
descendants. God renews this basic promise with Isaac: "to you and to
your descendants I will give all these lands, and I will fulfill the oath
that I swore to your father Abraham" (Genesis 26:3). Isaac in turn
includes in his blessing of Jacob this prayer: "May [God] give to you
the blessing of Abraham, to you and to your offspring with you, so that

5. R. Rendtorff, "Das Land Israel im Wandel der Alttestamentlichen
Geschichte," in *Judische-Volkgelobtes Land,* ed. W. Eckert, et al. (Munich: Kaiser,
1970), p. 153.

6. H. M. Orlinsky, "The Biblical Concept of the Land of Israel," in *The Land
of Israel: Jewish Perspectives,* ed. L. A. Hoffman (Notre Dame: Notre Dame University
Press, 1986), p. 34.

you may take possession of the land where you now live as an alien —
land that God gave to Abraham" (28:4). Then at Bethel God himself
promises Jacob: "The land on which you lie I will give to you and to
your offspring" (28:13). Later, in Egypt, Joseph says to his brothers,
"I am about to die; but God will surely come to you, and bring you up
out of this land to the land that he swore to Abraham, to Isaac, and to
Jacob" (50:24).

The land was promised and this promise was confirmed by an
oath sworn by God. So throughout their sojournings and time of slavery
in Egypt the people of Israel kept their eyes on the promised land
"flowing with milk and honey" (Exodus 3:17) and placed their hope
in the faithfulness and power of their covenant God. The promised land
was grasped by faith and in hope because for centuries it had been
occupied by others and was not yet ready for Israel's possession. From
the vantage point of slavery in Egypt it could be seen only from afar,
but already from the inception of the promise it had been grasped only
by faith. Therefore, when faith faltered on the boundaries of the land,
when fear of tall and strong people overwhelmed faith in the Lord's
promise and presence (Numbers 14), Israel was not allowed to possess
the land. Promised land is grasped by faith, not by strength. It is the
meek who inherit the earth, those who possess confident faith in the
God who always gives what he promises.[7] But when fear cancelled
faith, a generation was condemned to a wandering death in the wilderness. Only those who believed could enter the promised land (Numbers
14:30). Still the promise continued even though possession of the land
was deferred.

The boundaries of the promised land were never defined with
geographic precision. Various descriptions were given at various times
and under varying historical circumstances.[8] Perhaps one may conclude

7. W. Brueggemann comments on Numbers 14 (*The Land*, p. 39):

The land will be given not to the tough presuming ones, but to the vulnerable
ones with no right to expect it. The vibrations begin about the "meek" inheriting
the land, not the strident. This is a discernment that Israel would no doubt have
wished to reject. The world believes that stridency inherits, but in its vulnerability
Israel learns that the meek and not the strident have the future.

8. Cf. Genesis 15:17ff.; Exodus 23:31ff.; Numbers 34:1-10; Deuteronomy 11:24;
Joshua 1:2-4.

that the land is not only a territory but an idea as well. At least "the land" evoked various connotations and was associated with numerous blessings. For a people wandering in a wilderness and depending on miracles for food and water, a land described as flowing with milk and honey evoked the most hopeful anticipations. The land promised economic well-being: It was described as "an exceedingly good land" (Numbers 14:7), a land "watered by rain from the sky, a land that the LORD your God looks after. The eyes of the LORD your God are always on it, from the beginning of the year to the end of the year" (Deuteronomy 11:11f.). The land represented prosperity under God's watchful eye, fruitful fields and herds, an abundance of grain, wine, and oil, and numerous descendants. Such was the land promised by the Lord.

But above all other blessings, the land symbolized safety, peace, and rest. Oppressed in Egypt, buffetted by enemies during the wilderness wanderings, and continuously threatened by death, Israel desired a land that would provide safety, peace, and rest from its enemies. Moses promised the people of Israel that when God brought them into their inheritance, he would give them "rest from your enemies all around so that you live in safety" (Deuteronomy 12:10; cf. 25:19). The conclusion of the story of the conquest of the land tells us that "Thus the LORD gave to Israel all the land that he swore to their ancestors that he would give them; and having taken possession of it, they settled there. And the LORD gave them rest on every side just as he had sworn to their ancestors" (Joshua 21:43f.). Though Israel had fought to conquer the land, the battle was the Lord's and the land was his gift. Promises had been made and promises were kept. The Lord gave Israel the land and the rest that he had promised.

The Land: A Conditional Possession

Entrance into the land was denied to those who lacked faith, and Moses himself was denied entrance because of Israel's disobedience (Deuteronomy 4:21). Therefore, it is apparent that important conditions are attached to possessing the land. Just as faith and the obedience that flows from faith were necessary to enter the land, so faith and obedience are necessary to maintain possession of the land. It remains covenanted land, God's gift to Israel in fulfillment of covenant promises. It never loses its character as a gift, and Israel must never forget the "giftedness" of the land.

Israel cannot establish an independent claim to the land or assert a right to the land because possession of the land was not established by Israel's righteousness, military might, or greatness. Israel was not entitled to the land on the basis of its own righteousness because its sinfulness had been so great that were it not for Moses' intercession on the basis of the covenant with Abraham, Isaac, and Jacob, Israel would have been destroyed in the wilderness (Deuteronomy 9). Even though the army of Israel had destroyed many kings in the land and conquered many cities, its conquest of the land and the prosperity the land then provided were not due to Israel's power; rather, the people were to "remember the LORD your God, for it is he who gives you power to get wealth, so that he may confirm his covenant that he swore to your ancestors" (Deuteronomy 8:18).

The land and its blessings were promised gifts given to those whom the Lord had chosen to be his people. And especially here, at the point of Israel's election, no reasons for this election can be given that could serve as entitlements to the promised blessings. There simply was no reason in Israel for God's choice. Israel was a stubborn people, not righteous, "the fewest of all peoples" (Deuteronomy 7:7), not a great nation. The reason for God's choice resides in God alone. God freely loves Israel and keeps the oath that he made to Israel's ancestors (7:9). God's love is free, his choice unmerited, and the covenant blessings, including the blessing of the land, remain God's gifts of love to his chosen people.

It is not uncommon for Judaism to object to this emphasis on the land as a gift. Orlinsky, for example, objects vigorously to Christian scholars who stress the nature of the land as gift. He argues that the land is not "given" but "assigned." He has uncovered evidence that the Hebrew verb translated "given" is frequently found as a legal technical term in ancient real estate documents. Since the covenant functions as a legal instrument regulating the relationship between God and his people, we need not quarrel with Orlinsky on this point. But he gives a second argument, one that is more basic and far more controversial: The covenant, he says, is a contract like any other contract, an agreement between "equals" that creates a *quid pro quo* situation. Both parties to the covenant have legally binding obligations that lead to rewards. The covenant is thus a purely legal arrangement, and the covenant "blessings" are simply rewards to which one is entitled by fulfilling legal obligations.[9]

Clearly, the real issue is not whether God "gives" or "assigns" the land to Israel, but rather on what basis the gift or the assignment is made. What is at stake is the fundamental understanding of the covenant, a debate that is as old as the apostle Paul and that involves how we understand the Book of Deuteronomy.

The covenant is a legal instrument setting forth the stipulations for receiving the promised blessings. Consequently, Deuteronomy, the book of covenant renewal, is dominated by an emphasis on keeping the commandments. Moses warns Israel against serving other gods or doing what is evil in the sight of God lest the people soon be dispossessed of the land (Deuteronomy 4:25ff.). Maintaining possession of the land while violating the stipulations of the covenant is utterly impossible. Therefore the covenant contains lists of curses as well as of blessings. Curses of exile and destruction like that which fell on Sodom and Gomorrah will fall on Israel if it violates the commandments and forsakes the covenant of the Lord; blessings of prosperity and continuous possession of the land will fall on Israel if it keeps the commandments and walks in the Lord's ways (Deuteronomy 27–29). There is a legal basis for possessing the land, but this legal basis does not undercut the gracious character of the covenant made with Israel's ancestors.

God's covenant with Israel is dominated by themes of grace both in its origin and in its blessings. Never may Israel claim to have provided the basis for its own election. As we have seen, Deuteronomy exalts the themes of God's free choice of Israel, his unmerited love of a people stubborn and sinful by nature. That God established his covenant with the Israelites can be explained only by God's favor, not by their merit, and hence the establishment of the covenant was not a reward but a gift of love. Likewise, covenant blessings, including the land, are gifts of God's love. The land is first of all and always the Lord's, not Israel's. Amazingly, the people Israel are called "aliens and tenants" in the

9. Orlinsky, "The Biblical Concept of the Land of Israel," pp. 28, 42-43.

Lord's land since they have no permanent title to it and possess it with no absolute legal right to it (Leviticus 25:23). Thus the land never ceases being a gift, even when Israel possesses it.

The nature of the land as gift is reflected further in the fact that the land is divided by lot (Numbers 26:55), that its firstfruits must be given to the Lord, that the land also must observe a sabbath, and that land sold for debt must be returned to the original family in the year of Jubilee. Already before Israel entered the land Moses declared, "Heaven and the heaven of heavens belong to the LORD your God, the earth with all that is in it" (Deuteronomy 10:14). Israel is chosen to possess the land as an inheritance from the Lord, but its title remains in the Lord's hands.

Possession of the Lord's land requires that the possessors possess God's image and that the stewards of the land be like their Master. Israel must act as God acts: As God loved Israel, executed justice for the oppressed, and freed Israel from bondage in Egypt, so Israel must respond in love, practice justice in the land, free the oppressed, and be kind to sojourners in the land (Deuteronomy 10). Because God is holy, Israel must be holy, since the land itself partakes of the holiness of God (Leviticus 11:44f.). A holy land cannot tolerate an unholy people and it will vomit Israel out when Israel defiles the land just as it vomited out the wicked nations before Israel entered the land (Leviticus 18:28).

There are conditions for maintaining possession of the land, but these conditions are more the means by which a gift is retained and enjoyed than the self-fulfilled basis for establishing a claim to the land. God already made Israel holy by choosing Israel as his people (Deuteronomy 7:6), and then he requires that Israel be that holy people, those who reflect his holiness on earth. Without holiness the gift of the land cannot be possessed and prosperity, peace, and rest cannot be secured, because that land and the whole earth are the Lord's.

The Land: Lost and Promised Again

Israel did not live long in the land it reached by crossing through the Jordan. The Promised Land could not stomach the worship of idols and

the lack of justice and holiness, so it vomited Israel out.[10] Because Israel
played the harlot with other gods, it could no longer remain in the land
of the Lord (Hosea 9:1-3). Because there was no faithfulness, kindness,
or knowledge of God in the land, the land itself mourned (4:1-3).
Because Israel oppressed widows, orphans, foreigners, and poor people,
the nation was scattered with a whirlwind among other nations and the
land was left desolate (Zechariah 7:8-14). Instead of being the head and
moving upward (Deuteronomy 28:13), because of disobedience Israel
experienced its foes as the head who gloated over its downfall (Lamentations 1:5-7). Rest and peace fled because the Lord and his land resist
transgressors and destroy them.

Awful destruction fell upon the land, and Israel had to admit
that the Lord was in the right because the people had rebelled against
his word (Lamentations 1:8). Yet, amazingly, in the depths of mourning and lamentation because the Lord himself had become like an
enemy to destroy Israel (2:5), Israel still had hope, because

> The steadfast love of the LORD never ceases,
>   his mercies never come to an end;
> they are new every morning.
>
>   (3:22-23)

Though the land that was a gift had been taken away, the covenant
promises had not been cancelled. God is faithful. Within the covenant,
conditions for destruction had been set forth as well as conditions for
blessing, but destruction was never the final note. Moses had promised
that, when in exile Israel remembered the covenant and returned to the
Lord in obedience,

> then the LORD your God will restore your fortunes and have compas-
> sion on you, gathering you again from all the peoples among whom
> the LORD your God has scattered you. . . . The LORD your God will
> bring you into the land that your ancestors possessed, and you will
> possess it. (Deuteronomy 30:1-5)

10. These paragraphs owe much to Brueggemann's stimulating discussion of the
land as gift and not something to be grasped. Cf. his *The Land*.

Even when Israel failed and lost the land, the promise of possession did not cease. The promise that the land will be possessed is irrevocable. But if possession is to be maintained, God's people must become holy as God is holy.

The message of every prophet, even of those sent to announce approaching judgment and imminent doom, always includes a note of hope. Jeremiah, prophesying on the threshold of exile to Babylon and burdened by the coming wrath of God, which he was compelled to announce against his people, bought a piece of land as an objective sign of hope that "houses and fields and vineyards shall again be bought in this land" (Jeremiah 32:15). But first the Lord must give the people "one heart and one way" so that they will fear the Lord and serve him forever (32:39). Fear of the Lord must be placed in their hearts, and they must be cleansed from the guilt of their sins (33:8). Only then can the Lord bring them back to the land and make them dwell in safety. Only then will the desolate places be filled with "the voice of mirth and the voice of gladness, the voice of the bridegroom and the voice of the bride, the voices of those who sing" (33:11).

The amazing message of the prophets is that in spite of the faithlessness of his people, God is faithful and will act in mercy to restore the covenant blessings. God's covenant with Israel is as certain as the order of creation. As long as the fixed order of creation continues, so will God's covenant with Israel continue (Jeremiah 31:35-37). Just as no one is able to break God's covenant with day and night "so that day and night would not come at their appointed time," so no one can break God's covenant with David (33:20ff.). One of David's descendants will rule over the seed of Abraham, Isaac, and Jacob and will establish justice and righteousness in the land. This is God's irrevocable promise. Therefore, Israel can be assured and can confidently hope that God will restore its fortunes and have mercy on its people (33:14-26). The covenant promises are so irrevocably fixed that, if necessary, God himself will make it possible for the conditions to be fulfilled so that the land can again be possessed. He himself will cleanse his people and restore their holiness so that the holy land can accept their presence and shower them with blessings.

Ezekiel comes on the scene in the midst of exile with essentially the same message. The judgment announced by Jeremiah has occurred, the land has been lost, and even God himself has departed from the land (Ezekiel 10–11). Judgment has come because of God's holiness and Israel's lack of holiness. But now that judgment has occurred God will act to vindicate his holy name. Israel will be restored to the land, and God "will sprinkle clean water upon you, and you shall be clean from all your uncleannesses. . . . A new heart I will give you. . . . I will put my spirit within you, and make you follow my statutes and be careful to observe my ordinances" (Ezekiel 36:25-28). Only under such conditions of renewed holiness will the land prosper.

It is thus only God's gifts of grace that make it possible for Israel to inhabit the land. The inheritance cannot be possessed by human effort, not even by human righteousness, because "the righteousness of the righteous shall not save them when they transgress" (Ezekiel 33:12). There are no heirs to the promise without the mercy of God. Sin cancels every effort to grasp the inheritance. But the inheritance remains available as a gift because God gives the holiness that makes it possible for his people to live in the land of which it is said, "The LORD is There" (48:35). Land lost and land regained: lost through Israel's sin, regained by the mercy of God.

The Land, the City, and the Earth

The promise of the land looms large on the pages of the Old Testament, but as the exile approaches and actually occurs the hopes for the land comes to be focused on the city. The lament over the destruction of the land and the exile of Judah is expressed in Lamentations as a lament over Jerusalem. The people are identified as the daughter of Jerusalem, the virgin daughter of Zion. Jerusalem has become the essence of the land and the symbol of the people of God because it is in Jerusalem that God dwells.[11] Likewise Ezekiel, though he is concerned about the restoration of the entire land, devotes a large portion of his prophecy to a restored temple in a renewed city, because the essence of the hope for the gifted land is the assurance that God will dwell there.

11. "Jerusalem to the prophet is the quintessence of the land, corresponding to the people. . . . Jerusalem is called the mother of Israel, and she is also used as a synonym for Israel." Heschel, *Israel,* p. 15.

But it is especially in the prophecies of Isaiah that Jerusalem becomes the essence of Israel and of the land. Jerusalem lies at the center of the promises and becomes their content. The marvelous message of comfort given to Israel is addressed to Jerusalem first of all:

> Comfort, O comfort my people,
>> says your God.
> Speak tenderly to Jerusalem.

(Isaiah 40:1-2)

The promised salvation is on its way, return from exile lies ahead, and its hopes are focused on the comfort of Zion, that is, Jerusalem (51:3).

> So the ransomed of the LORD shall return,
>> and come to Zion with singing;
> everlasting joy shall be upon their heads;
>> they shall obtain joy and gladness,
>> and sorrow and sighing shall flee away.

(51:11)

Jerusalem will be rebuilt, and God himself will lead the procession to Zion. It will be "A City Not Forsaken" (62:12). Therefore, Jerusalem can be confident for its future since the herald "brings good news," "announces salvation," and "says to Zion, 'Your God reigns' " (52:7).

The scope and the glory of this future Jerusalem is hard to contain within the walls of a rebuilt city. As the prophecy of Isaiah unfolds from the near horizon of the promised return from exile to the far horizon of the new heavens and the new earth, the scope and glory of Jerusalem expands to embrace the entire earth. This city's children will be more numerous than those of Jerusalem before the exile, and she will need to enlarge her "habitations" to contain them because her descendants will "possess the nations." Her husband is the God of the whole earth (Isaiah 54:1-5), and he will vindicate Jerusalem before the nations. The wealth of the nations will come to her (55:5; 60:5; 61:6). The promised salvation will be a time of joy and singing, an end to oppression and violence; in fact, the curse on creation itself will be reversed and "all the trees of the field shall clap their hands" (55:12f.). Behind this renewed and enlarged glory of Jerusalem stands the glory of the Lord, for "the LORD will arise upon you, and his glory will appear over you" (60:2). The Jerusalem of the future will be indeed the City of God, and her inhabitants will be called "The Holy People, The Redeemed of the LORD" (60:14; 62:12).

When will this be? What Jerusalem does the prophet envision? Is it the earthly city, the heavenly Jerusalem, or the Jerusalem of the new creation? The prophet does not make such distinctions. Jerusalem is simply Jerusalem, but it will be in truth God's city, the center not only of the land of Canaan but of the entire world. It will be a city the like of which has not been experienced in human history because it will experience the reversal of creation's curse, will be inhabited only by those who are holy, and will have no need of sun or moon because God will be its light and glory (Isaiah 60:19). Has this Jerusalem which God creates as "a joy, and its people as a delight" already become a part of the new creation (65:17ff.)? Does the eternal nature of God's renewed covenant with Jerusalem indicate the beginnings of the new that makes all things new (59:20f.)?

Much disagreement about the answers to these questions could have been avoided if Isaiah had clearly distinguished the phases through which Jerusalem will pass. But prophets in their visions tend to see the whole sweep of history rather than its discrete parts. Even prophets are not given the insight to know the times or the seasons. Jerusalem is for Isaiah a single entity embracing the city to which the exiles returned and the city that will embody the salvation promised to the whole earth. This future city of salvation is a universal city, and just as the former Jerusalem represented the land of Canaan, so the Jerusalem of the future will be the quintessence of the new earth.[12]

Although God did not allow his prophets to make as many distinctions as we would like them to have made, is it possible that we may be able to make a few more? Perhaps we can, since just as the apostle Paul gained insight into the mystery of God's will through the fulfillment of that will made visible in the ingathering of the Gentiles (Ephesians 3:4-6), so we may look at the history of redemption subsequent to Isaiah to discover how God is actually fulfilling his promises

12. R. Smith asserts that Jerusalem "became in the biblical materials a symbol for the kingdom of God." *Micah-Malachi* (Waco: Word, 1984), p. 231.

concerning the land and the city. What kind of fulfillment happened from the time of the return from exile to Jesus? How does fulfillment of the promises in Christ affect the promised inheritance of land and city? Perhaps we may even ask (and will do so more fully in our final chapter) whether the return of Israel to the land in our own age sheds any light on the fulfillment of the promises concerning the land and the city. As we answer these questions important distinctions will be introduced into our understanding of the prophetic visions.

The Land: After Exile

Israel did repossess the land as God had promised. Beginning with Cyrus's edict, which opened the way to a return from exile, many Israelites returned from Babylon to rebuild the temple and the city. Under the leadership of Ezra, Nehemiah, Zerubbabel, and Joshua and with the needed encouragement of the prophets Haggai and Zechariah, the foundation of the temple was laid, the city walls rebuilt, and the temple completed. God himself returned to Jerusalem and promised prosperity, comfort, and a "sowing of peace" (Zechariah 1:16f.; 8:1-13). Yet, in spite of such promising beginnings, the land did not blossom as Isaiah had prophesied, neither were safety, peace, and rest ever secured. Violence was never far away, oppression almost never ceased, and it became apparent that the conditions for possessing the land had not been met.

God was on the side of the returning exiles. He declared that he purposed no longer to do evil to the returning exiles as he had done to their ancestors for provoking him to wrath. On the contrary, his purpose now was to "do good to Jerusalem and to the house of Judah." But in order to experience that good Israel would have to speak the truth, avoid evil, and practice the justice that makes for peace (Zechariah 8:14-17). Both Ezra and Nehemiah struggled zealously to form a people obedient to the covenant and separated from their pagan neighbors, a people who kept the sabbath, oppressed no one by receiving interest, and followed the Torah. But in spite of covenant renewal ceremonies, Israel failed to keep the covenant, and the land of promised freedom became a land of slavery. Ezra complained to God that they were slaves in the land that

God had given to their ancestors to enjoy (Nehemiah 9:36), and slaves they continued to be. Foreigners dominated their affairs from the return from exile until the destruction of Jerusalem by the Romans in A.D. 70. There was one brief period of independence won by the Maccabees and maintained by their descendants from 142 to 65 B.C., but even this period of freedom proved a disappointment as conflicts and even internecine warfare erupted under their own kings. Ezra's complaint that the people were slaves in the Promised Land became an accurate description of the post-exilic period. Politically Israel was in bondage to foreign powers.

Where was the promised land of rest and peace? Where was the prophesied Jerusalem filled with the glory of God and a blessing to the nations of the world, the Jerusalem that would "enjoy the wealth of nations" (Isaiah 61:6) rather than having its wealth devoured by the nations? It had not yet appeared. The fulfillments received after the exile were less than what had been promised.

Why should that be the case? Certainly, God's word never fails. Why then did fulfillments that had begun not continue to their fullness? The covenant allows only one possible answer. In spite of Israel's post-exilic zeal for the law, which produced the synagogues, the reform under Ezra, the Maccabean revolt, and the struggle for independence against Rome, righteousness had not been achieved (cf. Romans 10:2f.). Without righteousness and holiness the land could not really become in its fullness the Promised Land. As Jesus said, "unless your righteousness exceeds that of the scribes and Pharisees, you will never enter the kingdom of heaven" (Matthew 5:20). Jesus' and Paul's prophetic critique stems not from something outside God's covenant with Israel but precisely from the demands of the covenant itself. It is identical with the testimony of the prophets, who declared that righteousness achieved by humankind is always insufficient as the basis for inheriting the promises because human sin destroys its sufficiency (Ezekiel 33:12). The proclamation of the New Testament gospel of salvation comes as God's answer to this human insufficiency. It proclaims a righteousness that comes as a gift from God, an atonement through the cross of Christ that cleanses from the guilt of sin and bestows holiness through the Holy Spirit, and thus supplies the conditions necessary for inheriting the land or entering into God's kingdom. The *Promised* Land cannot be taken by force, secured by royal decrees or political treaties, nor merited by human righteousness. Holiness alone causes the land to flourish and to be what God has promised it will be — but holiness is beyond the human grasp.

The Land: A New Testament Perspective

The New Testament appears to be strangely silent about the land. The promise of the land is central to the Old Testament, but it appears that in the New Testament it lies on the periphery. The land as such is hardly ever mentioned, at least not explicitly. Does this indicate that the New Testament gospel is essentially different from the message of the Old Testament? Are the promises of the gospel spiritual and transcendant (heavenly) and intended to be contrasted with the earthy landedness of the Old Testament promises? Although in the history of the Christian Church some have so interpreted the matter, such a drastic contrast has always been considered incorrect, and its radical affirmation has been judged heretical. But if, on the contrary, the message of the New Testament stands in continuity with the promises of the Old Testament covenant, what has happened to the promise of the land?

Is it possible that the apostle Paul, educated in the law, would be uninterested in the promise of the land? One common interpretation of Paul argues that together with the law the land has become irrelevant. While for Judaism the law itself needs the land for its complete fulfillment, now that Christ has fulfilled the law the land has become irrelevant.[13] For Paul all the Old Testament promises are now fulfilled and have become personalized in Christ. Territory is insignificant and place does not matter. All that is significant is "in Christ." Thus, it is argued, the promises have been "deterritorialized," and Paul's silence

13. Judaism teaches that "the God of Israel can in fact be served by Jews anywhere and everywhere, but *fully and perfectly* only in the Land of Israel, where additional landbound commandments obtain." R. S. Sarason, "The Significance of the Land in the Mishnah," in Hoffman, ed., *The Land of Israel*, p. 136. Tradition also held that Moses said that "many precepts were commanded to Israel which can be fulfilled only in the Land of Israel. I wish to enter the land so that they may all be fulfilled by me." C. Primus, "The Borders of Judaism," in Hoffman, ed., *The Land of Israel*, p. 102.

concerning the land reflects a conscious rejection of any concern with territory at all. His interpretation of the promise is "a-territorial" because the promises have been "personalized" and "universalized" in Christ.[14]

Obviously, the "in Christ" relationship is the key to Paul's understanding of the fulfillment of the promises. But we still need to ask about the contours of this life in Christ. Certainly it is no longer restricted to the literal boundaries of the land promised to Israel, but is it in fact without territorial hopes or interests? If, as some suggest, Paul considers the promises fulfilled in Christ to be spiritual realities only with no territorial significance, then is it not surprising that in writing to the Ephesian church Paul recites "the first commandment with a promise": "Honor your father and mother . . . so that it may be well with you and you may live long on the earth" (Ephesians 6:2f.)? Significantly, Paul's quotation modifies the original Old Testament form of the promise by omitting the phrase, "that the LORD your God is giving you," a phrase referring to the land of Canaan (Deuteronomy 5:16).[15] By omitting this specification, Paul declares that now in Christ the promise applies to any land. The promise has indeed been universalized, but it has been universalized precisely with reference to land. What was once a blessing promised to God's people in the particular land of Canaan, given by God as a gift, is now promised to God's people living anywhere on the earth, which was given by God as a gift.[16]

Thus, there is at least this one hint that Paul's relative silence about the land should not be construed as an implicit declaration that the land has become irrelevant and that the promise of land should be forgotten. A universalized land is not an irrelevance; it is, in fact, what the prophets

14. Cf. Davies, *The Gospel and the Land,* pp. 173-179.

15. Although some have tried to restrict Paul's meaning to Jews in the land of Canaan, while others have gone to the opposite extreme of applying it to happiness in heaven, neither of these interpretations makes any sense of the quotation in the context of the Ephesian church. Cf. J. Eadie, *Commentary on the Epistle to the Ephesians* (Grand Rapids: Zondervan, 1977, reprint of 1883 edition), pp. 441f.

16. This is Calvin's position: "Moses expressly mentions the land of Canaan. For the Jews there could be no happy or desirable life outside it. But as the same blessing of God is today shed on the whole world, Paul has properly left out mention of a place, the particular discrimination of which lasted only till the coming of Christ." *Commentary on Ephesians* (Grand Rapids: Eerdmans, 1965), p. 213.

anticipated. Consequently, interpreters should exercise caution in treating Paul's supposed silence about the land as a radical negation of the Old Testament promise.

The Epistle to the Galatians is a case in point. Here Paul is deeply concerned with the promises made to Abraham, but he does not explicitly mention the land. Should it simply be assumed that the promise of the land has been rejected by Paul? The evidence does not point in that direction. Interestingly, the central phrase on which Paul's entire argument rests, "And to your offspring" (Galatians 3:16), is found only in promises that contain the promise of the land.[17] Paul's argument, however, concerns not the content of the promises (which is simply assumed) but the identity of its recipients and the means by which the promises will be inherited. Paul declares that Christ is the corporate embodiment of Abraham's seed, the One who represents and defines the authentic covenant lineage. In Christ it has been revealed that the inheritance of the promises is not by law but by promise, that the inheritance is a gift of God's grace (as was Canaan in the Old Testament) to those who believe. All those who have faith as Abraham had faith, who now believe in Jesus Christ, are "Abraham's offspring, heirs according to the promise" (3:29).

Heirs of what? Of "the promises," according to Galatians, and, according to Romans 4:13, these promises to Abraham and his descendants can be summarized in the promise "that he would inherit the world." For Paul, the promise to Abraham had a cosmic sweep, including not just the territory of Canaan but the entire inhabited world.[18] Whereas Judaism tended to place a national and restricted territorial stamp on the promises to Abraham, Paul perceives in Christ their universal scope,[19] a universalism that Isaiah had associated with the future

---

17. Cf. Genesis 13:15; 17:8; 24:7. But even apart from this fact, Paul treats the promises as a unity.

18. Cf. *Theological Dictionary of the New Testament* (Grand Rapids: Eerdmans, 1964-76) III, p. 888.

19. C. K. Barrett quotes J. Bonsirven's comment concerning Jewish neglect of the universal promise:

It seems that the universalist promise, "In thee shall all the families of the earth be blessed," was scarcely ever taken up. The commentaries do not develop it; or else it undergoes this significant transformation — all the blessings that God

Jerusalem. Just as this future Jerusalem, heir to the nations, had become
for the prophets a symbol of the kingdom of God, so Paul now perceives
the kingdom as the content of the inheritance. On every occasion but
one when Paul uses the verb "inherit," its object is the kingdom of
God.[20] The promise that the land will be inherited has become the
promise that the kingdom of God, which embraces all nations, the entire
creation, and even the cosmos itself, will be inherited. In Christ believers
already possess all things, and that includes "the world" (I Corinthians
3:21f.). Paul's attention is focused not on the land of Canaan but on the
new creation and on the powers that hold this present creation in sub-
jection (Romans 8:17-25).

Has Paul rejected or even forgotten the promise of the land? By
no means.[21] Instead, the horizons of the land have been shaped by the
revelation of Jesus Christ. His previous Jewish focus on a particularistic
fulfillment has been transformed into a Christian universalism focused
on the new creation. Just as in Christ the temple had become a universal
dwelling place and the seed of Abraham had been transformed into a
universal people, so the promise of the land already embraces the world.
Christ is already established in his universal rule, but there is a time
and an order for the complete manifestation of the fulfillment of the
promises (I Corinthians 15:20-28). An eschatological reservation
hovers over the earth. The final enemy has not yet been defeated, the
final resurrection has not yet occurred, and thus the creation has not yet
experienced its full release from bondage to freedom. Yet, because
Christ is the means by which the inheritance is received and by which
the conditions for possessing the earth are met, a time has been set aside
for the proclamation of the gospel, a time of grace, in which the Father
and the Son delay the manifestation of their claim to the earth and delay

bestows upon the earth, the rain, and even creation itself, were given for
Abraham's sake.

From First Adam to Last: A Study in Pauline Theology (New York: Scribner, 1962),
p. 34.

20. Galatians 5:21; I Corinthians 6:9f.; 15:50. The exception is Galatians 4:30.

21. J. Hester concludes from his study of the term "inheritance" that "the land
plays a very real role in Paul's concept of Inheritance in spite of the fact that he never
mentions it in his letters." *Paul's Concept of Inheritance* (Edinburgh: Oliver and Boyd,
1968), p. 82.

the final elimination of evil. But the renewal is already real in Jesus Christ and has been manifested in his resurrection from the dead. The goal of the creation and its history has appeared within history. Therefore, the gospel goes to the nations with its urgent appeal to believe. This eschatological reservation will be lifted by the return of Christ.

A similar universalizing of the promise is found in the Epistle to the Hebrews. The promised rest, symbolized by the land, was never really enjoyed in the Old Testament, at least not for long. The rest joyfully proclaimed by Joshua became only a temporary blessing later lost. Thus within the history of Israel in the Old Testament the original occupation of the land became only an anticipation of a rest still to be enjoyed. As faith was required then, so Hebrews declares that now faith in Christ is required to enter God's rest (Hebrews 4). This rest is not achievable within the territorial boundaries of any specific land on earth because it is a blessing associated with a heavenly country and city, a land and a city whose builder and maker is God (Hebrews 11). Thus, for the author of Hebrews, the land promise is focused on the city, whose nature and destiny we will consider in the next section of this chapter.

The Gospels, like Paul, speak more implicitly than explicitly about the land. But since the land can be focused in the city and the city is a symbol of the kingdom of God, the Gospels are permeated by a concern for the land. The kingdom, however, is a universal reality, and its embrace of the land is universal in scope. This kingdom has been established by Christ because he already possesses "all authority in heaven and on earth" (Matthew 28:18). The citizens of that kingdom receive the blessings promised to those who receive the land in the Old Testament: comfort, satisfaction of hunger, righteousness, laughter, and peace (Matthew 5:1-11; Luke 6:20ff.). The meek and the poor — those who place their trust and confidence in God and even in the midst of poverty and oppression expect everything from God — inherit the kingdom and the earth.

But the Gospels, again like Paul, place an eschatological reservation over the inheritance. Although the kingdom has been inaugurated by the ministry of Jesus and established by his death and resurrection, its full manifestation has been deferred. Since that kingdom means the overthrow of the oppressor, the defeat of evil, and the blessed rule of God, the gospel of that kingdom must first be proclaimed to the nations before the final end can come. Because the kingdom is a gift received in Christ, his disciples are exhorted to manifest its presence by giving to the poor and seeking the things of that kingdom (Luke 12:31ff.). Even during the time of the eschatological reservation the kingdom is present in humble fashion among the nations of the world. Such a gospel is not a "spiritualized" adaptation of an earthly promise, but the very means by which the Old Testament promise will be fulfilled.

Even the supposedly "spiritual" Gospel of John never completely loses contact with the earth. Though unlike the Synoptic Gospels John speaks infrequently of the kingdom of God and focuses instead on eternal life as its chief blessing, and even though this eternal life is already a present blessing prior to the resurrection of the body, the Gospel of John insists on the resurrection of the body as the culmination of the life that Jesus gives (John 6:39, 44, 54). Thus there is a tension between the promise of eternal life enjoyed under the conditions of present existence and the life of the age to come, but the tension is only temporal and will be resolved on the last day. However much the future blessings are experienced in the present as spiritual blessings, entrance into the full experience awaits the resurrection because the resurrection accomplishes the final entrance into the land. Thus the Gospel of John also shares the basic biblical perspective: The meek will inherit the earth because the earth already belongs to Jesus Christ.

The City: New Testament Fulfillment

The hopes for the land were centered on the city already in some of the Old Testament prophets. Jerusalem dominated the landscape of the future as the essence of the land and the symbol of the people of God. The blessings of peace, prosperity, and joy were contained within that city. The New Testament shares that focus.[22] The virtual absence of explicit references to the land is not caused by neglect of a central theme

---

22. This same dominance of Jerusalem is found in the Jewish literature of the intertestamental period, that is, the Apocrypha, the Pseudepigrapha, and the Qumran writings. Davies observes concerning this literature that "just as Jerusalem became the quintessence of the land, so also the Temple became the quintessence of Jerusalem." *The Gospel and the Land,* p. 152.

of the Old Testament. Instead, following the lead of several Old Testament prophets, the New Testament concentrates the future on Jerusalem and the temple. In this city the inheritance of land promised to Abraham, Isaac, and Jacob finds its fulfillment.

Why Jerusalem should become the essence of the matter is quite obvious. Jerusalem held a unique status among the cities of Israel and the world. God himself had chosen Jerusalem for his dwelling place (Psalm 132:13), and it was called the City of God, a city that God establishes forever (Psalm 48:1f., 8; 132:14). Such eternity is ascribed to no other city since it is a gift that flows from God's presence in the city. God promised to dwell in the midst of Israel forever (Ezekiel 43:7), and therefore the temple in which God dwells is the symbol of Jerusalem's eternal quality. Because God dwells in this city, Jerusalem is called also "the City of the Great King." Jerusalem is a royal city, "the throne of the LORD" (Jeremiah 3:17), the city from which God will rule the nations and to which the nations will gather. Because God dwells in it, Jerusalem is also the Holy City (Isaiah 52:1), and citizenship in that city means salvation. Jerusalem will be holy and its citizens will be holy, and consequently its citizenship rolls contain the names of those destined for life (Isaiah 4:3). Surprisingly, this role of Zion's citizens is not restricted to Israelites but includes peoples from the nations of the world. God will also register them on the citizenship rolls of Jerusalem (Psalm 87).[23]

Obviously, Jerusalem embodied the promise of the land. All that had been promised concerning the land — security, peace, and prosperity — depended on Jerusalem's status as the City of God. For only where God dwelled would there be that essential quality of holiness necessary for possessing the land. No wonder, then, that all attention was focused on Jerusalem. Israel's hopes for salvation, for freedom and peace, were wrapped up in the destiny of that city.

However, tragic events enveloped that city in New Testament times. The "eternal" city was destroyed like any temporal city in the history of the world. The war machine of the Roman Empire overran the City of Peace. Salvation fled from the walls of Jerusalem as chaos

23. For a helpful development of these themes concerning Jerusalem, see J. De Young, *Jerusalem in the New Testament* (Kampen: Kok, 1960).

and destruction reigned. What had happened to the promises? Why were they not fulfilled in the geographical Jerusalem of history? The New Testament answers these questions in several places.

The first answer is found in the Gospels. The promises were not fulfilled in geographical Jerusalem because its people responded to Jesus just as they had responded to the prophets God had sent throughout their history: "Jerusalem, Jerusalem, the city that kills the prophets and stones those who are sent to it" (Matthew 23:37). The consequence of this hostile response to Jesus is loss of land since the kingdom of God would be taken from them (21:33-44). The leaders in Jerusalem did not understand how to receive the inheritance of the land or know the conditions necessary to receive the promised peace (Luke 19:42). God had visited Jerusalem in the person of his Son, and Jesus had desired to gather the children of Jerusalem "as a hen gathers her brood under her wings," but they were unwilling for that to happen. Consequently, Jerusalem stood forsaken, devoid of the promised presence of God, and exposed to horrendous judgment (Matthew 23:37f.; Luke 23:28ff.). Even the temple would be destroyed, and days of vengeance would come (Matthew 24; Luke 21). In place of prosperity, there would come awful destruction; in place of peace, violence; in place of joy, weeping. Jesus wept over the future that would fall on Jerusalem (Luke 19:41ff.).

A surprising response to the question about Jerusalem is found in Galatians 4. The surprise is occasioned both by the unusual form of the allegory there and by what that allegory says about Jerusalem. Its teaching assumes the thesis of Galatians 3 that the inheritance promised to Abraham was given by a promise and received by faith and that the law could not be the means for receiving the inheritance because it can only pronounce a curse on human sin. Paul directs the allegory against those who think that through submission to the law the promised inheritance will be achieved. Two covenants are represented by two women. Hagar represents the covenant stemming from Sinai, and her children are children of slavery. There is no surprise in associating the children of Hagar with slavery. With that even Paul's opponents would agree. The surprise is that Hagar represents Sinai and "corresponds to the present Jerusalem, for she is in slavery with her children" (Galatians 4:25). In other words, Paul declares that the city of Jerusalem in his own day, which as a symbol of Judaism requires submission to the law as the means for gaining righteousness and inheriting the promises, has become a city of slavery. No longer is Jerusalem the promised city of freedom. Historical Jerusalem has lost its significance as the promised Holy City, the city of salvation.

What happens to the marvelous promises associated with Jerusalem? Astonishingly, the apostle Paul speaks of another Jerusalem, represented by Sarah as the mother of Isaac, but this Jerusalem is not yet visible, not yet on earth. This Jerusalem is "above" and is the promised city of salvation. All the promises of salvation are now associated with this Jerusalem because "she is our mother." Hence this Jerusalem is the fulfillment of Isaiah's prophecy that the future Jerusalem would have more children than pre-exilic Jerusalem had had, for its citizens are already being gathered on earth (Galatians 4:26f.). All who accept the promise through faith in Christ are the children of this free woman and inherit the promises given to Abraham and focused on Jerusalem.

Thus, for Paul, the historical disobedience of Jewish Israel has shattered the salvific significance of historical Jerusalem. The unbelief of Jewish Israel has shattered the unified picture of Jerusalem found in the prophets into two distinct Jerusalems: the geographic city in history, now a symbol not of salvation but of slavery under the law, and "the Jerusalem above," whose citizens are already being gathered on earth to inherit the promises. In this contrast, only the Jerusalem above can be considered the City of God.

A third response to the question about Jerusalem is found in the Epistle to the Hebrews. Here also a distinction is made between the earthly Jerusalem and the Jerusalem that is heavenly and is to come. The author understands this as due in part to the fault of Israel since the very establishment of the new covenant implies as much (Hebrews 8:8). But attention is then focused on the better things that God intended: The Old Testament saints did not receive what was promised during their historical pilgrimage on earth because "God had provided something better so that they would not, apart from us, be made perfect" (11:40). Fulfillment of the Old Testament promises of land and city in God's plan required the inclusion of the New Testament saints. Consequently, the earthly Jerusalem is no longer the embodiment of hope. The embodiment of hope is now the heavenly Jerusalem, which God designed and built (11:10, 16). As in the Gospels, the guilt of the earthly Jerusalem comes into view in the crucifixion of Jesus. Because Jesus was crucified outside the gate of the city, the earthly city is no longer the eternal city. Eternity belongs only to the city that is to come (13:14).

Old Testament prophecy about the future Jerusalem is affected by the history of Jerusalem, and the New Testament takes that unfolding history of redemption very seriously. What the prophet Isaiah did not and could not distinguish in his prophecies concerning the Jerusalem of the future now becomes clearer. Even though for some time the earthly Jerusalem was the central focal point of the redemptive promises, the response of that city to the coming of Jesus shattered that focus. Israel's historical disobedience, however, did not shatter the promises. All of the promises associated with Jerusalem continue in force, but the earthly city can no longer be the agent and object of that fulfillment. God himself must build the city of fulfillment and create the citizens who meet the conditions for inhabiting that city. The city that God builds is now above — where Christ is — and the citizens who inherit that city are those who believe in Christ and keep the covenant.

An underlying premise of New Testament teaching is that the promises that once were attached to the earthly Jerusalem are now attached to the heavenly and New Jerusalem. Believers in Christ have been born in Zion because Jerusalem is "our mother." Because their names are on its citizenship rolls, "our citizenship is in heaven" and their "names are in the book of life" (Philippians 3:20; 4:3). The author of the Book of Revelation clearly equates the book of life with the citizenship roll of Jerusalem, proclaiming that "nothing unclean shall enter [the city] . . . but only those who are written in the Lamb's book of life" (Revelation 21:27). These phrases constitute a clear reference to Isaiah 52:1, which promises that no longer would the unclean or uncircumcised enter the holy city, and Isaiah 4:3, which promises that everyone who "remains in Jerusalem will be called holy, everyone who has been recorded for life in Jerusalem." Thus the New Testament affirms that believers from every tribe and nation are citizens of Jerusalem and heirs of its promised salvation. Jerusalem has become a universal city and, as such, a symbol of the new earth. The fulfillment of the promise of land is under way, and the meek *will* inherit the earth.

Names for Jerusalem reflecting the presence of God there are also ascribed to the heavenly and the new Jerusalem. As part of the contrast between the old and the new covenants, Hebrews proclaims that Christians "have come to Mount Zion and to the city of the living God, the heavenly Jerusalem" (Hebrews 12:22). The Jerusalem that will come down out of heaven is called the City of God, and its citizens are those who conquer by faith (Revelation 3:12). This city is also the Holy City because God dwells in it, even though now there is no temple there, because the city itself has become the temple (Revelation 21). This city is the goal of human history into which the nations enter and by whose light the nations will walk (21:24). It is the Royal City from which God reigns, the city whose presence on earth means that peace and prosperity will transform the land, the city in which God's servants will reign forever (ch. 22).

Thus the New Testament is more interested in the promise of the land than it appears at first glance. To discover this interest one must keep in mind two basic principles. First, like some of the Old Testament prophets, and like Judaism in the Intertestamental Period, the New Testament focuses on Jerusalem as the essence of the promise of the land. Second, since fulfillment happens in Jesus Christ, an eschatological reservation hovers over the final fulfillment. Possession of the land and the appearance of the city are not yet seen. The present fulfillment is found only in Jesus Christ. Thus, since the conditions for inheriting the land are fulfilled only in Jesus and since he is the temple where God dwells, the New Testament locates Jerusalem where Jesus is. Jesus is in heaven and so is Jerusalem. Claims to citizenship are established by faith in Christ, and hence the members of the Church, the body of Christ, are also citizens of that city. Both the Church and the new Jerusalem are called the bride of Christ, indicating that the members of the Church and the citizens of that city are the same (II Corinthians 11:2; Revelation 21:2, 9; 22:17). Christ has only one bride. Thus even the New Testament teaching concerning the Church is not divorced ultimately from the promise of the land and the city.

The New Testament has neither forgotten nor rejected the promise of the land. Earthly Jerusalem has been transcended, but the present location of the city in heaven is viewed within the continuing history of redemption, which will culminate on the renewed earth. The heavenly Jerusalem will descend as the new Jerusalem, but not until its citizens have been gathered from among the nations of the world. Judging from this perspective of fulfillment, one may conclude that the original land of Canaan and the city of Jerusalem were only an anticipatory fulfillment of God's promise. As such they function in Scripture as a sign of the future universal city on the renewed earth, the place where righteousness dwells.

But does the New Testament simply defer the promise of land to the future? Are no aspects of this promise realized in the present? This is a very large question to which we will give a very brief answer. While the promise waits for the descent of the New Jerusalem, the Church is commissioned to function as an anticipation of that city. Jesus appointed his disciples to be a city on a hill whose light cannot be hid (Matthew 5:14). This is the function of the New Jerusalem: The light they manifest originates in the glory of God, which has risen on them (Matthew 4:16; Isaiah 60:1-3). This light is revealed to the world by the good deeds and righteous conduct of Jesus' disciples, and the purpose of their commissioning is that thereby "the Lord GOD will cause righteousness and praise to spring up before all the nations" (Isaiah 61:11; Matthew 5:1-20). Thus the New Jerusalem asserts its claims and manifests its presence in the present time. From it — through the disciples of Jesus — the law of God is already being issued to the nations, and the nations are coming to learn God's way (Isaiah 2:1-4). The mission of the Church to the nations, making disciples and teaching them to observe all that Jesus commanded (including the law of God in the Sermon on the Mount), fulfills the role of Jerusalem among the nations.[24]

Consequently, the blessings of Jerusalem are already available in the present time, and Jerusalem is already to some degree being established on the earth. But the demonstration of its presence is only in the form of a sign. The full reality has not yet been manifested. Still, a sign is a part of the reality to which it points, like the first flower of spring or the first snowflake of fall. The New Jerusalem has not yet come, and yet it is already here in the form of a sign as Jesus' disciples proclaim and live the righteousness that will fill the new earth. Enjoyment of the promise of the land has already begun, but only as a sign anticipating the future.

24. This theme of the role of law and righteousness in the mission of the Church will be developed below in chapter V.

CHAPTER V

Jesus and the Law:
A Question of Fulfillment

The coming of Jesus Christ created a significant challenge to the proper understanding of the Old Testament: Who is Israel, what is the role of the temple, and what happens to the promise of the land? At stake in each of these challenges lies the question of the role and function of the law. What happens to the law when Jesus comes? Jesus said, "Do not think that I have come to abolish the law and the prophets; I have come not to abolish but to fulfill" (Matthew 5:17). What does this saying mean? What is this fulfillment that does not abolish?

The Christian tradition gives no unanimous answer to this significant question. Some traditions believe that the law has come to an end and no longer has anything at all to do with the Christian believer. The law is for the Jews, but the Christian is under grace and completely free from the law. The law has no place within the arena of the gospel. Other traditions, however, believe that fulfillment in Christ does not support such a radical separation of law from gospel. While the believer is free from the curse of the law, the positive righteousness of the law must still characterize the life of the Christian. The issues are complex and these differences of opinion have existed for centuries. In this chapter we will focus exclusively on the perspective presented by the Gospel of Matthew. There will be opportunity in the following chapter for some brief comments on Paul's view of the matter.

We have chosen the Gospel of Matthew not only because it directly addresses the question of the law and its fulfillment but also because it

113

is focused on the theme of righteousness. To enter the kingdom of heaven, one must have a righteousness that exceeds that of the scribes and Pharisees (5:20), must perform good works so that others may glorify God (5:16), must be perfect as God is perfect (5:48), and must seek God's kingdom and righteousness (6:33). The doing of righteousness looms so large in Matthew's Gospel that without righteousness entrance into the future kingdom is denied, even if one has prophesied and performed miracles in Jesus' name (7:21-23). The kingdom of God belongs only to those who produce its fruits (21:43), and for Matthew the fruit of the kingdom is the doing of righteousness.

Matthew's passion for works, for moral integrity and ethical conduct, sounds perilously like creating one's own perfection. If, as Matthew teaches, nothing passes from the law, not even an iota or a jot, if one's righteousness must exceed meticulous scribal righteousness, if one must be perfect like God, if such standards hold in the final judgment, who then will be able to stand? Matthew's emphasis on righteousness has bothered many interpreters, leading several radical critics to suggest that Matthew has imported Judaism into his Gospel and causing Marcion, a second-century heretic, to throw Matthew out of the canon because of its close ties to the law and the Old Testament. Even if such radical positions strike us as unnecessary, all Christian interpreters have to face Matthew's radical emphasis on the necessity of works and the doing of righteousness. What does this emphasis reveal about Matthew's view of the law and its fulfillment?

To illumine Matthew's view of the law and its fulfillment, we shall develop in some detail three central themes: First, what is the relationship of law and grace, and is righteousness for Matthew a gift or a demand or both? Second, what happens to the law in the age of fulfillment? Third, is the law and its righteousness still foundational for the good existence of the Church and the world?

Law and Grace in the Gospel of Matthew

Matthew's Structures of Grace

Whereas Matthew's emphasis on righteousness is apparent to all, his structures of grace are more implicit and thus more difficult to discover.

Consequently, many have suggested that Matthew simply assumed that his readers had already heard the gospel and that he did not have to mention it. That is a possibility. If the Gospel of Matthew was written for the church at Antioch sometime after A.D. 65, after Paul had already been in that city, the church there would have been acquainted with his presentation of the gospel. This assumption was commonly made by interpreters from the days of the ancient Church until the present. For example, commenting on the Sermon on the Mount, John R. W. Stott claims that "the whole sermon in fact presupposes an acceptance of the gospel (as Chrysostom and Augustine had understood), an experience of conversion and new birth, and the indwelling of the Holy Spirit."[1] However, the language of conversion, new birth, and the indwelling of the Holy Spirit is not found in Matthew as it is in other parts of the New Testament.

St. Augustine also thought that Matthew's emphasis on good works assumed a structure of grace. Augustine discovered this structure in the gifts of the Spirit given to the anointed Branch of Jesse in Isaiah 11:2ff., "the spirit of wisdom and understanding, the spirit of counsel and might, the spirit of knowledge and the fear of the LORD." Since the activity of this anointed Branch would produce righteousness on earth, Augustine proposed that behind the virtues required in the Beatitudes stand these gifts of the Spirit of God. Matthew's emphasis on virtue or good works thus assumes this foundation of grace.[2] Augustine's proposal contains profound theological wisdom, but the question remains whether Matthew merely assumes a structure of grace or actually develops one.

Actually a definite structure of grace is found in the first chapters of Matthew's Gospel. There, before the Sermon on the Mount, the focus falls on the person and mission of Jesus Christ. Jesus is the son of Abraham and David, the Son of God, he who fulfills the promises of the Old Testament. Jesus is God's gift of grace, the one through whom the renewal of Israel occurs. We described this christology in our second chapter as a christology of fulfillment, an Israel–Son of God christology.

1. *Christian Counter-Culture: The Message of the Sermon on the Mount* (Downers Grove, IL: InterVarsity, 1978), p. 37.
2. Cf. U. Luz, *Matthew 1–7: A Commentary* (Minneapolis: Augsburg, 1989), p. 244.

Jesus is presented by Matthew as the corporate representative of Israel in whom and through whom the promises to Israel are being fulfilled. By means of this renewal of Israel the promises reach out to the entire world. Jesus in his person and mission is the embodiment of the faithfulness of God. He is Emmanuel, "God with us."[3] This gift of God precedes and makes possible Matthew's demand for righteousness.

Significantly, Jesus describes his mission as fulfilling all righteousness (Matthew 3:15). John's baptism symbolized God's standard of righteousness, and sinners who failed to meet that standard had to repent before being baptized. But Jesus had no sin and no need of repentance. Instead, he declared that he would fulfill the righteousness symbolized in John's baptism, that he would actively carry out that righteousness and thereby establish the righteousness of God's kingdom on earth.[4] Consequently, after the temptations in the wilderness, in which Jesus recapitulates the temptations of Israel in the wilderness and displaces Israel's former disobedience with his own obedience, he announces that light has dawned and the kingdom of heaven is at hand (4:15-17).

All of this precedes the demands of the Sermon on the Mount and constitutes a profound eschatological christology, a christology of fulfillment. This beginning of the Gospel also anticipates its end, and Matthew's early christology of fulfillment anticipates a further fulfillment in the cross and resurrection. Jesus' obedience to the will of God involves also the drinking of the cup, the blood of the covenant poured out for many for the forgiveness of sins (Matthew 26). It entails him remaining on the cross in the face of temptation in order to receive God's own deliverance because it is the meek who shall inherit the

---

3. Luz also finds an emphasis on grace in Matthew's christology. "The one who forgets that the Sermon on the Mount does not come until after Matt. 1–4 and, in the meaning of Matthew *can* not come any earlier, has misunderstood it." *Matthew 1–7*, p. 215. Georg Strecker argues the contrary position: The person of Jesus is not significant for understanding the nature of the Sermon on the Mount. But if Matthew's christology does not lay the foundation of grace for Jesus' demands, then his demands cannot be the liberating gospel that Strecker claims they are. Strecker, *The Sermon on the Mount* (Nashville: Abingdon, 1985), pp. 33ff.

4. That Jesus' baptism and his announcement of fulfilling all righteousness take place in the wilderness is also significant. The wilderness is the symbol of Israel's disobedience, the place of sin and lack of righteousness, and thus Jesus' announcement anticipates the fulfillment of Isaiah 32:15-20; 35.

earth. And the fruit of Jesus' righteousness is the earthshaking announcement that the turning point of the ages has dawned, the inauguration of the general resurrection (27:51-54), and Jesus' reception of all authority (28:18). Matthew's stress on the doing of righteousness is surrounded by the righteousness made possible by Jesus' life, death, and resurrection. The themes of fulfillment point to the grace of God that precedes and makes possible the demand for righteousness.

Any approach to Matthew's rigorous ethical demands that overlooks this foundation in fulfillment will inevitably turn Matthew's world upside down. Matthew's Christian world, built on a foundation of fulfillment in Christ, with its consequent demand for righteous living in God's kingdom, will be turned into a new edition of old Israel, with scribes trained for the kingdom producing meticulous rules with ever larger barriers hedging in God's righteous will. As it is, eschatology has become the barrier to legalism, but any Christian tradition that loses touch with biblical eschatology will return to forms of legalism. Matthew's demand for obedience is never merely for obedience to a command, for Christian obedience is always a participation by hope in the new reality of the kingdom of God.[5]

The Beatitudes and Righteousness: Gift or Demand?

The Beatitudes precede Jesus' explicit demand for greater righteousness in the Gospel of Matthew. The Beatitudes are blessings in form, but how should these blessings be understood? Are they a bestowal of gifts, or are they veiled demands for ethical conduct? Although the Beatitudes have been commonly interpreted as alternative forms of law demanding virtuous conduct, contemporary interpreters have discovered their eschatological thrust.[6] This eschatological shape, which reflects blessing

---

5. Following the teaching of Romans 8, Calvin asserts that even nature obeys not merely because of God's commands (what we today call natural law) but because of the hope of renewal. Eschatology makes even the world go round! For Calvin's eschatological perspective as a barrier to legalism, see D. Holwerda, "Eschatology and History: A Look at Calvin's Eschatological Vision," in D. K. McKim, ed., *Readings in Calvin's Theology* (Grand Rapids: Baker, 1984), chapter 18.

6. Scholars distinguish between wisdom-cultic beatitudes and prophetic-

and gift, is significant for understanding Matthew's perspective on righteousness.

Many interpreters agree that the promises of Isaiah 61 shape the first four Matthean beatitudes. This means that even in the Beatitudes Matthew continues his christology of fulfillment. In the Beatitudes Jesus presents himself as God's anointed Servant who bestows the promised blessings. Like a benediction, the Beatitudes actually bestow blessings on the afflicted and the poor. If Isaiah 61 is the promise fulfilled in the first beatitude, then "poor in spirit" refers not only to spiritual poverty and sorrow for sin but also to circumstances that include social, political, and economic affliction.[7] The poor of Isaiah 61 are the afflicted ones. To such Jesus announces that the blessings of the kingdom are already at hand, blessings not only of forgiveness of sins but also of righteousness and justice, even though the fullness of these blessings awaits the future consummation.

This theme of righteousness as blessing is continued in the fourth beatitude: "Blessed are those who hunger and thirst for righteousness, for they will be filled." Righteousness is a broad biblical category embracing the actions of both God and humanity. While there is in Matthew a strong emphasis on righteousness as the standard of conduct that God has willed for humanity (5:10, 20; 6:1), even Matthew cannot be restricted to righteousness as a demand for virtuous conduct. For in the fourth beatitude those who hunger and thirst for righteousness are evidently desiring something that lies beyond their ability to achieve or produce. Furthermore, the passive form of the promised consolation, "they will be filled," makes it obvious that righteousness will come as a gift from God.

What is that promised righteousness? A look at Isaiah 61 proves helpful. On the one hand, righteousness entails a restored relationship with God:

---

apocalyptic beatitudes. The former border on parenetic exhortation, calls to obedience, whereas the latter are statements of future vindication and reward and are intended to give assurance and encouragement in the face of trouble. Matthew's Beatitudes are prophetic-apocalyptic and thus not an alternate form of the law. Cf. R. A. Guelich, *The Sermon on the Mount* (Waco, TX: Word, 1982), pp. 63-65.

7. Cf. Guelich, *op. cit.,* p. 75: "For Matthew, the *poor in spirit* are those who find themselves waiting, empty-handed, upon God alone for their hope and deliverance while beset with abuse and rejection by their own social and religious context."

> I will greatly rejoice in the LORD,
>   my whole being shall exult in my God;
> for he has clothed me with the garments of salvation,
>   he has covered me with the robe of righteousness.
>
> (v. 10)

This robe of righteousness is the gift of salvation, a restored covenant relationship with God.

On the other hand, the righteousness of the covenant is never simply a gift passively received. Isaiah describes restored Israel as "oaks of righteousness, the planting of the LORD, to display his glory" (61:3), and promises that "the Lord GOD will cause righteousness and praise to spring up before all the nations" (v. 11). Thus God's gift of righteousness becomes an expression of historical obedience before the nations. Those who hunger for righteousness look to God for his gift of righteousness, which makes possible their own acts of historical obedience.

This same emphasis on righteousness as both gift and task is found elsewhere in the Sermon on the Mount. Jesus exhorts his disciples and the crowd to seek first his Father's kingdom and righteousness (Matthew 6:33). The kingdom is obviously God's gracious redemptive rule, which has come as a gift in Jesus Christ. God's righteousness is the righteousness that God himself manifests both in his mercy and in his demands. Righteousness is, then, virtually a synonym for the kingdom of God as the arena of salvation and justice. Significantly, Jesus' exhortation to seek God's kingdom and righteousness is given as a contrast to seeking food and clothing. This contrast does not mean that the Gospel of Matthew is not interested in the material necessities of life. Instead, in harmony with Old Testament covenant teaching, Matthew emphasizes that these material necessities provided by creation are actually gifts from the God of righteousness. The foundation for economic prosperity is righteousness. Here again Matthew's focus falls on righteousness as both a gift from God and a duty to perform, the consequence of which is the provision of all things necessary for life.

Jesus' blessings in the Beatitudes are directly linked to the kingdom of God and its righteousness, which have already arrived but await final manifestation. The Beatitudes bestow a present and a future blessedness. Because Jesus' blessings are themselves eschatological fulfillments of Old Testament promises, the ethical conduct described in the Beatitudes is already a response to the manifestation of God's kingdom, and that conduct in turn becomes a manifestation of the righteousness that entrance into God's kingdom requires. Both with righteousness and with the kingdom of God, the movement of grace goes from divine action to human response through the person and work of Jesus Christ. Obedience is itself eschatological. That is, it is motivated, enabled, and shaped by hopeful participation in the new reality of the kingdom unleashed in history by the righteousness of Jesus.

Matthew's christology of fulfillment brings humanity in Christ across the threshold into a new era. Still, this crossing of the threshold does not rupture the ties to what was right and true in the past. The law of righteousness is maintained without legalism, and the demand for righteousness becomes an easy yoke and a light burden (Matthew 11:30). Such are the strange anomalies of the kingdom of God, but without an appreciation of Matthew's eschatological christology these anomalies can be neither understood nor experienced.

The Law in the Age of Fulfillment

If the new era has already dawned, can the law of the old era still survive? What happens to the law of the Old Testament when the eschatological light shines in the darkness? Does this light merely illumine and clarify what the law has always intended and apply that true understanding to new and changing circumstances? Or does the light actually discriminate between law and law, casting aside some as no longer operative or valid while maintaining others unchanged? Or does the Messiah perhaps introduce a radically new law which is essentially different from the old law?[8] Many interpreters believe that the

8. While acknowledging that the Jews believed the Torah would continue into the messianic age with only minor adaptations and clarifications, W. D. Davies claims, nevertheless, that Matthew had in mind at least "the substance of a new Messianic Torah." *The Setting of the Sermon on the Mount* (Cambridge: Cambridge University Press, 1964), pp. 170-188. However, this position seems quite speculative in view of the lack of any contemporary evidence that anyone held such expectations. Robert

law has been set aside by Jesus, or that at least the law is no longer central to Jesus' teaching nor very significant for his followers.[9] But is this the best understanding of the Gospel of Matthew?

We have noted at various times that Matthew's Gospel is filled with themes of fulfillment. That perspective is found in Matthew 5:13-16, which is the section between the Beatitudes and Jesus' direct pronouncements on the law. Here Jesus appoints his disciples to be a city on a hill whose light enlightens the nations. This light takes the form of good deeds reflecting the righteousness that the light of God always is. Clearly, then, the task of the disciples is to be the eschatological city whose light is the reflection of the presence of the glory of the Lord (Isaiah 60:1) and which is to teach the nations God's ways so that they might live by them, "For out of Zion shall go forth the law, and the word of the LORD from Jerusalem" (Isaiah 2:3, *RSV*).[10] If this eschatological interpretation of Matthew 5:15 is correct, then the law that Jesus announces in the Sermon on the Mount is the law from Zion, intended for the nations. Jesus' law is then not simply a direct repetition of Sinai, with Jesus as the New Moses, but an expression of the eschatological law going forth from Mount Zion. How Mount Zion relates to Mount Sinai, how eschatological law relates to the law of the old covenant, is then the question.[11]

Banks demonstrates that Judaism had no expectation of a new Torah in *Jesus and the Law in the Synoptic Tradition* (Cambridge: Cambridge University Press, 1975), p. 81.

9. William Carl has examined recent Books of Worship produced by mainline Protestant churches and laments his discovery that in a little more than a decade the Decalogue has dropped out of sight in these liturgies. "The Decalogue in Liturgy, Preaching, and Life," *Interpretation* 18 (1989), pp. 267-281.

10. Approaching Matthew 5:14-16 from the perspective of his work on Isaiah, G. von Rad believes that no other interpretation is possible than to see the disciples as fulfilling the role and task of the Jerusalem of prophecy. *The Problem of the Hexateuch and Other Essays* (New York: McGraw-Hill, 1966), pp. 232-242. Various New Testament interpreters suggest that von Rad's position is possible, but some think Jesus' saying is too general to establish that position. Cf. R. H. Gundry, *Matthew: A Commentary on His Literary and Theological Art* (Grand Rapids: Eerdmans, 1982), p. 77; J. B. Meier, *Matthew* (Wilmington: Glazier, 1985), p. 44.

11. T. L. Donaldson has argued that various mountain scenes in Matthew contain themes related to the Zion eschatology of the Old Testament. Cf. *Jesus on the Mountain: A Study in Matthaean Theology* (Sheffield: JSOT, 1985). Although I agree that the Sermon on the Mount is best understood against the background of Old Testament eschatological expectations associated with Mount Zion, this topic will not be developed

The Rich Young Man and the Law

The significant issues that surround the question of the continuity and validity of the law arise conveniently from Matthew's presentation of the story of the rich young man (Matthew 19:16-22). The young man asked about the good that had to be performed to possess eternal life. Jesus answered that he should keep the commandments against murder, adultery, stealing, and false testimony, and to honor one's parents. Matthew adds to this the commandment to love one's neighbor as oneself. When the young man said that he had kept these and wondered what he still lacked, Jesus said, "If you wish to be perfect, go, sell your possessions, and give the money to the poor . . . ; then come, follow me."

Some suggest that Jesus confronted the young man with a double standard.[12] They argue that, on the one hand, Jesus does not abandon the Decalogue and the love commandments and thus requires what is essentially the ethics of both good Judaism and even good paganism. On this level the life of virtue required by Jesus does not differ from the life of virtue required by the law. But on the other hand Jesus wants his disciples to go far beyond the law by aspiring to perfection. Is such a double standard the best understanding of this story? Is Jesus' distinctive teaching a radically higher ethic that goes far beyond anything the law requires?

Others argue that Jesus is neither holding out the requirement of obedience to the law nor even radicalizing the law's demands, that he is actually requiring something altogether new, something that surpasses the law, namely, that his disciples follow him. But if this is the only demand that Jesus makes, why does he mention the law at all? Robert Banks argues that Jesus' reply "at first appears to be an absolute endorsement of the Mosaic law. It soon becomes clear, however, that it is only used as the first step in the discussion and that his instruction is to surpass its demands and, in the end, leave it quite out of sight."[13] In this view the law is

---

further because our interest lies only in the relationship of Jesus' commandments to the law of the Old Testament.

12. The position is advocated by R. Fuller, "The Decalogue in the New Testament," *Interpretation* 43 (1989), p. 246.

13. *Jesus and the Law,* p. 177.

understood as functioning only as an introduction for the intensely personal claim that Jesus imposes on his disciples, a demand, that is, that they follow him. Discipleship, then, entails following the demands of Christ and not, or not so much, the demands of the law.

Both of these proposals assume that it is possible to separate the two parts of Jesus' answer and that these two parts cannot form an essential unity. However, close attention to Matthew's insertion of the love commandment, which is not found in either the Markan or Lukan accounts of this story, makes a different interpretation more likely.[14] According to Matthew, the love commandment has hermeneutical significance for interpreting all the commandments. In Matthew 22:40 we read "On these two commandments hang all the law and the prophets," and in Matthew 7:12 "In everything do to others as you would have them do to you; for this is the law and the prophets." The point of these sayings is not that the commandment to love is the one that counts while others do not, but rather that love of God and love of neighbor is the expressed will of God that lies at the root of each and every commandment. Any interpretation of any commandment that is not informed by the love commandment misses the will of God expressed in the specific commandment. Fulfillment of the law must be measured by conformity to this "root idea."[15] Jesus' use of the love commandment radicalizes the commandments, but not by going beyond what they actually say or by adding demands that, though they are in harmony with the law, still go far beyond anything the law requires. Instead, it radicalizes the commandments by understanding each specific demand as an articulation of the fundamental will of God, which is that we love God above all and our neighbors as ourselves. Consequently, when the rich young man affirmed that he had kept all the commandments, he gave evidence that he had not

14. On either of the two current theories of synoptic relationships, the existence of the love commandment in this account is significant. If Mark is Matthew's source, then Matthew inserted it; if Matthew is Mark's source, Mark omitted it. In either case, the presence of the love commandment must be significant for understanding Matthew's account.

15. "Root idea" recalls Latin *radix,* "root," from which is derived "radicalize." My use of "radicalizing" in connection with the commandments always refers to the "root idea" and not to a going beyond, as others suggest.

understood the radicalization of all commandments that results from the hermeneutical use of the love commandment.

Because the young man had not actually understood the righteousness that the law requires, Jesus introduced the covenant category of being perfect (Matthew 19:21). The meaning of perfection is illumined by the Old Testament.[16] There it applies to the person whose "heart" is "wholly true to the LORD our God" (I Kings 8:61, *RSV*) and to one who is blameless before the Lord: "Noah was a righteous man, blameless in his generation; Noah walked with God" (Genesis 6:9). In such texts perfection is a relational category describing the condition of one's heart, one's fundamental allegiance. It refers to the undivided heart, the heart wholly true to God. Such a blameless person, perfect before God, would also be perfect in his relationships with others because the Old Testament covenant relationship always includes both — "to do justice, and to love kindness, and to walk humbly with your God" (Micah 6:8).

So when Jesus instructs this young man to sell what he owns and give to the poor, he is issuing a specific commandment that does indeed go beyond any *literal* commandment of the Old Testament. But this commandment is one that in this particular case applies to the young man the radical requirement of love implicit in all the commands. The second table of the law, which Jesus quotes, demands that the young man love his neighbor as himself. Although Jesus' commandment is radical in its demands, it applies the true understanding of the authentic righteousness contained in the law and the prophets to the specific situation of the rich young man.

Finally, is Jesus' commandment to follow him a climactic demand that goes well beyond any Old Testament requirement?[17] Not necessarily. According to Matthew, Jesus is the Son of God, the Emmanuel, God-with-us (Matthew 1:23). If so, Jesus' command to follow him may be a fulfillment of the Old Testament requirement to walk with God,

16. This understanding of perfection is based on the argument that in the Septuagint *teleios* ("perfect") is a translation of the Hebrew words *šālēm* ("wholly true") and *tāmîm* ("blameless").

17. Douglas Moo asserts that Jesus' demand does go beyond any requirement of the Old Testament. His general position on Jesus' relation to the Old Testament law is similar to that of Robert Banks, mentioned above. D. Moo, "Jesus and the Authority of the Mosaic Law," *Journal for the Study of the New Testament* 20 (1984), p. 13.

and such a walk requires that one be perfect as God is perfect and love one's neighbor just as God bestows his gifts indiscriminately on humankind (Matthew 5:48).

Even though that may be part of the answer, there is still room to ask why a discussion of the demands of the law ends in a demand for discipleship. The answer has to do with the fulfillment of the law, which we will discuss further in the next section. Thus, by way of summary, in the story of the rich young man, Jesus maintains the validity of the Old Testament law, radicalizes its demands by using the Old Testament law of love as the hermeneutical key to the law, and insists on discipleship.

The Law in the Sermon on the Mount

Our interpretation of Jesus' attitude toward the law in his encounter with the rich young man is confirmed by the more explicit treatment of this question in the Sermon on the Mount. Here Jesus declares that he has come not to annul or abolish the law and the prophets but to fulfill them, and he requires of his disciples the greater righteousness. The question that we will pursue here is this: What levels of continuity and radicalization exist between the law of the Old Testament and Jesus' teaching in Matthew 5? The answer will be derived first from an examination of the antitheses in Matthew 5:21-48 and second from the explicit statements about fulfillment in Matthew 5:17-20.

The Antitheses: Matthew 5:21-48. The introductory formula for the antitheses sheds some light on Jesus' intention: "You have heard that it was said to those of ancient times. . . ."[18] Who are these people of

18. H. Ridderbos considers it almost indisputable that this should be translated *"by* them of old time" and not *"to* them of old time" and that it refers only to "those who had explained the law in the so-called *halacha.*" His arguments are not grammatical but based on contextual considerations. *The Coming of the Kingdom* (Philadelphia: Presbyterian and Reformed, 1962), pp. 297f. However, a dative of agency with a verb of saying would be unusual. Therefore, most interpreters today favor taking "those of ancient times" as a simple indirect object. This translation broadens the scope of the persons addressed but still includes the teachers of the law, as in Ridderbos's view. Cf.

long ago? The category cannot be restricted to any particular period. It undoubtedly reaches back as far as the giving of the law to Israel at Sinai, but it would also embrace all those who received and passed on the tradition from Sinai until the time of Jesus. What would these ancient ones have heard? In the Jewish tradition Sinai is not limited to the giving of the written law because, it was believed, the oral law was also given to Moses at Sinai. Therefore, when Jesus says "You have heard," he is not referring simply to the written law of Moses, but rather to that law as interpreted and understood in the tradition. The contrast between what "was said" and what Jesus says is not between Jesus and Moses but between the tradition's understanding of Moses and Jesus' interpretation of the law of Moses.

Thus the introductory formula helps us to understand the focus of the contrast, but it does not fully explain the nature of the contrast. As far as the formula is concerned, the contrast could be understood either in a very mild sense, in which Jesus goes beyond the letter of the law to its ultimate intention and breaks with the tradition's casuistry and more literal understanding of the law, or in a more radical sense involving a revoking or abrogation of the law or at least of significant parts of it. The only way to discover the nature of the contrast is by examining the antitheses themselves.[19]

Almost all interpreters agree that in the first two antitheses there is no abrogation of the Old Testament law. Here Jesus only intensifies or radicalizes the positive intention of the commandments against murder and adultery. However, today some interpret the matter differently. As we have already noted, Robert Banks argues that Jesus is not using the law and expanding it. And Douglas Moo suggests that Jesus is actually going beyond the intent of the law because there simply is no evidence for placing anger and lust under the prohibitions of the Decalogue. Jesus is enunciating "principles neither derived from, nor intended to extend, the meaning of the laws which are quoted."[20]

This position falters for two reasons. First, if Jesus is uttering

---

J. P. Meier, *Law and History in Matthew's Gospel* (Rome: Biblical Institute Press, 1976), p. 133.

19. Cf. J. P. Meier, *op. cit.,* pp. 134f.

20. D. Moo, *op. cit.,* p. 19.

independent commandments unrelated to the limits of the Old Testament commandments, then he himself breaks his own commandments.[21] Jesus did become angry at people (Mark 3:5), and he called some people "blind fools" (Matthew 23:17). Only if Jesus' teaching is seen as illustrating the ultimate intention of the law can one argue that he did not violate his own commandments. There is an anger that arises not from the hatred of others that is prohibited by the law but from the law's commandment that we love each other.

Second, this approach by Banks and Moo seems too literal in its view of the law, even too legalistic. It seems to assume that if the law does not literally say "don't be angry" and "don't call people fools" and if such prohibitions cannot be derived from the law by simple grammatical exegesis, then Jesus' sayings about anger and calling someone a fool cannot be interpretation of the law. This approach thus misses seeing the law as an organic whole. If it is an organic whole and not just a collection of disparate commandments, then the relative weight of a specific commandment and its intentionality can be determined only in the context of the whole. That is why the question about the greatest commandment is critical for Jesus' interpretation of the law. Knowing which of the commandments is the greatest is essential for a proper understanding of specific commandments because the greatest commandments shape the whole law and determine its essence. Proper interpretation of specific commandments can never violate the essence of the whole law.

Therefore, although Jesus is not engaged in simple grammatical-linguistic exegesis, he is honoring the integral wholeness of the law and is articulating the radical or full-orbed demand of love of neighbor that the specific laws point to.[22] His commandments neither transcend the law nor have independent status. Instead, they are commandments

21. R. Banks says that Jesus did break his own commandments but that this only indicates that Jesus' teachings are principles whose application "depends upon the circumstances in which they come into play." *Op. cit.,* p. 245. How this differs from situation ethics that Banks seeks to oppose is not so clear.

22. The position advocated here is typically at home in the Reformed tradition. The Heidelberg Catechism interprets the entire Decalogue from this perspective. Earlier Calvin had organized his commentary on the laws of Moses under the headings of "Love of God" and "Love of Neighbor."

limited by the Old Testament commandments that they illustrate.[23] The law of love functions hermeneutically in Jesus' interpretation of the law and the prophets.

The third antithesis involves the law of divorce (Matthew 5:31f.). Since divorce is not commanded in Deuteronomy 24:1-4, Jesus' teaching does not abrogate an Old Testament commandment. The question is only whether Jesus revokes an Old Testament permission. Whether he does depends on interpretation of the exception clause, "except on the ground of unchastity." If "unchastity" is restricted to incest as defined by Leviticus 18, then a Mosaic permission is, in fact, abrogated by Jesus. But if "unchastity" is interpreted more broadly, then Jesus, like the law, recognizes the destructive impact of certain sins on the marriage relationship, in which cases divorce remains a possible response. If this interpretation is correct, then Jesus' teaching was a stricter understanding of marriage and divorce than was current in his day.

Nevertheless, in either case, Jesus' teaching reflects an appreciation of the law as an organic whole. He knows that Moses' permission is a concession to Israel's hardness of heart because he knows from the law God's original creation intention for marriage. Genesis 1 and 2, not Deuteronomy 24:1-4, should function as the norm for maintenance of the marriage relationship. God's creation will, not Moses' permission, should control understanding of the righteousness that governs marriage and divorce.

Some interpret the fourth antithesis, which is about oaths (Matthew 5:33-37), as a summary of citations or allusions from the Old Testament law.[24] If it is, then Jesus' commandment, "Do not swear at all," becomes a revocation of the Old Testament permission and command. The problem with such an interpretation is that Jesus' examples (vv. 34-36) seem to be directed against a misuse of oaths constructed to avoid truthfulness. All the examples are oaths based on something other than the name of God and, therefore, oaths considered not binding. If this is correct, then Jesus' commandment, as in Matthew 23:16-22,

23. H. Ridderbos speaks of Jesus' commandments in the antitheses as examples of the application of the law that should not be interpreted as new or independent commandments divorced from the law. *The Coming of the Kingdom*, pp. 309f.

24. I.e., Exodus 20:7; Leviticus 19:12; Numbers 30:2; Deuteronomy 23:22.

simply underscores the truthfulness required by the law, whether under oath or not. Jesus is criticizing any approach to the law that by its excessive literalness avoids the will of God. His rejection of oaths refers primarily to private oaths and actually intends to intensify the genuine intention of the Old Testament commandment regarding truthfulness.

The fifth antithesis (Matthew 5:38-42) speaks of retribution and is the one most frequently claimed as a clear revocation of an Old Testament commandment.[25] In the Old Testament the law of retribution is, in fact, not just a permission granted but an obligatory commandment, and it appears that Jesus considers this commandment nonbinding and, in effect, revokes it. Turning the other cheek is the opposite of seeking retribution. However, even here the issues are not so simple. Many have observed that the intention of the law of retribution was to limit revenge and that Jesus is thus radicalizing the intention of the law by outlawing revenge altogether. In addition, one could conclude from the examples given that Jesus is opposing the use of the law of retribution by private parties. But since such usage was never intended, the practices Jesus opposes are actually attempts to circumvent the will of God.

If this is the case, this antithesis reflects again Jesus' unerring sense of the fundamental will of God, to which all specific laws point. He rejects conduct justified by an appeal to a specific commandment severed from its relationship to the entire will of God. In his own teaching Jesus honors the law as an organic whole and disallows any attempt to play off one law against another. The law of retribution is an expression of the fundamental law of love in the arena of justice. Any interpretation or application of the law of retribution that ignores this fundamental will of God will be an expression of revenge and not of retributive justice.

While all these considerations must be taken into account in understanding Jesus' sayings about nonretribution, there is at least one additional consideration that is crucial. Jesus has come to fulfill the law. He does this in his teaching by giving expression to the true meaning

---

25. For example, J. P. Meier asserts that "Jesus revokes the *jus talionis* of Ex. 21:24; Lev. 24:20; and Dt. 19:21. This is perhaps the clearest and least disputable case of annulment in the antitheses." *Op. cit.,* p. 157.

of the law, but he also fulfills the law in his life and death. Consequently, he invites his disciples to take up their crosses and follow him (Mark 8:34), to lose in order to gain. In the light of such fulfillment, is it possible that in the counterexamples to the law of retribution (Matthew 5:39-42) Jesus points his disciples to the justice of God expressed in the cross? The cross expressed the justice of God that does not overturn retributive justice but actually fulfills it. Nevertheless, the cross also manifested a divine justice that is neither anticipated by nor demanded by the law of retribution.[26] By asking his disciples to "turn the other cheek," surrender their cloaks, walk the second mile, and give to the beggar who cannot repay, Jesus invites them to go beyond the law of retribution in their lives. Disciples who imitate Jesus live from the awareness that in the cross all demands of retributive justice have been met. Thus the law of retribution is not actually revoked by Jesus but is fulfilled in his cross.[27]

If this perspective is correct, then in the interpretation of the antitheses it is important to remember that Jesus is more than a teacher giving correct insights into the law. If Jesus functioned only as a teacher, then once the correct interpretation were known it would be possible to have the law and follow it apart from Christ. But if Jesus' own fulfillment of the law is essential for both understanding and obeying the law's righteousness, then the disciple encounters the law only in Christ and is called to follow the fulfilled law in him. The focus falls on Christ, and the law is relevant for his disciples only in the form and manner by which it achieves fulfillment in him. Christ becomes the focal point of continuity with the Old Testament law and of its radicalization both in his teaching and in his person. That is why Jesus invited the rich young man, and every disciple, to *follow* him (Matthew 19:21). Only by following Christ can the disciple both understand and receive the capacity to perform the greater righteousness. This christological focus on the law is the death knell of all legalism and the beginning of the imitation of Christ.

26. For a similar perspective on retribution and the cross, see O. O'Donovan, *Resurrection and Moral Order* (Grand Rapids: Eerdmans, 1986), pp. 74f.

27. Hebrews 12:24 speaks of "the sprinkled blood [of Jesus] that speaks a better word than the blood of Abel." Only in the cross is Abel vindicated and the guilty forgiven by a justice that supersedes all other justice, because the justice exhibited in the cross both fulfills the law of retribution and transcends it.

The final antithesis (Matthew 5:43-48) is usually not considered an abrogation of the Old Testament because the phrase "hate your enemy" is not found there. Some have argued that the phrase came from Zealot teaching or Qumran. Others argue that Old Testament Israel was, in fact, expected to hate its enemies because they were also God's enemies, and thus the phrase could be considered a logical inference from Old Testament data. However one interprets this matter, it is apparent that Jesus' universalizing of "neighbor" occurs in a situation of fulfillment. Though hints of universalizing can be found within the Old Testament — for example, in Leviticus 19:34 the obligation to love includes the resident alien — it is the arrival of the universal kingdom of God that removes all particularistic limits, both national and geographical, and whatever shaping effect they had on the stipulations of the law. Jesus presents the proper understanding of the Old Testament in terms of its deepest intention, but this intention enters on its complete realization only through the fulfillment of the law and the prophets in Jesus Christ with the consequent arrival of the universal kingdom of God. The scope of the disciples' love of neighbor must reflect the scope of God's own love.

We have discovered that the antitheses do not require the conclusion that Jesus cancels or abrogates the Old Testament law. Instead, his teaching radicalizes the law in terms of its original intention. Consequently, the righteousness that Jesus requires stands in continuity with the righteousness required by the law of the Old Testament. This discovery is supported as well by Jesus' explicit pronouncement concerning his mission to fulfill the law.

Jesus' Pronouncements on the Law. In Matthew 5:17-20, Jesus makes three pronouncements concerning the law. First, he announces that he has not come to abolish the law and the prophets but to fulfill them (v. 17). With regard to the prophets, Jesus' announcement is not so difficult to understand, even though Matthew's own presentation of the fulfillment of certain prophecies may be very complex. Fulfillment of prophecies means simply that the reality promised in the prophetic word becomes an actual event in human history. What then is the fulfillment of the law? Obviously this fulfillment happens when the righteousness articulated in the law similarly becomes reality in human history. The law is an articulation, under the specific circumstances in which Israel lived, of the righteousness that will cover the face of the earth. Therefore, fulfillment of the law entails a realization in history of the righteousness articulated in the law. To bring that about was the intention and achievement of Jesus' mission.

Second, Jesus declares that historical fulfillment does not negate the ongoing validity of the law (vv. 18f.). Even the insignificant parts of the law, the iota and dot, retain an ongoing validity "until heaven and earth pass away" and "until all is accomplished." The first limit refers to the permanence of the creation, which endures until the new heavens and the new earth. The second limit sounds much like the phrase in Matthew 24:34, "until all these things have taken place," a reference to the fulfillment of God's redemptive purposes. Both limits point to the fulfillment of God's redemptive purposes at the close of the age. Therefore, according to Jesus, the law retains its validity in the Christian era and retains it as a whole and in all of its parts. That is, of no part of the law can it simply be said, "This is rescinded, this is cancelled."[28]

This lasting validity of the law and prophets must be understood in the light of Jesus' declaration that he has come to fulfill the whole of Scripture (Matthew 5:17). Fulfillment is itself an affirmation of the validity of the law and not cancellation of it. Of course, fulfillment may have the effect of altering the shape of specific commandments or even of setting them aside because the righteousness they articulate is now experienced in a different form. For example, the new people of God are now incorporated by baptism and not by circumcision (Matthew 28:19). Therefore, even though Jesus affirms the ongoing validity of the law until the close of the age, the Christian has no direct access to

28. Some argue that for Matthew the fulfillment of Scripture and the turning point of the ages occurs in the death and resurrection of Jesus and, therefore, the iota and dot last only until then (e.g., J. P. Meier, *op. cit.,* p. 168). If the only temporal limit in Jesus' saying were "until all is accomplished," this view would be very attractive because it would easily resolve the whole question of the law in the Christian era. However, the parallel temporal limit, "until heaven and earth pass away," is not fulfilled with the death and resurrection of Jesus. Even Meier acknowledges that one should not be too radical about the end of the law's applicability because Matthew acknowledges that the old aeon continues and still awaits the close of the age (p. 39).

that validity apart from the fulfillment in Christ. The fact that something is required by a specific Old Testament commandment does not directly dictate the shape of Christian obedience. The shape of that obedience is understood only by following the teachings and actions of Jesus Christ. Consequently, Jesus instructs his disciples to attend to what he says: "But *I* say to you," "Everyone then who hears these words of *mine* and acts on them," "teaching them to obey everything that *I* have commanded you," and "Come, follow *me.*" Only as fulfilled and radicalized in the teaching and life of Jesus does the Old Testament law retain its validity until the close of the age.[29]

In his third pronouncement concerning the law Jesus describes the required righteousness as exceeding that of the scribes and Pharisees (Matthew 5:20). He criticizes both the scribes and Pharisees' understanding of the righteousness that the law requires and their failure to practice what they preach (23:3). The greater righteousness announced by Jesus requires conformity to the entire will of God rather than observance of minimal standards derived from the letter of commandments treated in isolation.

Jesus' relationship to the normative Old Testament thus reflects both continuity and radicalization. His disciples are not yet finished with the structured righteousness of the law and the prophets. Yet this structured righteousness of the Old Testament must always be interpreted and applied in the light of fulfillment in Christ.

The Keys of the Kingdom and the Law: Matthew 16:18f.

Jesus' commissioning of Peter (and the apostles) in Matthew 16:19 provides added confirmation of this understanding of the relationship of Jesus to the law in the Gospel of Matthew. Jesus gave his apostles the keys of the kingdom and promised "whatever you bind on earth will be bound in heaven, and whatever you loose on earth will be loosed in heaven." Just before this commissioning, Peter had confessed Jesus as "the Messiah, the Son of the living God." In response, Jesus establishes his Church on the foundation of this apostolic confession, prom-

29. Cf. Ridderbos, *op. cit.,* pp. 306-308.

ising that the Church will not be vanquished in the warfare that will
follow.

There would indeed be warfare between "the gates of Hades" and
the Church built on the rock. These metaphors used by Jesus are difficult
to grasp because normally gates resist but do not vanquish or overcome,
and the rock seems to be a metaphor of defense rather than offense.[30]
Thus the picture is not of a Church on the attack against the gates of a
city but rather of a Church whose foundation resists the storms that beat
upon it (Matthew 7:25). Consequently, today most interpreters understand Hades' "gates" as a symbol of the entire city with its rulers and
inhabitants, that is, the realm of the dead together with its demonic
rulers.[31] Jesus is depicting a scene in which the powers of the underworld burst forth from their city to attack the Church, a scene similar
to Revelation 9:1-11, where an angel is given the key to the bottomless
pit and unleashes hordes of demonic forces, which like locusts wreak
havoc on the earth. In this apocalyptic warfare against the forces of
death and Hades, Jesus promises that the Church will prevail.[32]

How do the keys of the kingdom and the power to loose and bind
contribute to this victory of the Church? Traditionally interpreters have
taken their clue for interpreting Matthew 16:19 from the use of the same
phrase in Matthew 18:18. There the power to loose and bind is simply
the power to exclude from membership in the community, a proclam-
atory and disciplinary authority, which permits access into or declares
exclusion from the kingdom of God. With that understanding applied
to 16:19, the assurance of victory comes from the fact that no one who

30. The common interpretation (since the seventeenth century), that the gates
are defensive and are unable to resist the Church's attack, falters on the grammar of
the sentence. The verb with the genitive is always active in meaning, "vanquish," and
not passive, "resist successfully." Cf. J. Jeremias, *Theological Dictionary of the New
Testament* (Grand Rapids: Eerdmans, 1964-76) VI, p. 926. Interestingly, Calvin's interpretation stressed the active warfare of Satan against the Church and interprets
"gates" as a reference to every kind of power and weapons of war.

31. Most today understand "gates" as a metonymy, a part-for-the-whole, representing a city. Here Hades and the entire underworld and abode of the dead are viewed
as a city.

32. This interpretation of "gates" and of binding and loosing owes much to an
article by Joel Marcus, "The Gates of Hades and the Keys of the Kingdom," *Catholic
Biblical Quarterly* 50 (1988), pp. 443-455.

has the sign of God's kingdom on his or her forehead should be over-come by the demonic hosts. Then the assurance of victory is focused exclusively on the individual members of the Church.

But another interpretation is possible and is worth pursuing. Joel Marcus has suggested that there are by implication two sets of gates that unleash their powers on earth.[33] The key that opens the gate to the kingdom not only lets people in but also unleashes the power of God's rule into human history, where the battle is raging. Then the use of the keys of the kingdom becomes in effect God's response to the Church's prayer, "Your kingdom come. Your will be done, on earth as it is in heaven." Is this a possible interpretation? When Peter or the Church opens the gates of the kingdom, do they thereby allow God's sovereignly redemptive will to be expressed on earth, that will of God which in the end will exercise effective rule in human history by overthrowing the forces of evil?

The answer to this question resides to some extent in the meaning of "binding" and "loosing." They are rabbinic terms referring to "authoritative halakhic decisions concerning what is prohibited and what is permitted" by the law.[34] Therefore, they are concerned with the true interpretation of the law, since it is the law of God or the will of God that determines what is bound and what is loosed. The opening of the gates of the kingdom brings to earth the secret of the true interpretation of the law.

What the Church binds and looses, according to Jesus, will have been bound or loosed in heaven. The grammar is difficult, but if taken literally it implies that the action in heaven precedes the action on earth.[35] Because the heavenly action comes first, the Church's authority is neither autonomous nor arbitrary. Instead it must correspond to what has already been decided in heaven. But how can the Church know what has been decided in heaven? It can only know this from the revelation that Peter and the Church have received, namely, that Jesus

---

33. *Ibid.,* p. 447.

34. *Ibid.,* p. 449. Cf. also F. Büchsel, *Theological Dictionary of the New Testament* II, pp. 60f.; D. Hill, *The Gospel of Matthew* (Grand Rapids: Eerdmans, 1984), p. 262. While virtually all grant that this is the meaning of "binding" and "loosing," applications vary greatly.

35. Marcus, *op. cit.,* p. 448.

is the Christ, the Messiah. In other words, the law must be interpreted in the light of that confession and in the light of the fact that the law and the prophets are fulfilled in Christ. Everything has already been bound or loosed in heaven in terms of Jesus the Messiah. For that reason the gift of the keys in Matthew 16:19 was still historically in the future, to be given after the fulfillment in Christ. Until that time the authority resided with Christ and could not be shared with the disciples.

What does this authority to bind and to loose actually mean? Obviously the apostles had no authority to bind what Jesus had loosed or to loose what Jesus had bound. For that reason they used the teaching or commandment of Jesus to settle issues in the Church, at least on matters that Jesus had spoken on.[36] Jesus did loose his disciples from the laws of clean and unclean with reference to food (Matthew 15:17), at least temporarily from fasting (9:14f.), and from the temple tax (17:26), thus implying release from all temple obligations. Although the disciples did not understand such implications during Jesus' ministry, later they applied temple, priestly, and sacrificial categories to the Church and Christian life. There is also an implicit release from circumcision as the rite of entrance into the kingdom (28:19). In addition, the apostles were to teach what Jesus had commanded.

Thus the authority to bind and to loose refers to interpretation and application of the law and the prophets in light of the confession that Jesus is the Messiah, the one who in his teaching and actions fulfilled that law. Jesus describes the disciple as a scribe trained for the kingdom of God and a householder who brings out of his treasure things old and new (Matthew 13:52). The treasure is Jesus Christ, the fulfiller of the law and the prophets, whose fulfillment is the original binding and loosing. In the light of that fulfillment, the Church continues to interpret the righteousness of the law and the prophets as a norm for Christian living. If the Church is to successfully ward off the demonic hosts and the forces of death, it cannot ignore the law and the prophets. Until the end of the age, the law and the prophets provide valid instruction in the way of righteousness.

This view of the law implies that the law is not a static entity. The law is the articulation of the dynamic will of God moving toward fulfillment, an articulation capable of adaptation and change. Thus, for

36. A good example of this is seen in I Corinthians 7:10, 12, 25.

example, the New Testament way of righteousness releases Jesus' disciples from the necessity of circumcision even though every relevant Old Testament text insists on its necessity. It releases the Church from the structures of the seventh-day sabbath because that reality finds its supreme fulfillment in Christ's resurrection on the first day of the week. It releases Christians from the law's proscription of lending at interest when under new economic circumstances Christian scribes perceive that that total prohibition is no longer required by the demand of love.[37]

This task of assessing how the ongoing validity of the Old and New Testament Scripture should be applied is never ending until the close of the age. If the Church fails to include in this task the application of the law and the prophets, it will be weakened in its struggle against the forces of evil and death in our time. In our fears we should not resort to simplistic literalisms in our binding and loosing since that may well result in an inferior righteousness. The complexities of assessing continuities and discontinuities and determining radicalization and fulfillment may seem formidable, but Christ assures the Church that he will be in its midst (Matthew 18:20). As the Church performs Christ's mission, he promises to be with it until the close of the age (28:20). Only then will the Church's struggles and debates over such matters come to an end. Until then the gates of the kingdom of God have swung open, fulfillment has happened, righteousness has been sown on the earth, and the powers of death cannot win.

The World's Foundations:
The Law as an Impetus to Mission

If the kingdom of God has entered human history, what are the obligations and responsibilities of its citizens for the world and its history? Is

---

37. This example comes from John Calvin, who argued that every commandment was but a specific form of the commandment to love and that under the newer economic patterns lending money at interest for production purposes contravened the demands of neither love nor justice. Thus Calvin overthrew the Church's long tradition against lending at interest, which had been based on Scripture's universal prohibition of interest. Cf. Calvin's commentary on Exodus 22:25. Later Calvin expressed some concern that his approval of lending at interest might lead some to lend money that should have been given to the poor.

the righteousness of the kingdom of God intended for the nations? Is the morality taught in the Scriptures intended also for the world, or is it a private morality for Christians only? The Sermon on the Mount has often been interpreted as a special or private morality for Christians only, or only for certain classes of Christians (those taking vows of humility, poverty, and chastity), or as binding only on the Jews in the millennium. If any of these is correct, then there are two distinct types of righteousness and two entirely different systems of morality, one for life in the kingdom of God and another for life in the creation that exists prior to or outside of the arrival of that kingdom. But does a dual approach to the question of righteousness do justice to scriptural teaching?

A Single Universal Righteousness: Old Testament Teaching

The thesis developed in this chapter moves in a different direction. We have argued for continuity between the righteousness set forth in the Sermon on the Mount and the righteousness of God revealed in the Old Testament law and prophets, a continuity that exists even in the radicalization of righteousness found in Jesus' teaching. On the basis of such continuity, the clear Old Testament conviction that the righteousness of God that shaped Israel's ways was intended to shape the ways of all nations continues to be valid.

For example, after speaking of Israel's evil neighbors and prophesying that God in judgment would pluck those neighbors from their lands, the prophet Jeremiah announces: "And then, if *they* will diligently learn the ways of my people, to swear by my name, 'As the LORD lives,' as they taught my people to swear by Baal, then they shall be built up in the midst of my people. But if any nation will not listen, then I will utterly uproot it and destroy it, says the LORD" (Jeremiah 12:16f.). The covenant righteousness required of Israel was not private or exceptional but universal and foundational because "righteousness and justice" are the foundation of Yahweh's throne and "steadfast love and faithfulness" continuously go before him (Psalm 89:14). As Creator and Redeemer, God rules a cosmic order structured by righteousness, justice, steadfast love, and truth, that is, faithfulness. Nations and peoples may try to control creation and history by power, by armies and great strength (Psalm 33:16f.), but their plans are frustrated by Yahweh because his plan and counsel stand firm, "the thoughts of his heart to all generations" (33:11). That plan of the Lord frustrates the plans of the peoples because

> the word of the LORD is upright,
>> and all his work is done in faithfulness.
> He loves righteousness and justice;
>> the earth is full of the steadfast love of the LORD.
>
> (33:4f.)

Thus the Old Testament reveals a cosmic order of righteousness that is normative for all peoples.[38] This order is known in Israel, and it is Israel's privilege to be God's planting in the earth, a sign of God's righteousness, which is rooted in creation itself and expected to become fully visible in the eschatological future. The covenant demand for righteousness and justice in Israel is rooted in a larger order of righteousness that has its origin in God himself, is reflected in the creation, and is expected in the future. Consequently, Israel was established to be a sign between the times until

> Steadfast love and faithfulness will meet;
>> righteousness and peace will kiss each other.
> Faithfulness will spring up from the ground,
>> and righteousness will look down from the sky.
>
> (Psalm 85:10f.)

Israel itself, as well as the nations, is judged by that God-ordained order, and someday the order of creation and the order of history will coincide and the eschatological kingdom will have dawned. Such is the majestic Old Testament conviction, which is still valid for the New Testament people of God. What occurs in the New Testament is not a fundamental

---

38. An important stimulus to my reflections on law, cosmic order, and history has been Rolf Knierim's "Cosmos and History in Israel's Theology," *Horizons in Biblical Theology* 3 (1981), pp. 59-123.

change in the order of righteousness, but rather a fundamental over-coming of the fatal division between human knowing and doing, a release from suppression of the truth, and an enlightening of the mind to perceive the things of the Spirit.

However, can one claim that this Old Testament concept of a single righteousness, which is both universal and foundational, is also a fundamental assumption undergirding the Gospel of Matthew? The difficulty in demonstrating this lies in the fact that usually the most fundamental assumptions of an author are neither stated openly nor conveniently contained in single texts. Up to this point the argument that Matthew indeed makes such an assumption is derived from Matthew's presentation of Jesus' relation to the law of the Old Testament. Jesus' teaching stands in continuity with the essential righteousness of the Old Testament. But there are also other bits of evidence pointing in the same direction, suggesting that for Matthew also the righteousness that God requires of his people is embedded in the order of creation itself and is, therefore, a righteousness required of the nations of the world — a righteousness by which, indeed, God will judge all the nations. Such righteousness is not private or exceptional, but universal and foundational for the existence of the world. There are structures, perspectives, and even texts in Matthew that allude to just that foundational assumption, that point to it, or that are only fully comprehended when interpreted in its light.

A Single Universal Righteousness: Matthean Teaching

Does the Gospel of Matthew differ from the Old Testament's teaching of a single foundational righteousness rooted in creation and intended for the nations of the world? The original audience of the Sermon on the Mount is instructive. Usually this sermon is thought to be addressed only to the disciples. But such an interpretation is possible only if Matthew 5:1 is separated from the summary introduction in 4:23-25, which speaks of the gathering crowds, and if the concluding comment in 7:28f. is ignored: "Now when Jesus had finished saying these things, the crowds were astounded at his teaching, for he taught them as one having authority, and not as their scribes." Jesus taught his disciples, who were committed to him, but also the crowds who did not believe in him. He taught the crowds and had compassion on them "because they were harassed and helpless, like sheep without a shepherd" (9:36). If Jesus' teaching in Matthew has as its primary content the structured righteousness of God's kingdom, it is a teaching intended also for a world that has not perceived that righteousness and has no ability to live by it. Jesus' teaching is not secret lore intended only for the ears of a favored few. The unbelieving world must also hear the structured righteousness by which God measures the world.

Jesus clearly articulates this perspective in the Great Commission (Matthew 28:19f.). His overarching command is to disciple the nations. This is to be done by baptizing them, an action that entails their repentance, forgiveness of them, and cleansing of them from sin on the basis of the redemptive actions proclaimed in the gospel; yet discipling is done at the same time by teaching them to live by all that Jesus commanded. The disciples are commissioned to continue his original activity in the Sermon on the Mount, teaching not only those who follow Jesus but also the crowds — with a view to having the crowds join the ranks of the disciples. The gospel of the kingdom is not limited to an announcement of the central salvific events in order to elicit repentance and faith. It also includes teaching the nations the structured righteousness of the kingdom of God.

Additional evidence concerning Matthew's fundamental assumptions about righteousness can be found perhaps in the structure of the Sermon on the Mount. Several interpreters have suggested that the sermon's three parts bear a striking similarity to a saying of Simeon the Just, a rabbi of the Maccabean period: "The world stands on three things: the Torah, the temple service, and deeds of kindness."[39] These are the pillars on which the world rests and by which it is sustained. If Matthew intended this parallel in structuring the Sermon on the Mount, then for Matthew the foundations of the world are the greater righteousness demanded by the law as interpreted in Jesus' antitheses (Matthew 5:21-48), the righteous-

---

39. Mishnah Aboth 1.2. This parallel was observed by Davies, *op. cit.*, pp. 305-307, and developed by D. C. Allison, "The Structure of the Sermon on the Mount," *Journal of Biblical Literature* 106 (1987), pp. 423-445.

ness manifested in cultic or worship activities (6:1-18), and the righteousness manifested in social and religious acts of benevolence (6:19–7:12).
These three pillars of righteousness are the foundation of the world. Since
we have already examined the first of these and the third is quite similar,
we shall use the second to illustrate the point.

Usually we do not think of almsgiving, prayer, and fasting as the
doing of righteousness, but that is precisely the heading given to these
activities in Matthew 6:1. Since these activities are part of the Lord's
will for his people, they constitute part of the righteousness that is
required. Because they are activities done unto the Lord, they must be
done in secret, not with public display designed to seek approval from
others. Such activity performed in private with a view to the Lord
constitutes one of the pillars of righteousness that sustain the world. At
its center lies the Lord's Prayer.[40] This prayer summarizes the central
petitions of God's people, who seek his kingdom and the accomplish-
ment of his will on earth while they depend fully on him for their daily
sustenance and for protection in the midst of continuing historical evil.[41]
The focus of the prayer is on the God-directed life, which seeks from
God himself the gifts and the blessings that make righteousness
possible. By so petitioning and so living, this new people of God reflect
the very purpose of creation itself as they live according to the righteous
order of creation. Their doing so is made possible by redemption in
Christ. The righteousness for which the disciples pray and the fruit
which that righteousness produces are the very foundation of the world's
existence and its redemption.

Even if one is not fully convinced by the proposed parallel with
Jewish thinking about the pillars of the earth, there are several familiar
passages that point in a similar direction. Jesus instructs his disciples
to seek first God's kingdom and righteousness "and all these things will

40. Luz argues that the entire Sermon on the Mount is constructed as a series of
concentric rings built symmetrically around the Lord's Prayer as its "central text." He
observes that in the main body of the sermon, Matthew 5:21–7:11, there are the same
number of lines in the Greek text before and after the Lord's Prayer. He concludes that
"according to Matthew, an interpretation of the Sermon on the Mount is a misunderstanding if it overlooks the fact that the center of its practice is prayer." *Op. cit.*, p. 215.

41. Cf. C. Brown, "Prayer," in *The New International Dictionary of New Testament Theology* (Grand Rapids: Zondervan, 1975-78) II, pp. 871f.

be given to you as well" (Matthew 6:33). It is interesting to notice the focus here on foundations. The preceding discourse is about food, drink, and clothing, which are not to be the object of one's striving and seeking. Instead, the command is to look to the foundations of the world's existence, to God's rule and to the structured righteousness of his kingdom. According to both Matthew and the Old Testament, we live in a world filled with God's steadfast love, in which food and drink are gifts from a loving Father who knows that we need them. They are like the manna that sustained Israel in the wilderness, the blessing of daily bread on those who seek God's will and kingdom.

The same theme is found in the fourth beatitude: "Blessed are those who hunger and thirst for righteousness, for they will be filled" (Matthew 5:6). The parallel beatitude in Luke speaks only of satisfying those who are hungry (Luke 6:21). Here again Matthew focuses on the foundation: Food and drink are the fruit of righteousness, God's righteousness and ours. Thus in the fourth beatitude, as in Matthew 6:33, Matthew epitomizes the Old Testament covenant instruction regarding the ultimate foundation of the fertility of the field, or expressed in more contemporary terms, the foundation of economic productivity. Israel was warned not to follow other avenues in search for economic success, such as worshiping the fertility deities and boiling a kid in its mother's milk (Exodus 23:19).[42] Instead, Israel was called to keep the covenant and its righteousness and thereby discover the truth that it is God who gives grain, wine, and oil. As a matter of fact, the earth as God's creation is ordered by righteousness, justice, steadfast love, and mercy (Hosea 2:19), and the earth as God's agent showers its abundance on those who seek God and observe the order that he has established. To follow other norms is to seek another God, and the result will be judgment, not only on Israel but on the nations, even if it takes seventy years to appear.[43]

42. The prohibition against boiling a kid goat in its mother's milk was a warning not to practice rites by which Israel's neighbors sought to gain fertility from their deities. Israel's God was not a nature deity capable of being manipulated by magic or fertility rites. Israel's God is a God of the covenant who sends blessings, including fertility, on those who keep his covenant.

43. The fall of the Communist system in Russia, which ignored God and his laws, is a case in point. It lasted seventy years (1917-87) before it openly began to unravel.

Thus the righteousness articulated in the Sermon on the Mount is foundational because it is rooted in God's created cosmic order.

From creation to consummation, the basic biblical questions are: Who possesses the earth, how can it be possessed, and when? While the "when" remains in the hands of God, the consistent answer to the first two parts of the question is that "the meek" will "inherit the earth" (Matthew 5:5).[44] The Sermon on the Mount proclaims the righteousness that is the answer to that basic biblical question, a righteousness that is necessarily universal and foundational rather than private and exceptional. This righteousness is concerned fundamentally with the possession of this earth, which is the Lord's. Therefore, it places Jesus' disciples in competition with or in prophetic opposition to all human systems, structures, and ideologies that advocate other ways. The meek will inherit the earth. This, too, the world must hear.

In this same sermon Jesus appointed his disciples to be the salt of the earth (Matthew 5:13). Whether this salt is interpreted as a seasoning, a preservative, or a purifier, the disciples are essential for the continuing existence and the good existence of the earth. They are appointed also to be "the light of the world," the light which is like a city on a hill that cannot be hid, the eschatological city of promise, the Jerusalem that is a light to the nations (v. 14). Light exposes, illumines, overcomes darkness, and maps out the way. This light is seen by the world as it is reflected in good works, the deeds of righteousness taught in the Sermon on the Mount. The world must know this righteous will of God; otherwise the people of the world will not know how to live on this earth and possess it. The earth cannot finally be possessed by power or by the powerful. Strikingly, in our time governments, which are of necessity power structures, have had to confront the dilemma that the power by which they maintain possession of the earth is the power that, if unleashed in all its fury, will destroy the very earth that we seek to possess. Perhaps in his providence God has created an opening for the gospel of the kingdom and its righteousness to be heard.[45]

44. This biblical theme has been developed above in chapter IV. For a striking parallel to Jesus' teaching in the Sermon on the Mount, see Psalm 37:1-11.

45. If Jesus' disciples fulfill Israel's role among the nations, then the situation among the nations may be especially ripe for a further fulfillment of Isaiah 2:3 and Zechariah 8:22f.

The Great Commission includes teaching the nations all that Jesus commanded (Matthew 28:20). The world rests on foundations: righteousness and justice, steadfast love and faithfulness. Perhaps in terms of what God expects of us, it can be described as resting on three pillars: the righteousness of the law, the righteousness of the cult or of obligations to worship, and deeds of mercy. Thus awareness of God's law and righteousness should impel the Church to mission. For the earth is the Lord's, and he has ordered it by his righteousness, a righteousness with which the Church has been entrusted.

Lest so much talk about law and righteousness sound like the salvation of the world rests in our hands, we must not overlook the righteousness of the second pillar, at the center of which lies the activity of prayer: "Your kingdom come. Your will be done, on earth as it is in heaven." It is God who places the world back on its foundations and gives it to those who humbly trust him. For that we patiently wait and confidently hope. Until then, Jesus' disciples are salt and light, living and proclaiming the gospel of the kingdom and its righteousness, not only to disciples, but also to the crowds and nations in the expectation that they, too, will believe and learn how to possess the earth.

Thus, according to the Gospel of Matthew, the law is indeed fulfilled in Jesus Christ, but the effect of that fulfillment creates no dichotomy between law and gospel. Authentic discipleship necessarily entails doing the righteousness expressed in the law, a righteousness rooted in creation itself. Hence Jesus calls his disciples to be a manifestation of righteous Israel, the light among the nations of the world.

CHAPTER VI

A Future for Jewish Israel?

Is there still a future for Jewish Israel? This is not primarily a question about the political fortunes of the modern State of Israel but of whether Jewish Israel still has a special place in God's history of salvation. Once Jewish Israel was the people with whom God established his covenant and to whom he made promises. Does that original covenant still hold? Can Jewish Israel still legitimately claim the promises?

If, as the previous chapters have shown, Jesus is the one through whom God's promises to Israel are fulfilled, can there still be fulfillment outside Jesus or beyond him? If, as the promised descendant of Abraham and David, Jesus represents the whole of Israel in his person and mission, can an ethnic or religious or ethnic-religious group existing outside him still have a special place in God's history of redemption? Can Jewish Israel still lay claim to being the elect people of God even after they refuse to believe the claims of Jesus, who manifests that election? Or must we conclude that their unbelief effectively cancels the legitimacy of their claim?

A Variety of Answers

The Gospels and Paul

Do Paul and the authors of the Gospels and Acts give the same answers? The Gospels speak of judgment for those who reject the claims of Jesus. For example, after demonstrating that the Old Testament promises made to Israel are fulfilled in Jesus, Matthew concludes that the kingdom of God will be taken from those who reject the authority of the Son of God and fail to produce the fruit of the kingdom (Matthew 21:43). Similarly, the Gospel of John vigorously rejects any appeal to Abraham and Moses by those in Jewish Israel who refuse to acknowledge the claims of Jesus. Instead, the Gospel insists that belief in Jesus is the only way to understand Moses and to appropriate the promises made to Abraham and his seed (John 5:46; 8:34-59). Therefore, the disciples of Jesus receive the promised blessings and are viewed as the true or renewed Israel, even if this is stated only implicitly (Matthew 13:16-17; John 3:16; 15:1-11).

If such is the teaching of the Gospels, can there be room in God's covenant for another Israel who still has the right to claim the promised inheritance? The Gospels and Acts teach that judgment has fallen on unbelieving Israel and that this judgment fulfills the prophetic word of Isaiah:

> Go and say to this people:
> "Keep listening, but do not comprehend;
> keep looking, but do not understand."
> Make the mind of this people dull,
>   and stop their ears,
>   and shut their eyes,
> so that they may not look with their eyes,
>   and listen with their ears,
> and comprehend with their minds,
>   and turn and be healed.[1]

(Isaiah 6:9f.)

---

1. Cf. Matthew 13:14f.; Mark 4:11f.; Luke 8:10; John 12:40; Acts 28:25-28.

Does this prophetic judgment of blindness and failure to repent that has fallen on Israel signal the end of Jewish Israel as the people of God? Have they forever lost the right to claim the promises of the covenant?

Many interpreters today insist that such is indeed the case. They believe that the proper understanding of the Gospels and Acts implies the end of the significance of Jewish Israel in the history of redemption, and that on this score only the apostle Paul teaches a perspective that is significantly different.[2] But is this so? Do the Gospels and Acts teach the definitive exclusion of Jewish Israel from the covenant?

It is important to observe that the Gospels and Acts never explicitly make a definitive judgment on the *future* of unbelieving Jewish Israel. Instead, they focus on the *present* manifestation of unbelief, the judgment that necessarily falls on such unbelief, and the consequent *present* loss of covenant blessings. However harsh these judgments sound, the wording and its harshness is borrowed from the Old Testament prophets, especially Isaiah. Covenant prophets had always spoken forcefully to those in Israel who did not believe and obey, because from its very beginning the covenant contained the promise of blessing and the threat of curse. Failure to believe and obey brought on Israel judgment, not blessing, death, not life. The New Testament message is pervasively the same. Because the covenant promises have been fulfilled in Jesus, failure to believe and obey brings judgment and loss of covenant blessings.

But are these judgments final? Will they ever be lifted? Will life someday appear where only death and judgment reign? On this possibility the Gospels and Acts are mainly silent.[3] They do not *explicitly* address the future of unbelieving Israel as the apostle Paul does. How-

2. For example, J. C. Beker, *Paul the Apostle: The Triumph of God in Life and Thought* (Philadelphia: Fortress, 1980), pp. 328-330; in regard to Acts, J. T. Sanders, "The Salvation of the Jews," in *Luke-Acts: New Perspectives from the SBL Seminar,* ed. C. H. Talbert (New York: Crossroad, 1984), pp. 104-146.

3. There is possibly a positive answer to these questions in Matthew 23:39 and Luke 21:24, but not all interpreters agree. If a positive answer lies implicitly in these verses, then the difference from Paul is not very great. Similarly, today many interpret Acts as leaving open the question of the future of unbelieving Jewish Israel. Cf. J. Jervell, *Luke and the People of God* (Minneapolis: Augsburg, 1972); D. Juel, *Luke-Acts: The Promise of History* (Atlanta: John Knox, 1983); J. B. Chance, *Jerusalem, the Temple, and the New Age in Luke-Acts* (Macon: Mercer University Press, 1988).

ever, one must not overlook the fact that the apostle Paul also describes the *present* status of unbelieving Jewish Israel as under the reality of the judgment of God (Romans 11). While Paul differs from the Gospels and Acts in explicitly addressing a question that they do not address, he is strikingly similar to them in announcing present judgment in words borrowed from the Old Testament covenant. Interpreters should not isolate the Gospels and Acts from the Old Testament covenant background and then extrapolate answers to the question of the future of unbelieving Israel, a question that lies beyond the conscious horizons of the authors. If their language of judgment assumes Old Testament covenant perspectives, there is nothing in the Gospels and Acts that either biblically or logically entails an absolute or definitive rejection of Jewish Israel.

The Church's Attitude, Past and Present

We have already described in chapter I how the Church's attitude toward the future of Jewish Israel has varied widely over the centuries. The variety of New Testament pronouncements has been seized on to support different views. Already in the second century of the Church's existence the dominant view had come to be that the significance of Jewish Israel as a people had been forfeited. Although granting that individual Jews could participate in the promises by conversion to Christianity, this view taught that the Jewish people as such no longer had a special role in God's plan of salvation. They were no longer the elect people. Instead, the Church had totally superseded Israel.

This supersessionist perspective became dominant in the Church, but it was not the only point of view. Not only were premillennial views concerning Jewish Israel always present in the Church, even though frequently opposed, but also some of those whose views were mainly supersessionist concerning the relationship of the Church and Jewish Israel acknowledged a mystery that the Church must respect. Paul's teaching in Romans 11 about the Israel that was an enemy of the gospel but still the elect of God formed a barrier to any simple logical deduction that Jewish Israel had been completely rejected by God.

This Pauline teaching about the continuing election of Jewish

Israel has become in our century the foundation for all theological thinking about the relationship of Jesus and Israel or of the Church and Israel. The tragic events of the Holocaust and the reestablishment of the state of Israel have forced the issue to the forefront of the Church's consciousness. As I have briefly described in chapter I, many churches have made declarations affirming this continuing election of Jewish Israel. However, there is as yet no consensus concerning the theological consequences that should be derived from this continuing election. Is there one covenant or two? Is Jewish existence as the elect people of God in history self-contained, without any necessary or essential relationship to Jesus Christ? Does the Church have any obligation to evangelize Jews? On such questions there is wide disagreement among the churches and their theologians.

Thus any informed reflection on the question of Jesus and Israel must examine this Pauline mystery of a people who reject the gospel but are still called the elect of God. What does Paul teach in Romans 9–11? Since these chapters are the only ones in the New Testament which explicitly consider the future of Jewish Israel, any attempt to speak about that future must examine the argument of these chapters. In Romans 9–11 the apostle Paul develops a theologically complex answer, which we will attempt to highlight only in its central concerns.

Understanding Paul's Anguish

Can God Be Trusted?

Why should the apostle Paul be concerned with the destiny of Jewish Israel? Since the discussion in Romans 1–8 presents the fact that all have sinned (both Jew and Gentile), that justification is by faith alone, and that salvation is received only in Christ and through the Spirit, why should Paul suddenly be so deeply concerned with the status and future of unbelieving Jewish Israel? Centuries of Protestant interpretation, which made individual justification Paul's central teaching, had no ready answer for Paul's deep concern. For if one assumes that Romans 9–11 is focused on individual justification, on the election and judgment of separate individuals, then the apostle had an obviously logical answer

to his question. He should have answered: "If one does not believe in
Jesus Christ," as most of his fellow Jews did not, "then it follows that
that person is not elect." While Romans 9–11 has been interpreted in
that fashion, such a view assumes an answer that Paul did not and could
not accept because his concern arose precisely from Israel's election.
But how can the election of Jewish Israel be maintained in the face of
such widespread unbelief? Such is the apostle's dilemma, and, like
Moses in the wilderness (Exodus 32:32), Paul expressed himself willing
to suffer judgment on behalf of his kinsmen if that would bring about
their salvation (Romans 9:3). His offer was not motivated merely by
ethnic or racial identity, by solidarity with his own people; rather, like
Moses, Paul was motivated by concern for the honor of the God who
had chosen Israel. How would the honor of God, who is always faithful
to his promise, be maintained in the face of an unbelieving Israel?

Today most interpreters agree that the horizons of Paul's argument
in Romans 9–11 extend as wide as God's history of redemption in the
world. Paul is concerned with the role of Jewish Israel in that history.
His basic question is whether the role of Jewish Israel comes to an end
in an era when God is bringing his salvation to the nations of the world.
Now that Gentiles are flocking into the people of God, has the definition
of that people been so altered that Jewish Israel no longer qualifies? It
was beginning to look that way to Paul, but was it conceivable that God
could simply abandon his Old Testament people? Such are the questions
that Paul seeks to answer in Romans 9–11, and they arise from all that
has preceded in chapters 1–8.[4]

One important connection to Paul's previous discussion is found
in the immediate context. Romans 8 functions as a celebrative climax

4. There are various opinions concerning the precise relationship of Romans
9–11 to the preceding argument. Today most agree that there are not only various
interconnecting themes but also an essential connection to the basic thrust of Paul's
total argument. Cf. H. N. Ridderbos, *Aan de Romeinen* (Kampen: Kok, 1959), pp. 203f.;
C. E. B. Cranfield, *The Epistle to the Romans* (Edinburgh: Clark, 1979) II, pp. 445-448;
R. David Kaylor, *Paul's Covenant Community: Jew and Gentile in Romans* (Atlanta:
John Knox, 1988), pp. 159-162. Even E. Käsemann, who suggests concerning Romans
9–11 that "apart from ch. 16, no part of the epistle is so self-contained as this,"
nevertheless acknowledges the necessity of not divorcing justification from salvation
history. *Commentary on Romans* (Grand Rapids: Eerdmans, 1980), pp. 253ff. It is this
salvation-historical perspective that has altered the interpretation of Romans 9–11.

to the proclamation contained in chapters 1–7. In chapter 8 Paul celebrates both the present freedom granted by the Spirit in Christ and the hoped-for freedom of the entire creation at the resurrection, freedoms firmly grounded in and guaranteed by the electing love of God. The apostle has absolute confidence that nothing in the entire creation can separate believers from this electing love of God and the salvation given in Christ Jesus. Thus Romans 8 ends on a note of absolute certainty rooted in the actions of God in Christ.

Why then should there be such an abrupt change in mood from celebrative certainty to personal sorrow and anguish at the beginning of Romans 9? The reason is obvious. When Paul looks away from Christ to the reality of Jewish unbelief he wonders whether he has a right to be so confident. And he wonders, in the face of such massive resistance to the gospel, is election such a reliable guarantee? After all, Jewish Israel was the original object of election, the recipient of numerous blessings and privileges; but now in the presence of Jesus and the gospel, most did not believe. Is election such a sure thing? If Israel can apparently fall away, what happens to Christian confidence in God's electing love in Christ? Without a satisfactory answer to the unbelief of Jewish Israel, the certainty expressed in Romans 8 stands in jeopardy. Consequently, Paul necessarily raises the question of the status and destiny of Jewish Israel in the light of its prior election. The validity of his gospel depends on the answer.

Keeping Paul's Conclusion in View

When complex arguments are analyzed, it is sometimes necessary to look at the conclusions lest the analysis contradict the author's intentions. The history of the interpretation of Romans 9–11 demonstrates how easily one can misconstrue Paul's argument: Sometimes interpreters have developed a view of election that leads to conclusions that disallow Paul's own.

While Paul's anguished concern stems from unbelieving Jewish Israel and its existence under the hardening judgment of God, his remarkable conclusion announces the ultimate salvation of Jewish Israel. The reason for his certainty is expressed in Romans 11:28f.: "As regards the gospel they are enemies of God for your sake; but as regards election they are beloved, for the sake of their ancestors; for the gifts and the calling of God are irrevocable." Thus the apostle's confidence concerning the salvation of unbelieving Jewish Israel rests precisely on the same foundation as his certainty concerning the salvation of those who are in Christ. This unshakable foundation is that ultimately nothing can thwart the purposes of God's electing love. With the Old Testament prophets, Paul affirms that even the faithlessness of God's people cannot cancel God's faithfulness, because God will heal their faithlessness (Hosea 14:4). While in the midst of history there may be reasons for sorrow and anguish in the face of unbelief, at the end God's faithfulness to his promises will be manifested and his people can rejoice. Of course, Paul's argument is not focused primarily on the destiny of individual unbelievers but rather on the mutual destiny of Jewish Israel and the Gentile world in the history of redemption.

Understanding Paul's Answer: Romans 9 and 10

The Faithfulness of God

The beginning of Paul's discussion focuses on the faithfulness of God. If the promises made and the covenants established with the patriarchs are given to Israel, and if the Christ descends according to the flesh from their race, how is it possible that it is precisely this privileged Israel that, for the most part, do not believe in Jesus Christ? Is it conceivable that God does not keep his promises?

For the apostle Paul, and for anyone brought up on the Old Testament, such a thought is utterly inconceivable: "It is not as though the word of God had failed" (Romans 9:6). God's word always produces in human history what it says. His promises never return to him without first achieving in the life of his people what he promised (Isaiah 55:10f.). Thus if the word of God has not yet accomplished what it promised, there must be something else to be considered. So the apostle considers the recipients of the promise. To whom were the promises made? Were they given to all Jews indiscriminately, simply on the basis of genetic or racial connections to the patriarchs? To this question Paul, together with the rest of Scripture, gives an emphatic No. The basis for claiming the promises of salvation has never been simply physical descent from the patriarchs. God's covenant with Israel is not fundamentally a matter of ethnic ancestry.

The principle Paul uses in support of his emphatic No is that "not all who are descended from Israel belong to Israel, and not all are children of Abraham because they are his descendants" (Romans 9:6f., *RSV*). Paul does not invent this principle but derives it from Old Testament history (vv. 7-12). The line of Abraham's true descendants runs through Isaac, not Ishmael, and through Jacob, not Esau. The reason for this selection lies not in those selected but in the will and choice of God. Neither Abrahamic genetic lineage by itself nor any action of the persons involved can account for their inclusion in God's covenant promises. All that true Israel can ever say about its existence as God's people is that it was chosen by God and is the recipient of his love and mercy.

Such is the lesson contained in Paul's quotation from Malachi: "I have loved Jacob, but I have hated Esau" (Romans 9:13; Malachi 1:3). Since Malachi wrote at the end of the Old Testament, he is speaking not so much of the individuals he names but of the peoples these ancestors represent. Malachi asserts that the disparity in history between Israel (Jacob) and Edom (Esau) can be explained only by God's undeserved love for Israel. Israel had returned from exile but Edom remained under the judgment of God. While God's judgments can be accounted for in terms of human responsibility (cf. Amos 1:11-15 for Edom and 2:4-8 for Judah and Israel), the restoration of Israel and its continuing existence in history is due exclusively to God's unmerited love for Israel. Israel was restored from exile not because its people were inherently better than those of Edom but solely because God loved Israel (cf. Hosea 11). Thus, not only in Israel's origin but also in its continuing existence, it lives from God's special favor. As God's people, Israel is an objective manifestation of God's electing love. Such is Israel's nature and essence, and God's promises are given only to those who acknowledge and possess that nature and essence.

Paul's initial answer is thus not based primarily on numbers.[5] He

---

5. If one assumes that Paul's argument is only concerned with numbers, that Israel is either the *whole* of ethnic Israel or only the true *remnant* of Israel, then it is

is not accounting for the present status of unbelieving Israel by arguing that true Israel was always less than the total number of Abraham's or Isaac's physical descendants. Although that is true, Paul is establishing primarily the essence of what it means to be Israel. In essence Israel is, and has always been, the people who were called into existence by God's love and who continue to live from his love. Promise, call, gift, and love are the actions of God embracing and sustaining Israel, and Israel must always respond with a faithful acceptance of that which God promises and gives. If Israel forgets its essential nature, if Israel tries to establish another basis for its existence, then it lives outside the promise and gifts of God.[6] While God's word and promise can never fail, Israel in its historical existence frequently forgets its essential nature and fails to respond in faith as it should (Romans 4:11f.).

The Sovereignty of God and the Disobedience of Israel

God's sovereignty and human disobedience are thus for Paul two key realities shaping the course of the history of salvation. The relationship between these two realities creates dilemmas that our finite minds can never fully resolve. Nevertheless, in spite of such unresolved dilemmas, the central emphases of Paul's discussion are sufficiently clear to resolve his personal anguish and produce at the end a hymn of praise.

The sovereignty of God lies at the center of Paul's discussion. Only God's sovereign mercy can account for Israel's origin and continued existence in history. If Israel had depended on human will and

---

difficult to maintain the unity of Paul's argument. I agree with Elizabeth Johnson, who argues that "Paul has a single understanding of Israel in Romans 9–11 that is drawn not from ethnic or historical characteristics, but theological ones." *The Function of Apocalyptic and Wisdom Traditions in Romans 9–11* (Atlanta: Scholars, 1989), p. 141. Paul develops this theological understanding at the beginning of his argument. Cf. also Ridderbos, *Aan de Romeinen,* p. 209, who entitles Romans 9:6-13, "The Nature of Israel's Election."

6. For example, the haggadic tradition, which projects the enmity between Jacob and Esau into the time before they were born as the reason for God's choice of Jacob, represents a different understanding of Israel's election than that presented by Paul.

achievement for its existence, it would long ago have ceased to exist. So, in Romans 9:14-29, the apostle celebrates God's sovereign will, his sovereign mercy and compassion, as the only source of life and salvation for the people of God. In fact, God's sovereignty is stressed so exclusively that it sounds almost arbitrary and capricious. Yet God is neither capricious nor unjust because he is the God who has freely chosen to be merciful. This message of sovereign grace freely given by a merciful God is not problematic for the believer, but is rather a source of joy and hope. Salvation resides in the hands of a merciful God.

God is as sovereign and just in his judgments as in his mercy. While neither Paul nor the prophets have any difficulty pointing out adequate reasons for such judgments, the relationship between God's sovereignty and human accountability is not easily grasped. Consequently, one can easily be diverted by difficult questions. But Paul focuses on the remarkable fact that the judgments of God are designed to further his purposes of grace and salvation. God's judgments occur "so that [his] name may be proclaimed in all the earth," and "in order to make known the riches of his glory for the objects of mercy" (Romans 9:17, 23). Remarkably, God's judgments serve his sovereign grace. This was true in the case of Pharaoh's hardening, which served God's liberation of Israel, and now in the case of Israel's hardening, which serves the salvation of the Gentiles (11:11ff.). Thus while Paul discusses wrath and judgment, salvation continues to be his theme. Even God's final manifestation of wrath is delayed in favor of his long-suffering patience, which seeks to secure the salvation of his selected people from among both Jews and Gentiles (9:22-24). For the apostle Paul, salvation rests solely in the hands of the sovereign God, who accomplishes his will in mercy and judgment, and most remarkably in judgment serving mercy.

How do these emphases advance the discussion concerning the status and destiny of unbelieving Israel? If God is sovereignly merciful, why has Israel become unbelieving and rejectors of God's mercy in Christ? Paul's answer flows naturally from what he has already established concerning the essential nature of Israel. The Israel of his day, for the most part, failed to believe because they had lost a proper understanding of what it meant to be Israel. They thought that righteousness could be secured by their own works. For Paul righteousness includes salvation and all that it entails, from God's justification of the individual to the final renewal of creation.[7] Israel failed to imitate the faith of Abraham, which acknowledges and receives this salvation, which is promised in the covenant as a gift from God. Paul uses the stone prophecy from Isaiah (Romans 9:33) to clarify the present situation of Israel. Just as ancient Israel preferred to trust in their own political and military strategies to guarantee their security in times of national crisis, so the Israel of Paul's day trusted that their own works were sufficient to secure salvation. Neither trusted in the sovereign action of God for their salvation, and neither placed their trust in the foundation stone on which God would build his house and his kingdom. As a result the stone intended for security and salvation became for Israel a stone of stumbling.[8] The people of Israel were not looking for such a foundation stone because they thought they had no need for it. So they stumbled over Jesus, the stone that God had laid in Zion as the foundation for his kingdom of righteousness, because they thought that the kingdom could be established without him. But such an Israel, one that fails to respond in faith to God's actions that establish salvation, lives in denial of its own essential nature as the people of God.

Amazingly, the essential nature of Israel is seen in Gentile believers, those who have not been God's people before and were not even pursuing righteousness. These Gentiles believed in Christ and were not put to shame by stumbling over the stone that God had intended for security and salvation. These Gentiles, who had no capability of establishing a rightful claim to the promises of God on the basis of their own

7. For this broad understanding of righteousness see C. Brown and H. Seebass, "Righteousness," in *The New International Dictionary of New Testament Theology,* ed. C. Brown (Grand Rapids: Zondervan, 1986) III, pp. 352-373. Righteousness is essentially the covenant blessings promised by God and the covenant conduct of God and his people, which is necessary for realizing those blessings.

8. Paul combines two stone texts from Isaiah 8:14f. and 28:16. A similar use of the stone motif, with the addition of Psalm 118:22, is found in I Peter 2:4-8. For both New Testament authors, the Stone is Jesus Christ. This New Testament use of the stone motif probably originated with Jesus himself in the parable of the vineyard (Mark 12:10; Matthew 21:42; Luke 20:17f.). Cf. J. Jeremias, *Theological Dictionary of the New Testament* (Grand Rapids: Eerdmans, 1964-76) IV, pp. 271-279; B. Lindars, *New Testament Apologetic* (London: SCM, 1961), pp. 177-179; E. E. Ellis, *Paul's Use of the Old Testament* (Edinburgh: Oliver and Boyd, 1957), pp. 87-89.

achievement, had now become the people of God.[9] God had bestowed on them the same electing love that had originally called Israel into existence. The exclusivism of Jewish Israel's claim to salvation by keeping the law (Torah) had been shattered by the sovereign grace of God.[10]

Salvation by Faith, Not by Works

Why is salvation by works demanded by the law not possible? Certainly Judaism also confesses the grace of God in giving Israel the law, but its understanding of this grace places Israel in the position of attaining righteousness and salvation by doing what the law requires. All that is required for attaining the future salvation is at least a minimal keeping

9. What does Paul's use of Hosea 2:23 and 1:10 in Romans 9:25f. demonstrate? Although the prophecy of Hosea originally had in view God's reacceptance of Israel after exile, one need not assume that Paul was ignorant of this original meaning. Instead, the apostle uses Hosea to highlight the freedom of God's grace given to those who have no claim upon it. Thus Hosea supports Paul's argument in Romans 9 concerning the essential nature of Israel. Cf. Ridderbos, *Aan de Romeinen*, p. 223.

10. Recently, several have suggested that Paul's major criticism concerns Judaism's exclusivism and not its "self-righteousness." While Paul indeed opposes a Jewish exclusivism that excludes Gentiles, the basis of his opposition lies at a deeper level. While E. P. Sanders is correct in suggesting that Christian interpreters should not accuse Judaism of practicing a superficial legalism or of advocating a psychological attitude of self-righteousness, since such is absent from Jewish literature, it still remains true that Judaism has no place within its perspective on salvation for a crucified messiah. The reason for this exclusion is the belief that repentance and doing the works of the Torah are a sufficient basis for salvation. Cf. G. F. Moore, *Judaism in the First Centuries of the Christian Era* (Cambridge: Harvard University Press, 1927-30) I, pp. 491ff. Obviously, such a belief also has the consequence of excluding Gentiles unless they become adherents of Judaism (proselytes) who observe Torah. But Paul's primary criticism of this belief lies in its necessary rejection of Jesus Christ. Cf. J. G. Gager, *The Origins of Anti-Semitism: Attitudes Toward Judaism in Pagan and Christian Antiquity* (New York: Oxford University Press, 1983); E. P. Sanders, *Paul, the Law, and the Jewish People* (Philadelphia: Fortress, 1983). While Gager and Sanders agree that the issue for Paul is Jewish exclusivism and the noninclusion of the Gentiles, they have a major disagreement. Gager holds that Paul does not criticize Judaism as such and hence does not require of Jews faith in Christ, whereas Sanders holds that Paul called Jews also to faith in Christ. Gager's thesis has been briefly summarized in chapter I above.

of the law, if not a doing of good that outweighs the evil.[11] With that understanding of the relationship between law and salvation the apostle Paul disagrees. Out of his encounter with the crucified and exalted Jesus, Paul received an awareness of human sinfulness that rendered impossible the belief that salvation could be achieved by the works of the law. Even though Paul never criticizes the law as such because it is a holy, just, and good expression of the righteousness God requires, nevertheless, in Christ Paul knows, both personally and theologically, that the law cannot produce in human conduct the righteousness it demands (Romans 7:1–8:11). The fault lies not in the law but in sinful human beings, and God's remedy for this humanly insurmountable fault is Jesus Christ. This deepened understanding of human sin allows only for a salvation that is a gift from God, a righteousness not based on works but received by faith in Christ (5:17). While the apostle's personal understanding of righteousness was drastically altered first of all by his visionary encounter with Jesus Christ, he discovered this same teaching of a righteousness based on faith in Moses and the prophets (10:5-20). God has always been pleading with Israel for faith, for belief in the gospel (10:15-17).

Paul's provocative summary of this teaching is contained in Romans 10:4: "Christ is the end of the law, that everyone who has faith may be justified" *(RSV)*. What does the apostle mean by describing Christ as the end *(telos)* of the law? Basically, there are two possibilities: Christ is "the end of the law" either by being the termination or cessation of the law or of some part of it or by being its goal, culmination, or fulfillment. In the ancient church and still at the Reformation, interpreters favored goal/fulfillment. But today the interpretive pendulum has swung in favor of termination/cessation.[12] This issue is very

---

11. E. P. Sanders's *Paul and Palestinian Judaism* (Philadelphia: Fortress, 1977) has convinced many that Judaism also believes in salvation by grace through faith. However, Sanders does not adequately discuss Judaism's understanding of the relationship of grace and merit, which is quite different from that found in the teaching of Paul. Paul's view of grace stands radically against any notion of merit. For a critique of Sanders on this point, see S. Westerholm, *Israel's Law and the Church's Faith: Paul and His Recent Interpreters* (Grand Rapids: Eerdmans, 1988), pp. 141-164.

12. For a summary of various positions, see R. Badenas, *Christ the End of the Law: Romans 10:4 in Pauline Perspective* (Sheffield: JSOT, 1985); B. L. Martin, *Christ*

complex. "End" is obviously a metaphor describing Christ's relationship to the law, but the term itself does not give all the information necessary to determine precisely how Paul viewed that relationship. Such information must be gathered from an examination of Paul's entire teaching on the law.[13] But since a full exposition of Paul's view would demand considerable space and since in this chapter we are interested only in the impact this teaching has on Paul's view of Jewish Israel, we will simply indicate our conclusions concerning Paul's view of the law.

Paul reveals two basic attitudes toward the law. First, when the sinfulness of humanity is in focus, Paul views the law as a judge pronouncing the sentence of death. The law itself cannot release from sin; in fact, it can only increase sin and stand in judgment over the sinner (Romans 5:20). The believer, who is united with Christ in his death and resurrection, has died to sin and is, therefore, no longer under the law as judge, no longer under the law's power to increase sin and to pronounce over the sinner the judgment of death. Freedom from sin in Christ means freedom from the law in its relationship to sin and the sinner (Romans 6). If this were Paul's exclusive perspective on the law, the meaning of "end" would be termination/cessation. The law in that respect has come to an end in Christ for the believer.[14]

However, there is in Pauline teaching a second perspective on the law. In Romans 8, after once again focusing on what the law could not achieve because of sin, the apostle teaches that the work of Christ and

---

and the Law in Paul (Leiden: Brill, 1989). Badenas argues for "goal," Martin for "termination," specifying the "enslavement, condemnation, and death which the law brings" (p. 144).

13. One should not expect consensus concerning Paul's teaching about the law. This issue has been a significant cause of division between major Christian traditions. Recently a new debate has been stimulated by the work of E. P. Sanders, op. cit.; H. Räisänen, Paul and the Law (Tübingen: Mohr, 1983); and others. For a summary of the issues and evaluation, see Westerholm, op. cit., pp. 46-101.

14. Cf. Martin, op. cit., for arguments in favor of this position. Seyoon Kim argues for the cessation of the law more broadly conceived: "Christ is the end of the law in the sense that he has superseded it as the will of God and has therefore terminated it as the means of salvation, so that righteousness may be granted to everyone who has faith." The Origin of Paul's Gospel (Grand Rapids: Eerdmans, 1982), p. 308. But Paul's use of Deuteronomy 30 in Romans 10:5-8 suggests that even the law points to the righteousness of faith and that, therefore, Paul does not grant what Kim assumes, namely, that the law was once the means of salvation.

life in the Spirit have as their goal the fulfillment of the just requirements of the law (Romans 8:2-4). There is for Paul a real sense in which the righteousness demanded by the law has not been terminated by the death and resurrection of Christ. Instead, that righteousness articulated and required by the law has achieved fulfillment in Christ, and now in Christ and through the Spirit that righteousness describes and shapes the Christian life.

If both of these perspectives form the background of Romans 10:4, then the interpretation of "end" as goal or fulfillment does the greatest justice to Paul's entire teaching. "Goal" enables one to speak both of that which ceases, because the goal has been achieved, and of that which continues because of an essential harmony between what leads to or prepares for the goal and the goal itself.[15] Paul knows which functions of the law and which forms of righteousness have ceased as well as the essential righteousness of the law that continues because the law has been fulfilled in Christ.[16] It is this fulfillment in Christ that provides unity to Paul's understanding of the law.

15. The criticism by Johnson, in her otherwise excellent thesis, that those who see both perspectives and thus favor "goal" as the best interpretation are "sitting on the fence" and trying "to have one's cake and eat it too" is too facile to be taken seriously. Certainly, metaphors by their very nature need not be restricted to a single perspective. In any case, every interpretation of Romans 10:4 seems to be a case of "having one's cake and eating it too" because every interpreter uses his or her prior understanding of Paul's view of the law as the obvious interpretation of this verse. Cf. Johnson, *op. cit.,* p. 152. Here she quotes R. Jewett, "The Law and the Coexistence of Jews and Gentiles in Romans," *Interpretation* 39 (1985), p. 353.

16. All agree that Paul does not require Gentiles to observe the cultic or ceremonial requirements of the law. Although Paul never explicitly develops a theology of Christ as the fulfiller of these aspects of the law, he does refer to Christ as "our paschal lamb" (I Corinthians 5:7), and some interpreters have seen a connection between circumcision and baptism in Colossians 2:11f. Still, Paul does not object to circumcision for Jewish Christians, nor does he object if one lives as a Jew among Jews (I Corinthians 9:20-22). What Paul does object to is an understanding of law observance that has no need for receiving righteousness by faith in Christ. For positive arguments in favor of "end of the law" as goal, see Badenas, *op. cit.;* for "goal" as including both fulfillment and cessation, see A. Bandstra, *The Law and the Elements of the World* (Kampen: Kok, 1964), pp. 101-106. J. S. Vos also favors inclusion of both aspects in Romans 10:4: "Christ is the endpoint of the law (as 'the law of works' the end, as 'the law of faith' the goal)." "De letter doodt, maar de geest maakt levend," in T. Baarda, et al., *Paulus en de andere joden. Exegetische bijdragen en discussie* (Delft: Meinema, 1984), p. 128.

How does this understanding of the law affect Paul's attitude toward Judaism and toward those who do not accept Christ as the end of the law? Obviously, he can no longer accept Judaism's traditional teaching that repentance and doing the works of the Torah (law) are sufficient for attaining the final salvation. While he permits Jewish Christians to observe parts of the Torah that he will *not* allow to be imposed on Gentiles, and while he continues to apply the category of election even to unbelieving Jewish Israel, he cannot allow a view of Torah observance that has no place for and no need of the crucified and resurrected Christ. While Paul received this view of law and righteousness by revelation on the Damascus road, he discovered that righteousness has always been received by faith since such was the teaching of the Old Testament (Romans 4:13ff.; 10:6ff.). The way of salvation for both Jew and Gentile is the same because both must call on the name of the Lord Jesus to be saved (10:9-13). Consequently, Paul faults Jewish Israel for their lack of faith. That is their primary disobedience (10:14-21).

One begins now to appreciate Paul's "great sorrow and unceasing anguish" over the status and destiny of the greater part of Jewish Israel. For even if God is faithful, what options does God himself have if Israel has not responded in faith? If the power of sin is so universally present that no one is righteous and no one can be justified by the works of the law (Romans 3:9-10), what is the present status of Jewish Israel, which continues to seek God's righteousness by trying to do what the law demands rather than by faith? If they persist in following that impossible way, can God do anything but reject such a "disobedient" people (10:21)?

Understanding Paul's Answer: Romans 11

The Remnant and the Rest:
Election and Disobedience

The apostle's remarkable answer is neither simple nor expected because in every stage of his answer he emphatically rejects the possibility that God has rejected even this "disobedient" people. The argument is astonishing, but this astonishment is created by an awareness of the overwhelming grace of a faithful God.

The first stage of the argument is the easiest to understand. In Romans 11:1-6, Paul introduces the idea of a believing remnant of Israel as evidence that God has not rejected his people. Paul himself and all other Jewish Christians constitute this remnant of Israel. Just as it had happened once in the days of Elijah, so now in the apostle's time only a remnant of Israel responded faithfully to God.[17] We must not misunderstand the thrust of this argument. We err if we assume that the significance of the remnant pertains only to the elect individuals who constitute the remnant. Paul is not implying that the remnant alone is Israel and no one else. If we assume that the people of God in Romans 11:1 is now restricted to the elect remnant, we undercut the rest of Paul's argument. Nowhere in Romans 11 does the apostle withdraw from unbelieving Jewish Israel the reality of being the people of God or the fact of their election. Instead, Paul points to himself and other Jewish Christians as evidence that God has not withdrawn his grace from Jewish Israel. This remnant is a sign that God is still faithful to his election of Jewish Israel. The remnant signifies to the whole of Israel the essential nature of true Israel and what Israel is always called to be because the Jewish Christian remnant exists as the Israel of God, whose status is based not on works but on grace.[18] For this reason the apostle stresses his own solidarity with Jewish Israel (Romans 11:1). Paul himself is the hopeful sign that God has not rejected his disobedient people because Paul also was in an active state of disobedience when God's grace was given to him.

But even if the believing remnant is a hopeful sign concerning

17. Is Paul developing a typological argument that he is the Elijah of the end time? Cf. E. Käsemann, *Commentary on Romans* (Grand Rapids: Eerdmans, 1980), p. 301. Markus Barth discovers an alternate symbolism. Since Paul is a member of the tribe of Benjamin, the only northern tribe attached to Judah, he could view himself as a representative of "all Israel." *The People of God* (Sheffield: JSOT, 1983), p. 82, n. 3. Most interpreters believe that Paul intends to draw a parallel only to the remnant.

18. Cf. Cranfield, *op. cit.,* pp. 547f.; Ridderbos, *op. cit.,* pp. 247-249. Calvin speaks of the election of a people as distinct from the election of individuals (*Institutes* III.21.7). While such a distinction has some validity, one must not make this distinction into a separation that denies the bonds of corporate solidarity. The remnant represents and is significant for the rest of Israel.

God's faithfulness to Israel, what is the status of those who do not manifest the signs of election? Paul answers: "the rest were hardened" (Romans 11:7). We must resist the temptation quickly to draw inferences from this statement, because what Paul declares is not new teaching. However difficult the language is for us to understand, God's hardening of his people because of their disobedience is announced already by the Old Testament prophets. From Moses to David to Isaiah, Israel finds itself at times under a judging action of God that keeps it unresponsive to the grace of God.[19] The prophetic language of judgment employs pictures of a deep slumber, a blindness that fails to see what God is doing, a resounding deafness. Consequently, Israel forgot the great redemptive events of the exodus (Deuteronomy 29:4), persecuted God's anointed servant (Psalm 69), and refused to worship God (Isaiah 29). Still, in the very context of these prophetic judgments there can be found words of hope for Israel: The deaf will hear, the blind will see, and those who err in spirit will come to understanding (Isaiah 29:18, 24). The harshness of the prophetic judgment is clearly intended to evoke repentance and faith, and consequently we cannot infer that these are absolute and final judgments beyond which there is no hope. Thus the apostle's answer to the question about the status of unbelieving Israel is precisely the same as that given by the Old Testament prophets during other times of Israel's disobedience.

This Old Testament perspective continues in the next stage of Paul's argument (Romans 11:11ff.). Here the apostle describes hardened Israel as having stumbled but not having fallen. Clearly Paul's distinction between stumbling and falling is intended to describe a judgment that is less than final. His description is borrowed from prophetic judgments that speak of a snare, a trap, a pitfall, or a stumbling block, as well as the prophecy concerning the stone in Zion that makes Israel stumble. Stumbling is not an irrevocable condition. The prophets speak of historical judgments of God on Israel that, because they are historical in nature, are always open to possible change. In addition, these historical judgments are not detached from God's plan of salvation, but instead actually further its purposes. Just as the hardening of Pharaoh

19. In support of his teaching, Paul quotes Deuteronomy 29:4; Psalm 69:22f.; 35:8; Isaiah 6:10; 29:10.

served God's purpose of grace (Romans 9:17), so the hardening of Israel serves the salvation of the Gentiles. Not only did Israel's unbelief become the historical occasion for Paul's ministry to the Gentiles (Acts 13:46; 28:28), but also in the face of such unbelief God necessarily turned to those who were not his people precisely to maintain the gracious character of salvation.[20]

Yet this turning to the Gentiles is not an end in itself. It contributes, rather, to God's ultimate intention to save Israel by making Israel jealous. The gathering of the Gentiles does not definitively displace Jewish Israel. Instead it serves God's purpose of achieving Israel's full inclusion. Steeped in Old Testament promises, the apostle cannot imagine that the eschatological completion of God's plan of salvation would not include the eschatological fullness of Israel. Thus the apostle teaches that God has not yet closed the book on unbelieving Jewish Israel because he still anticipates their full inclusion, an event analogous to resurrection from the dead (Romans 11:12, 14f.).[21] The door is still open to the future salvation of Jewish Israel in spite of the present judgment of hardening because of unbelief. Amazingly, God's hardening of his disobedient people is not his negation of their election.

How can the apostle hold in tension two realities that appear on the surface to be contradictory, namely, hardening and election? Part of our difficulty in grasping what the apostle is saying stems from our predominantly individualistic modes of thought. We tend to assume that benefits and blessings are received solely on the basis of individual worth, action, or merit. Perhaps we are beginning to understand today that individuals do not stand alone but are shaped, blessed, and even judged on the basis of an entire network of essential relationships to others, both family and nation. The strength and reality of the corporate relationships that define who we are as individuals is beginning to modify our traditional individualism. Such corporate relationships are the basis of Paul's eschatological hope for Israel. He sees a relationship

20. Cf. Ridderbos, *Aan de Romeinen,* p. 252.

21. E. Käsemann suggests that the phrase "life from the dead" designates what Paul elsewhere describes as the "resurrection of the dead" and thus refers to the parousia. He concludes, "Thus the conversion of Israel is for the apostle also the last act of salvation history." *Op. cit.,* p. 307. Cf. also M. Barth for a similar perspective, *The People of God,* p. 43.

between the present harvest of believers among Jewish Israel and his eschatological hope for the future of Jewish Israel. The believing remnant constitute the first fruits dedicated to the Lord and represent the entire "lump of dough" or the entire harvest (cf. Numbers 15:17-21). Just as Jesus Christ, as the first fruits of those who have died, represents and guarantees the resurrection of those who belong to him (I Corinthians 15:23), so the elect remnant of Jewish Israel represents and assures the eschatological salvation of Jewish Israel.[22] In addition, Paul's eschatological hope is rooted in Abraham and the patriarchs of Israel. Because of God's election they form the root of the olive tree of Israel, and their consecration to God — their holiness — means that the branches have the same character of holiness, being consecrated to God (Romans 11:16).[23] Thus for Paul blessings remain a future possibility for hardened Israel because of the corporate relationship to those who have received God's grace. Disobedience need not cancel future hope rooted in God's electing grace.

The metaphor of the olive tree becomes a summary statement of all that Paul has been saying. The olive tree exists only because God chose to plant Israel in the midst of the nations.[24] Because of unbelief among those who are Jewish Israel, Gentiles are grafted into the olive tree to share in the privileges that God gave to Israel. Gentile Christians become part of the olive tree, a part of the Israel whom God elected. Since their status has been created by grace and not by their own nature,

22. The more common interpretation of the two metaphors in Romans 11:16 (first fruits and root) understands both as referring to the patriarchs. For example, Ridderbos argues against interpreting "first fruits" as a reference to Jewish Christians on the ground that the parallelism in v. 16 suggests that the two parallel lines refer to the same reality (*Aan de Romeinen*, p. 257). On this interpretation v. 16 has no connection with the preceding verses. However, could not the position of v. 16 indicate that Paul is in transition from the corporate significance of the believing remnant to the corporate significance of the patriarchs for Jewish Israel? Cf. Cranfield, *op. cit.*, pp. 564ff.

23. Paul thinks along the same corporate lines regarding marriage and children: Children are holy, that is, consecrated to God as members of his people, by virtue of birth to a believing parent (I Corinthians 7:14). Such teaching reveals the inadequacy of modern individualism to understand fully God's plan of salvation.

24. The olive tree is a symbol of righteous Israel in Psalm 52:8 and Hosea 14:6. The metaphor of the planting of Israel is associated with the vineyard in Isaiah 5 and the oaks of righteousness in Isaiah 61.

any thought or attitude on their part that minimizes this grace by assuming another basis for membership in Israel will result in judgment. Specifically, Gentile believers may not assume any kind of superiority over unbelieving Jewish Israel, over the branches cut off, because all believers live exclusively from the sovereignly given grace of God. Because Israel exists solely on the basis of God's grace and because that grace promises even to heal Israel's faithlessness (Hosea 14:4), the apostle has reason for hope even for the branches that have been cut off. God, who is sovereign and gracious, can certainly, and perhaps even more easily than with the Gentile branches, graft them in again. Of course, for this hope to be realized, those under judgment and presently cut off will have to come to faith, for that is the only way to be Israel (Romans 11:23).

The Mystery of a Final Fullness

The climax of Paul's presentation is the revelation of a mystery concerning the salvation of the full number of the Gentiles and of all Israel. This mystery has proven to be, in fact, very mysterious for interpreters, as our discussion will indicate. Yet mystery has nothing to do with being mysterious. The biblical use of "mystery" refers to the counsel of God concerning his plan of salvation, which was hidden either because it had not yet been revealed or because a partial revelation had not been fully understood.[25] While it is possible that the apostle received this mystery by direct revelation, it is more likely that it was by prophetic insight into the plan of salvation unfolding before his eyes and illumined by the Old Testament.[26] Paul discovered that God's plan contained unexpected avenues and surprising complexities, but the clarity of his

25. Cf. R. Brown, *The Semitic Background of the Term "Mystery" in the New Testament* (Philadelphia: Fortress, 1968).
26. Ephesians 3 uses "mystery" in the same way. The apostle's insight into the mystery was based on the actual conversion of the Gentiles. While Ephesians 3 focuses on the present unfolding of God's plan not previously revealed, Romans 11:25 includes a future element. But Paul's discussion in Romans 11 also clearly reveals an insight based on the present unfolding of God's plan of salvation interpreted in the light of the Old Testament promises. Cf. Ridderbos, *Aan de Romeinen,* p. 261.

insight into the essential mystery of the movements of God's grace remains unclouded by the complexities that puzzle interpreters. After all, God's paths are beyond our ability to trace out (Romans 11:33).

One of the complexities is the meaning of "all Israel" (Romans 11:26). Who is this Israel that will be saved? While some argue that it refers simply to all the elect, both Jews and Gentiles, neither the previous nor the subsequent context supports this view. Although one can point to the olive tree metaphor as a symbol of Israel embracing both Jewish and Gentile believers, and to the fact that in Galatians 6:16 Paul refers to the Christian Church as "the Israel of God,"[27] the burden of the apostle's concern throughout Romans 11 has been the Israel that has been hardened and cut off. His concern has not been simply with the salvation of the elect, for on one level that raises no concerns (cf. Romans 11:7). His concern is, rather, focused on whether God's election of Israel is no longer in force because of unbelief. Paul agonizes over his fellow Jews who do not believe, and his hope for the salvation of all Israel includes precisely those who are presently categorized as "enemies of God" with regard to the gospel (11:28). Therefore, it is unlikely that "all Israel" refers simply to all elect Jews and Gentiles.

A more satisfying interpretation relates "all Israel" to Paul's earlier hope for the "fullness" of Israel (Romans 11:12, "full inclusion" in *RSV* and *NRSV*). Fullness need not mean the salvation of every individual who ever belonged to Jewish Israel. The Scriptures give adequate reason for believing that individual members can be excluded. Paul contrasts fullness with remnant, and in the eschatological future he sees no longer a partial remnant but a fullness of Israel. But since the present remnant is also contrasted with the rest of Israel who are hardened, it seems that the achievement of fullness requires a removal of the judgment of hardening. Unless the hardening that now blinds unbelievers to the grace of God in Christ is removed, there is no possibility of overcoming the disparity between the present salvation of a remnant of Jewish Israel and the anticipated future salvation of the

27. While some interpret the "Israel of God" in Galatians 6:16 as a reference to Jewish Israel, most do not agree. Since Galatians teaches that circumcision is not required and that all in Christ are descendants of Abraham, it seems more likely that the "Israel of God" is the church. Cf. E. P. Sanders, *Paul, the Law, and the Jewish People*, p. 174.

fullness of Jewish Israel. "All Israel" refers, then, to Jewish Israel in its eschatological fullness.

A second complexity concerns when and how this salvation of the fullness of Israel will happen. Paul's description of the mystery continues the theme of his earlier argument that the hardening of Jewish Israel has as its effect the salvation of the Gentiles. He now adds that this hardening will be in effect "until the full number of the Gentiles has come in," that is, has entered into salvation (Romans 11:25). We must emphasize that Paul is not focusing narrowly on the salvation of separate individuals and suggesting that every individual Gentile will be saved. The apostle is describing God's history of salvation, which embraces the whole of humanity, that is, Jewish Israel and the Gentile world. In both cases individuals may be excluded from participating in the promised salvation without destroying the validity of Paul's argument. The rejection of unbelieving Jewish Israel has in view the reconciliation of the (Gentile) world (11:15). Thus there will be a hardening of that part of Jewish Israel until the world has been reconciled to God and the eschatological fullness of the Gentiles has entered God's kingdom and received his salvation. The fullness of the Gentiles then constitutes the eschatological limit on the hardening of Jewish Israel, for at that moment the salvific intent of hardening will have achieved its goal.

Yet if that is all that the mystery reveals, then the salvation of Jewish Israel will be limited forever to a remnant and the eschatological fullness of Israel can be only the sum of all Jewish Christians throughout the ages. While some interpreters hold this view, this simple arithmetical approach to fullness, adding up the remnant of all ages, destroys the dynamic of Paul's argument.[28] Paul describes a reciprocal relation of the hardening of Israel producing the fullness of the Gentiles, which then in turn produces jealousy and the fullness of Israel. Thus even though Paul does not speak directly in Romans 11:25 of a removal of hardening from Israel, the thrust of his entire argument implies that it

28. A. A. Hoekema, following W. Hendriksen's *Israel in Prophecy,* argues that "all Israel" is "the sum total of all the remnants throughout history." He allows for a possible large-scale conversion of the Jews in the future, but not until after the full number of the Gentiles has been gathered in. *The Bible and the Future* (Grand Rapids: Eerdmans, 1979), pp. 145-147.

will happen. Only by a removal of this "blindness" can there be an entity described as "the fullness of Israel" and not just a remnant. Paul promises more than the continuing existence of a remnant. As the hardening of Israel serves the salvation of the world, so the salvation of the world is intended to evoke jealousy and hence the salvation of hardened Israel.

The apostle's hope for Israel's future is rooted in Old Testament prophecy (Romans 11:26f.):

> Out of Zion will come the Deliverer;
> he will banish ungodliness from Jacob.
> And this is my covenant with them,
> when I take away their sins.

This prophecy combines Isaiah 59:20f. and 27:9 with possible overtones from Psalm 14:7 and Jeremiah 31:33f., and its form is also very significant. The quotation follows the Greek (Septuagint) translation, which differs considerably from the Hebrew version of these verses. The Hebrew text reads, "and he will come to Zion as Redeemer, to those in Jacob who turn from transgression." While the existence of the different Septuagint reading may point to a pre-Christian dispute concerning the meaning of this prophecy, the Hebrew text allows the possibility that the promised salvation depends on the prior repentance of Israel. In fact, this is the position of normative Judaism: The messianic salvation is conditional on Israel's repentance, study of Torah, and good works. Until such repentance occurs sufficiently, the messianic salvation cannot arrive. E. E. Urbach states succinctly the consequences of this rabbinic position: "If repentance alone makes redemption possible and brings it near, then there is no need for the Messianic sufferings."[29]

Therefore, the interpretation of Isaiah's prophecy has critical consequences. In the Septuagint text, quoted by Paul, the emphasis falls completely on the action of God or the Messiah. The Deliverer himself will remove godlessness from Jacob. Such an emphasis not only coincides with Paul's personal experience, but it also harmonizes with the

---

29. *The Sages: Their Concepts and Beliefs* (Jerusalem: Magnes, 1979), p. 671.

apostle's teaching concerning the hardening of Israel, which must be removed by God himself if the fullness of Israel is to be saved. Salvation does not lie within Jewish Israel's own possibilities or achievements. It can only be the result of the divine initiative on behalf of Israel. The Lord himself will renew his covenant with Israel when he takes away Israel's sin.

Does this text tell us also when and how this salvation will occur? Two other questions must first be answered. Does the future tense of "will come" refer to an event that is still future, such as the return of Christ? Or, since that future tense is contained already in the original prophecy of Isaiah, does it refer to the first coming of Christ? The second related question is this: Is "Zion" the heavenly Jerusalem, from which Christ will return, or is it the earthly Jerusalem, from which the gospel has gone out to the entire world?[30]

Which possibility is correct is difficult to decide. A number of interpreters today favor the view that Paul envisions a future conversion of Israel associated with the return of Christ.[31] Since the gospel must be preached to all the nations before the end, since Israel's hardening lasts "until the full number of the Gentiles has come in," since the acceptance of Jewish Israel may be associated with the endtime resurrection of the dead (Romans 11:15), and since in general the salvation of the fullness of Jewish Israel is clearly future, then is it not likely that Paul understood Isaiah 59:20 as not yet fulfilled in the first coming of Christ? If this salvific event is best understood as completely future, then it also makes sense to interpret "out of Zion" as a reference to Christ's return to earth from the heavenly Jerusalem (cf. Galatians 4:26). But if this view is correct, then the salvation of the fullness of Israel, in distinction from the salvation of the fullness of the Gentiles, does not result directly or at least not primarily from the gospel and the preaching mission of the Church in the world. Instead the salvation of the fullness of Israel, in distinction from the remnant, will be accom-

30. Paul's description of the Deliverer as coming "out of" Zion differs from both the Hebrew text ("to Zion") and the Septuagint ("on behalf of Zion"). Perhaps Paul's quotation of Isaiah is influenced by Psalm 14:7.

31. Käsemann argues for this position and lists many who agree. *Commentary on Romans*, p. 314. Karl Barth and Markus Barth also both advocate this position (see chapter I above).

plished only when the One who is himself the content of the gospel reappears.

However convincing this first possibility may seem, others are convinced that such a view destroys the dynamic of Paul's prophetic vision. Earlier the apostle depicts an interrelated process set in motion by the unbelief of Jewish Israel, the acceptance of the gospel by the Gentile world, and an eventual jealousy on the part of unbelieving Jewish Israel that will lead to their inclusion. This view understands the proclamation of the gospel (Romans 10) as central to the salvation of both the Gentile world and Jewish Israel. While indeed the Deliverer himself will remove blindness from Israel, Paul does seem to teach that the removal of hardness from Jewish Israel will be associated with the active power of the gospel. Speaking of hardened Israel, the apostle writes that when a person turns to the Lord in response to the gospel, it is through Christ that the hardness is removed (II Corinthians 3:14-16). One need not assume that Christ removes blindness or hardness only by coming in person.

Therefore, it is possible that Paul understands the future tense of the Isaiah prophecy as fulfilled in the first coming of Christ, which set in motion the apostolic mission of the Church. Such a view of a single interrelated process leading to the salvation of Jewish Israel finds additional support in the parallel drawn in Romans 11:30-32. Salvation is always given to those existing in disobedience. Gentiles in their disobedience received God's mercy because of the disobedience of unbelieving Jewish Israel. Now disobedient Jewish Israel may receive mercy by the mercy shown to the Gentiles. This reciprocal and interrelated process clearly seems to establish the view that salvation is received in the same manner by Jews and Gentiles alike through the efficacy of the Word working in history. "So faith comes from what is heard, and what is heard comes through the word of Christ," that is, through the preaching of the gospel (Romans 10:17).

If one is convinced by this view that sees the conversion of Jewish Israel as related to the first coming of Christ and to the subsequent proclamation of Christ in the gospel, when will that conversion occur? The apostle did not develop a precise calendar of events because he himself did not possess one. Instead he was granted prophetic insight into the outcome of a process that the Lord had already set in motion.

That process already begun completely reversed his original expectations. In place of a conversion of Jewish Israel followed by the conversion of the Gentiles, Paul saw a Jewish Israel that was hardened while the Gentiles were coming to the faith. Still, this process, which *now* (Romans 11:30) brought God's mercy to the Gentile world, would have as its effect that unbelieving Jewish Israel would receive that same mercy. If the "now" found in some manuscripts in Romans 11:31 is included,[32] then Paul is clearly relating the conversion of Israel to the process inaugurated by the first coming of Christ and the subsequent preaching of the gospel.

Precisely when this process will result in the salvation of the fullness of Israel, the apostle does not say.[33] Obviously, the salvation of the fullness of Israel also includes those Jewish Christians who now believe along with the Gentiles. In that sense the salvation of "all Israel" is already under way. Yet, as we have said, the dynamic of Paul's argument points to the fullness of Israel as an eschatological reality that will exist without the mark of hardening that now characterizes Israel's existence and divides Jewish Israel into the remnant and the rest.[34] Paul's prophetic insight reaches from the time of his own preaching mission to the culmination of God's plan of salvation. While the "now"

32. There is some doubt whether "now" was found in the original text. Today, however, textual critics insert it in brackets to indicate that its inclusion is probably authentic. Cf. Nestle-Aland, *Novum Testamentum Graece,* 26th ed.; and Bruce M. Metzger, *Textual Commentary on the Greek New Testament* (New York: United Bible Societies, 1971), p. 527.

33. Whether or not Paul thought the end was near is not a question of major concern for interpreting this issue. His insight concerned the necessary process of disobedience preceding mercy as God's manner of accomplishing his plan of salvation.

34. John H. Stek's position (*To the Jew First: An Exegetical Examination of a New Testament Theme* [Grand Rapids: Board of Home Missions of the Christian Reformed Church, 1973], pp. 168-258) is in many respects similar to mine but with one significant exception. Stek also believes that "all Israel" does not refer to the elect of all ages. However true that may be theologically, it does not fit the context, which speaks of Israel as the seed of Jacob (Romans 9). However, because of the mutual interdependence of Jew and Gentile in salvation history, Stek does not believe that Paul's view "requires a final epoch in which the mass of Israel shall be turned to the Lord" (p. 252). My focus on the fullness of the Gentiles as the eschatological limit on the hardening of Israel implies a subsequent significant conversion of Israel.

points to a process of redemption already under way, it cannot be used to restrict Paul's vision to the present moment. There is an eschatological fullness of both the Gentile world and Jewish Israel that awaits consummation.[35] That moment describes the end of God's history of salvation since then his purpose will have been fully achieved. But the time for the arrival of that moment cannot be determined in advance. That moment remains, in the proper sense of the term, an eschatological reality that the Father keeps in his own hands.

From Sorrow to Doxology

Paul's wrestling with the future of Jewish Israel began with expressions of personal sorrow and anguish but ends in a hymn of praise. Doxology is the only fitting response to reflections on the sovereignty of God. When sovereignty is divorced from God's loving mercy, God may appear to be cruelly tyrannical. But when we understand with Paul that God uses his judgments to serve his purpose of grace, and even delays the final manifestation of his wrath to accomplish his purposes of salvation, then we, too, can sing a hymn of praise to this God who sovereignly accomplishes his will.

Many mysteries remain because the sovereign God cannot be called to account before the bar of human understanding (Romans 9:20ff.). The unimaginable "depth of the riches and wisdom and knowledge of God" (11:33) exposes the limits of the human mind. Not even the apostle himself can fathom either the judgments of God or his love

---

35. Because Paul does not declare that after the fullness of the Gentiles has come in, *then* all Israel will be saved, Ridderbos refuses to interpret this as a future *conversion* of Israel. He prefers the language of the salvation of Israel, but does say that "Israel as a nation will not again exhibit the image of the people of God before the Gentiles, too, have brought their full portion into it." Ridderbos criticizes G. C. Berkouwer who, in *The Return of Christ,* argues that Paul is simply concerned with the Israel of his day. Although the process of the mystery is already opening up in the present, Ridderbos argues that one should not overlook the future element in Paul's pronouncements, the fullness "as a not yet fulfilled eschatological, or if one will, apocalyptic reality, whereby the question of whether more or less 'near at hand' plays no special part." H. N. Ridderbos, *Paul: An Outline of His Theology* (Grand Rapids: Eerdmans, 1975), p. 35, n. 71.

or completely figure out his ways. Yet, however far the mind of God is beyond our ability to comprehend, we know from his revelation in the Scriptures and in Jesus Christ that his mind is focused on salvation (v. 32). Sometimes it does not appear that way to human onlookers living under God's sovereign disposition of human history, because within history human disobedience and the judgments of God produce anguish and sorrow. Still, even in the midst of human history, the believer catches a glimpse of the sovereign God's riches, wisdom, love, and knowledge as he works out his salvation to the ends of the earth.

Motivated by personal anguish over the destiny of his own people, the apostle Paul discovered anew the sovereignty of a merciful God. Standing with the Old Testament prophets, he regained the confidence that God remains faithful even when his people do not, and he remembered from firsthand experience that God's mercy is given precisely to disobedient people. Thus the *remnant* holds out hope for the *rest*. Finally, Paul concludes that everything in the entire creation and in the history of salvation originates in God, is sustained by God, and finds its meaning and eschatological fullness in him. Because God is the Creator, Sustainer, and Ruler, and the goal toward whom all things are headed, in the final analysis it is the sovereign God and his will that control, and nothing else. Whatever originates in the creative and redemptive will of God will find its final goal in him. With that confession the apostle Paul rests assured, and his personal sorrow and anguish find their resolution in a joyful song of praise to that God (11:36): "To him be the glory forever. Amen."

CHAPTER VII

Universal and
Particular Fulfillment?

What can be said about the future? Are we able to draw an elaborate scenario of what God has in mind for the future? Hardly, at least not on the basis of what we have discussed, and perhaps not even on the basis of all the texts in the Bible. Promise and prophecy are simply not detailed road maps that enable us to predict all the historical detail that will occur between promise and fulfillment. In addition, our focus has not been on the texts that are often interpreted as looking to the future, such as the text about the millennium in Revelation 20 nor the so-called "signs of the times" in Mark 13. Nevertheless, several of our discussions of basic themes have led into the future, namely our discussions of the future of Jewish Israel, Israel's land and the city of Jerusalem, and even the temple. Though we have focused on present fulfillment, each theme as an anticipation of a greater future has had implications for the shape of that future. Those implications are the topic of this final chapter.

We must be careful in discussing that future lest we assume that we can box God in by our elaborately drawn pictures, as if God would not be faithful if he departed in any way from the scenarios we have imagined. If there is one thing that we should learn from the fulfillment that has already occurred in Jesus Christ, it is this: God's fulfillment of his word is filled with such surprises that we can respond only with amazement. We should expect the unexpected and that it will surpass our expectations.

What no eye has seen, nor ear heard,
  nor the human heart conceived,
what God has prepared for those who love him.

(I Corinthians 2:9)

Even the initial fulfillment in Jesus Christ exceeded everyone's expectations, and apart from the revelation of the Spirit no one would have believed what they had seen. Whatever the final shape of fulfillment may be, we know that it will conform in the most profound manner with the deepest intention of God's word of promise. Of that we can be certain. God is faithful.

The expectation for the future held by the original disciples was literally turned on its head. Brought up in the expectations of Judaism, they believed that fulfillment would first occur within the limits of the particularism of the Old Testament promises about temple, land, and city. Only after such fulfillment would the Gentile nations participate in the salvation of Israel by flocking to the newly refurbished Jerusalem located in Palestine. But those expectations were literally turned upside down. The disciples had to rethink their eschatological scenario. It is this reversal of expectations that poses the basic question addressed in this chapter.

The question can be put in this way: If God still promises a future for Jewish Israel, will this new history be contained within the symbols and institutions of the Old Testament? After the promises of God have already entered on their universalistic fulfillment, which embraces the nations of the world, will God turn history back once more so that the promises can be fulfilled again within the particularisms of the Old Testament as they existed prior to the coming of Jesus Christ? In other words, will Israel as a *nation* become the sign of God's future, a symbol of hope for the salvation of the world? Will God refurbish Jerusalem and the land and reestablish a temple of stone as the sign of his presence? The dispensational understanding of the future and many premillennial scenarios say Yes. What are our conclusions?

Each theme discussed in this book has uncovered an amazing universalizing of the promises. Promises made originally to the particular people Israel in the Old Testament now in Jesus Christ universally embrace the nations of the world. Promises associated with a temple made of stone located in a particular place now find fulfillment in a universal temple composed of human persons living among the nations. And Jerusalem is already a universal city whose citizens are gathered from the nations of the world.

This understanding of the fulfillment of the promises has been called a "spiritualizing" of the promises, and critics of the position we have adopted especially like to use that term.[1] A spiritualizing of the promises is then declared to be inadequate, if not erroneous, a substitution of invisible, spiritual realities (in the heart of the believer) or transcendent realities (in heaven) for the visible, concrete, historical, flesh and blood realities of the Old Testament promises. However, the fulfillment we have described is not "spiritualizing" in that sense. The people of God, Israel, is still a flesh and blood historical reality, although now a universal people and no longer a single, particular people as in the Old Testament. The temple, although no longer restricted to a single geographic locale, is still a visible, historical reality, as visible and historical as human persons are. The land is still the actual land under our feet, but now it refers to the entire created earth. And Jerusalem, although not yet making its perfect appearance on earth as the goal and destiny of human history, is already reflected in its citizens being gathered from the nations of the world. Jerusalem has already expanded its borders and can no longer be contained within the geographic limits of the earthly city. Such a universalizing of the promises, which occurs in Jesus Christ and through the Holy Spirit,[2] stands in direct continuity with the Old Testament promises because it is already announced on its pages.

There are additional New Testament texts that participate in the universalizing of the Old Testament promises. Paul argues against the Judaizers in Galatia that the inheritance is not by law but by promise

1. Cf. J. F. Walvoord, *The Millennial Kingdom* (Findlay, OH: Dunham, 1959), pp. 59f.; C. L. Feinberg, *Millennialism: The Two Major Views* (Chicago: Moody, 1980), pp. 41-45.

2. "Spiritualizing" can have a positive meaning when it refers to the work of the Holy Spirit by which the promises achieve historical fulfillment. However, the real debate is not about "spiritualizing" in this sense, but about whether God *must* fulfill the promises under the particularistic restraints of the Old Testament even after these promises have already experienced a richer, universal fulfillment.

and that this is revealed in the nature of the true descendant of Abraham, Jesus Christ.[3] Because the promises are fulfilled in Christ, all who believe in him, whether Jew or Gentile, are "Abraham's offspring, heirs according to the promise" (Galatians 3:29). Abraham's family is a universal family defined in its essence by Christ, and the promised inheritance belongs to Christ and those who are his.[4]

Similar universalizing tendencies are seen in the Book of Acts. While some interpret the disciples' question, "Lord, is this the time when you will restore the kingdom to Israel?" (Acts 1:6), as an indication that the author of Acts believes that the kingdom *as understood within Judaism* is still a legitimate expectation, such an interpretation fails to see Acts itself as an answer to the disciples' question.[5] Obviously, the question of the disciples was motivated by the understandings of kingdom and Israel common to Judaism, but Acts clearly reinterprets the nature of both Israel and the kingdom by universalizing them. For example, Peter universalizes the recipients of the promise to Abraham's descendants by adding the phrase, "and for all who are far away" (Acts 2:39), a phrase that Paul uses of the Gentiles (Ephesians 2:13). Later Peter announces that, while the message has been sent to the Jews first, it is intended by God for all the families of the earth (Acts 3:25f.). How this universal intention of God is achieved is demonstrated in the design of the Book of Acts.

The temple of stone in Jerusalem, and consequently geographic Jerusalem itself, is relativized by Stephen in his "anti-temple" speech. He declares on the basis of the prophet Isaiah that God "does not dwell in houses made with human hands" (Acts 7:48). In the context of the New Testament such a phrase clearly underscores the arrival of the new temple not made with hands. God now dwells among the nations of the

3. "Judaizers" were Christian Jews who still maintained the essential positions of Judaism regarding the law (Torah) and circumcision.

4. The inheritance of which Paul speaks includes the land. See the discussion above in chapter IV.

5. A. J. Heschel believes that Jesus defers only the question of the time of the kingdom and implies nothing different concerning its essence. Those in the Christian Church who assert that the disciples were in error in their expectations and had to have their understanding altered are said by Heschel to be under the influence of Hellenism. *Israel: An Echo of Eternity* (New York: Farrar, Straus and Giroux, 1969), pp. 163-167.

world. Perhaps the most dramatic universalizing of the promises occurs in James's use of Amos 9:11f. at the Council of Jerusalem (Acts 15:15-18). James declares that the ingathering of the Gentiles is no less than the restoration of the house and kingdom of David.[6] In its restoration the kingdom of David embraces the nations, as had been prophesied by Amos. Amazingly, the house and kingdom that God promised to build for David's son turns out to be identical with the house that David's son builds for God (II Samuel 7:11-14). David's restored kingdom is the kingdom of God established on earth through the mission of Jesus Christ. Such is the inexorable unfolding of God's promises from particularism to universalism, a movement that necessarily shatters the particularistic limits that were originally in the disciples' minds when they asked about the restoration of the kingdom to Israel.

After such repeated indications that the promises have already entered into the phase of universal fulfillment announced by the Old Testament, should we expect a return to a literalistic fulfillment within the Old Testament limits of Israel's nationhood? Or is it rather the case that the particular promises concerning land and city, temple and people, will find their fulfillment only within the structures of the universal fulfillment inaugurated in history by the cross and resurrection of Jesus Christ?

Literalistic or particularist fulfillment has its problems. The basic problem is this: Is it possible to achieve fulfillment apart from the Messiah or the messianic age? Even Rabbi Heschel, though filled with joy and hope by the return of Jews to Israel, does not wish to claim too much for this return: "The State of Israel is not the fulfillment of the Messianic promise, but it makes the Messianic promise plausible."[7] Heschel's reservation about fulfillment arises from his acknowledgment of the basic problem. If earthly Jerusalem is supposed to be a replica of the heavenly city, how can that be achieved? Simple physical occupation of Jerusalem by Jewish Israel is insufficient. If Jerusalem and the state of Israel are supposed to be signs of "the redemption of all

6. This restoration promised in Amos 9 has its foundation in the original covenant promise to David in II Samuel 7:10-16. For a similar interpretation of Acts 15:15-18, cf. O. Palmer Robertson, "Hermeneutics of Continuity," in *Continuity and Discontinuity*, ed. J. S. Feinberg (Westchester, IL: Crossway, 1988), pp. 89-108.

7. Heschel, *op. cit.*, p. 223.

men,"[8] how should the present inhabitants conduct themselves? Can the true meaning of Jerusalem and Israel, according to the Old Testament, be achieved by human effort? Even though we have heard Jewish voices pleading, since the establishment of Israel in 1948, that Israel must be special among the nations of the world — more democratic, more humane, more just — it has discovered in its brief existence how impossible that really is. Reality does not seem to cooperate.

The problem is even larger. Heschel acknowledges that the burden for establishing hope and peace falls not only on Jews but on non-Jews as well.[9] Even according to the Old Testament the obligations are universal. But how can that be accomplished? The New Testament gives the answer. Reality is fractured not only on the individual level but on the corporate political and social levels as well. Sin is the reality that corrupts all human idealisms and the zeal necessary to accomplish them. Even the most zealous attempts to do the will of God cannot and will not succeed in turning the Jerusalem of dust and stone into a replica of the heavenly city. God himself must intervene to build that city and to overcome the reality that corrupts life in every city. Apart from such divine intervention the Old Testament knows that its promised hope cannot be realized.

The New Testament announces that this divine intervention has occurred in Jesus Christ, and it reveals that this hoped for universal peace cannot be established by the armies and coercive power necessary for the maintenance of a political nation. This universal peace will be established only through Christ's death and resurrection, the gift of the Spirit, and the proclamation of the gospel, which leads to Christ's final return. Thus the basic problem has already received its authentic resolution. Consequently, any so-called literalistic or particularistic fulfillment occurring outside or apart from this authentic resolution of the basic problem cannot be the genuine fulfillment that the Old Testament promises.

Even if it is not the genuine fulfillment of the Old Testament promise, can God still be using the recent political history of Jewish Israel to contribute to the fulfillment of his promises of salvation? Of

8. *Ibid.,* p. 225.
9. *Ibid.,* p. 222.

course he can. In fact, he has already used the establishment of the state of Israel to reignite messianic hopes after the Holocaust, in Heschel's words, to make "the Messianic promise plausible." And the sudden victory in the Six-Day War also caused many Jews to question their uniqueness: What does it mean to be a Jew and to be Israel? Nevertheless, we must observe that this Jewish messianic hope is not now or not yet focused on the authentic resolution announced by the New Testament, and the definition of Israel cannot be restricted to physical descendants of Abraham forming a political nation requiring armies for its maintenance. From a New Testament perspective it was Jewish nationalism and Jesus' refusal to lead a political revolt that led to his rejection as Messiah.

Therefore, however important politically and religiously the state of Israel is for the Jewish people, the essence of the meaning of Israel and the Davidic kingdom promised to them lies on another plane. That kingdom will not be achieved by politics as usual or even by an unusual politics, because it consists of a deeper reality that must be grasped by faith. This deeper reality of Israel and the Davidic kingdom has been disclosed through Jesus Christ. Consequently, the claim of Judaism that Israel in its land as such functions as "Jacob's ladder pointing to Jerusalem on high"[10] is contested by the New Testament's application of Jacob's ladder to Jesus as the Son of Man (John 1:51). What is at stake in these competing claims is a different understanding of Israel, of what is necessary to stand in the presence of God, and a different understanding of what needs to be accomplished if the peace of the kingdom of David and the City of God is going to be established in this world.

God will use history, as he always has, to lead both Jews and Gentiles to acknowledge the authentic resolution of their basic problem. Someday the fullness of Jewish Israel will be included with the fullness of Gentile believers in the one people of God. How all this will be achieved in terms of visible events, or how many Old Testament particulars God will rerun or allow to reoccur, I do not know. One perspective shapes all that I do know: There is one people of God, not two; one way of salvation, not two; one way to citizenship in the City of God, not two. The universalizing of the promises in Christ illumines

10. *Ibid.*

the authentic meaning of the particular promises. Therefore, any so-called particular fulfillment of Old Testament promises that bypasses Jesus Christ cannot be the genuine fulfillment that the Old Testament anticipates.

History is shaped by the promises of God. Once spoken, God's word of promise cannot return to him until it is filled with the promised reality (Isaiah 55:10f.). Until then it works its way dynamically through the history of the nations creating what is necessary to achieve its stated goal. History is filled with promise because God's word is sure.

For from him and through him and to him are all things.
To him be the glory forever. Amen.

(Romans 11:36)

Index of Authors

Index of Scripture References